BOSTON
SOCIETY
OF
ARCHITECTS
FOUNDED
A·D
1867

The Steaming Kettle
Government Center
Photo: Phokion Karas

Architecture Boston

produced and edited by
The Boston Society of Architects

introduction by
Walter Muir Whitehill

text by
Joseph L. Eldredge, F.A.I.A.

graphics by
Mark Driscoll

published by
Barre Publishing
Barre, Massachusetts

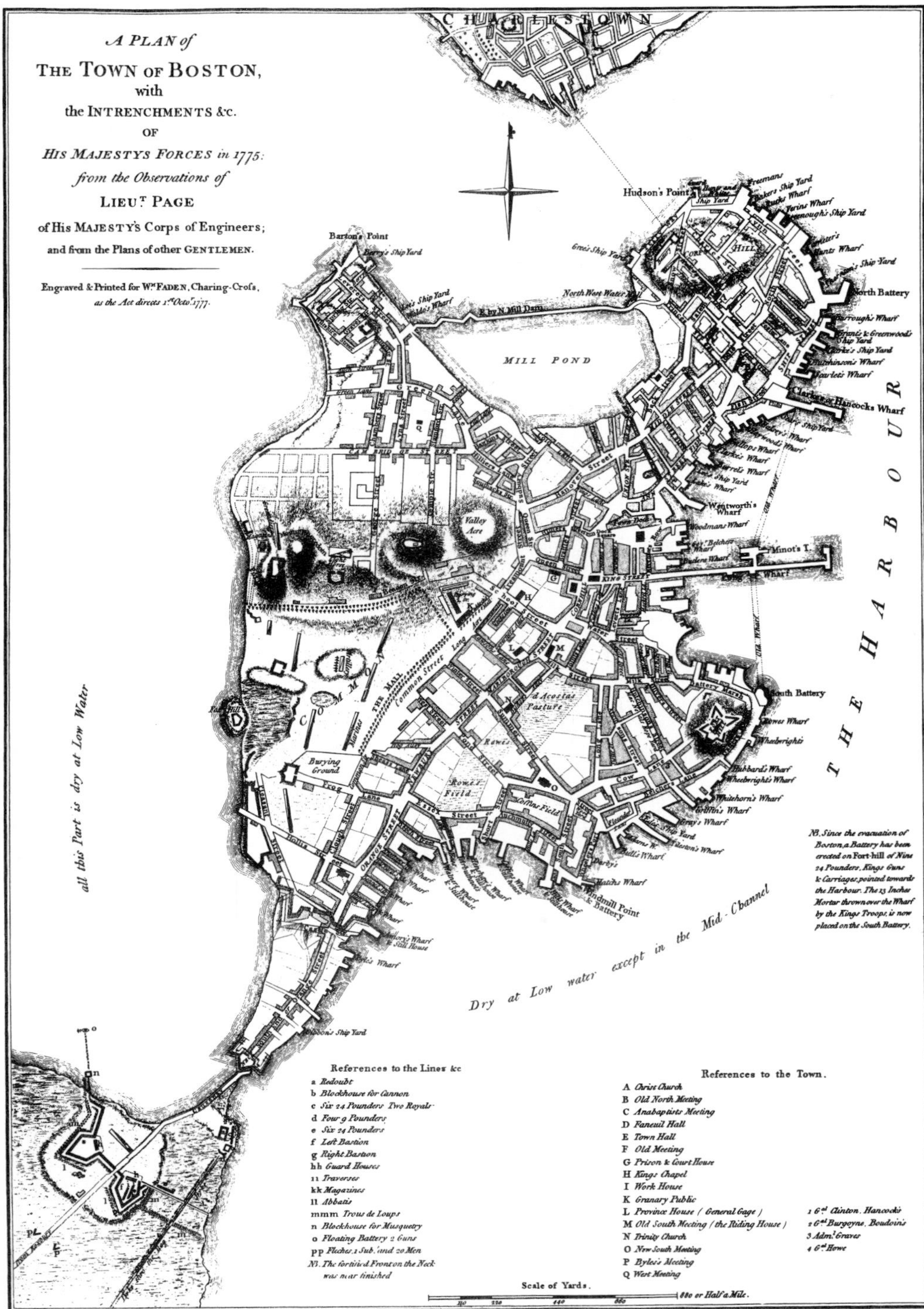

Lieutenant Page's Map prepared in 1775 of the Town of Boston, Population 16,000.

Published simultaneously in Canada by General Publishing Company Limited

First edition

Printed in the United States of America

Library of Congress Cataloging in Publication Data

Boston Society of Architects.
Architecture, Boston and Cambridge.

Bibliography: p.
Includes index.
1. Architecture—Boston—Guide-books.
2. Architecture—Cambridge, Mass.—Guide-books.
I. Title.
NA735.B7B67 1976 974.4'61 76-12589
ISBN 0-517-52501-1
ISBN 0-517-52502-X pbk.

Boston, its Environs and Harbour with the Rebels Works raised against that Town in 1775, from the Observations of Lieutenant Page of His Majesty's Corps of Engineers.

The Boston Skyline from Cambridge across the Charles River. *Photo: Phokion Karas*

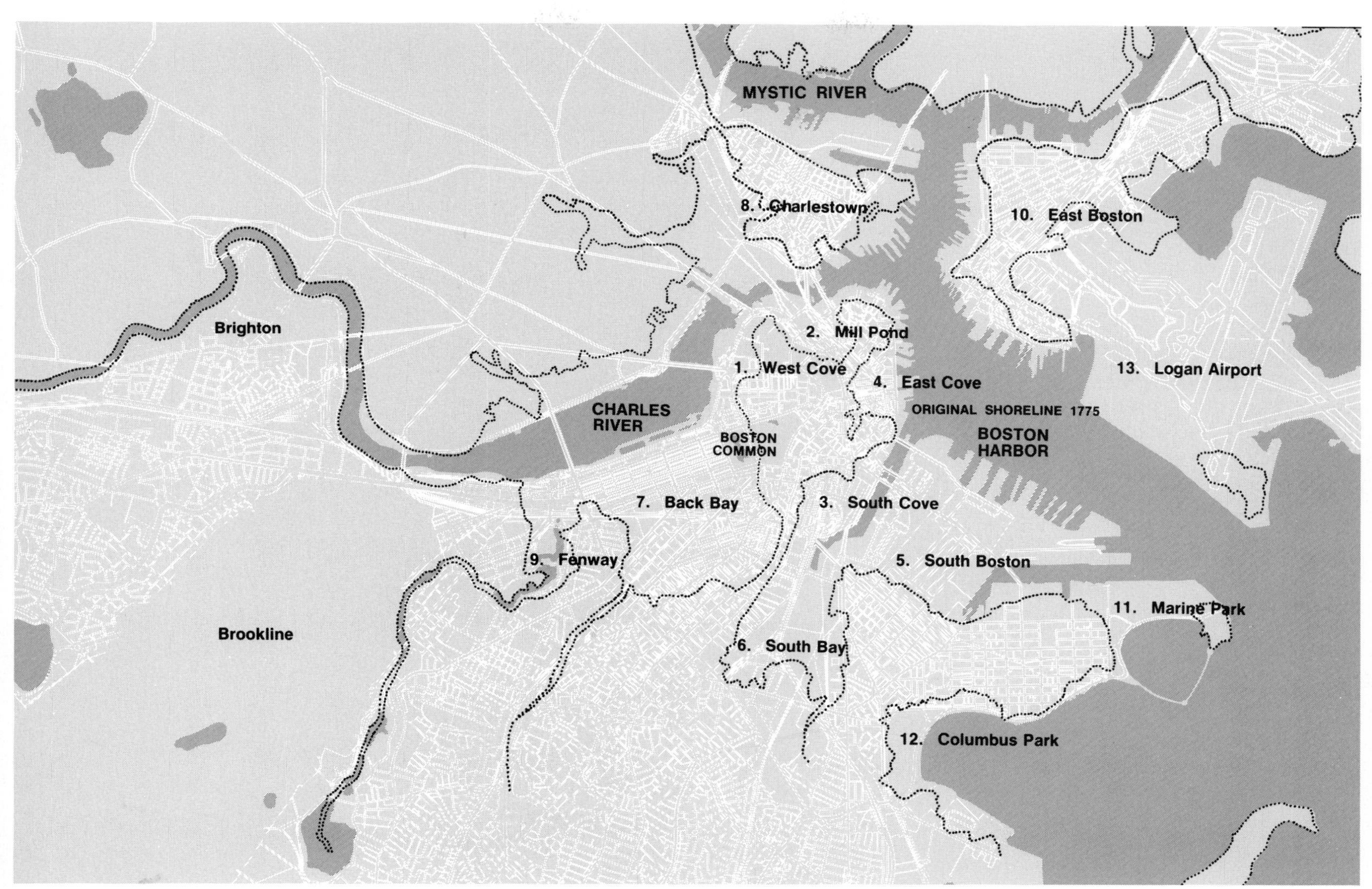

Original Shoreline and Present

Historic Land Fillings:

The city's history is marked by the encroachment of land upon water—the filling in of the coves, harbor, and the tidal flats. The original land area of 783 acres has increased to over three thousand acres today.

1. West Cove 80 acres 1803-1863
2. Mill Pond 70 acres 1807-1829
3. South Cove 86 acres 1806-1843
4. East Cove 112 acres 1823-1874
5. South Boston 714 acres 1836-present
6. South Bay 138 acres 1850-present
7. Back Bay 580 acres 1857-1894
8. Charlestown 416 acres 1860-1896
9. Fenway 322 acres 1878-1890
10. East Boston 370 acres 1880-present
11. Marine Park 57 acres 1883-1900
12. Columbus Park 265 acres 1890-1901
13. Logan Airport 150 acres 1922-present

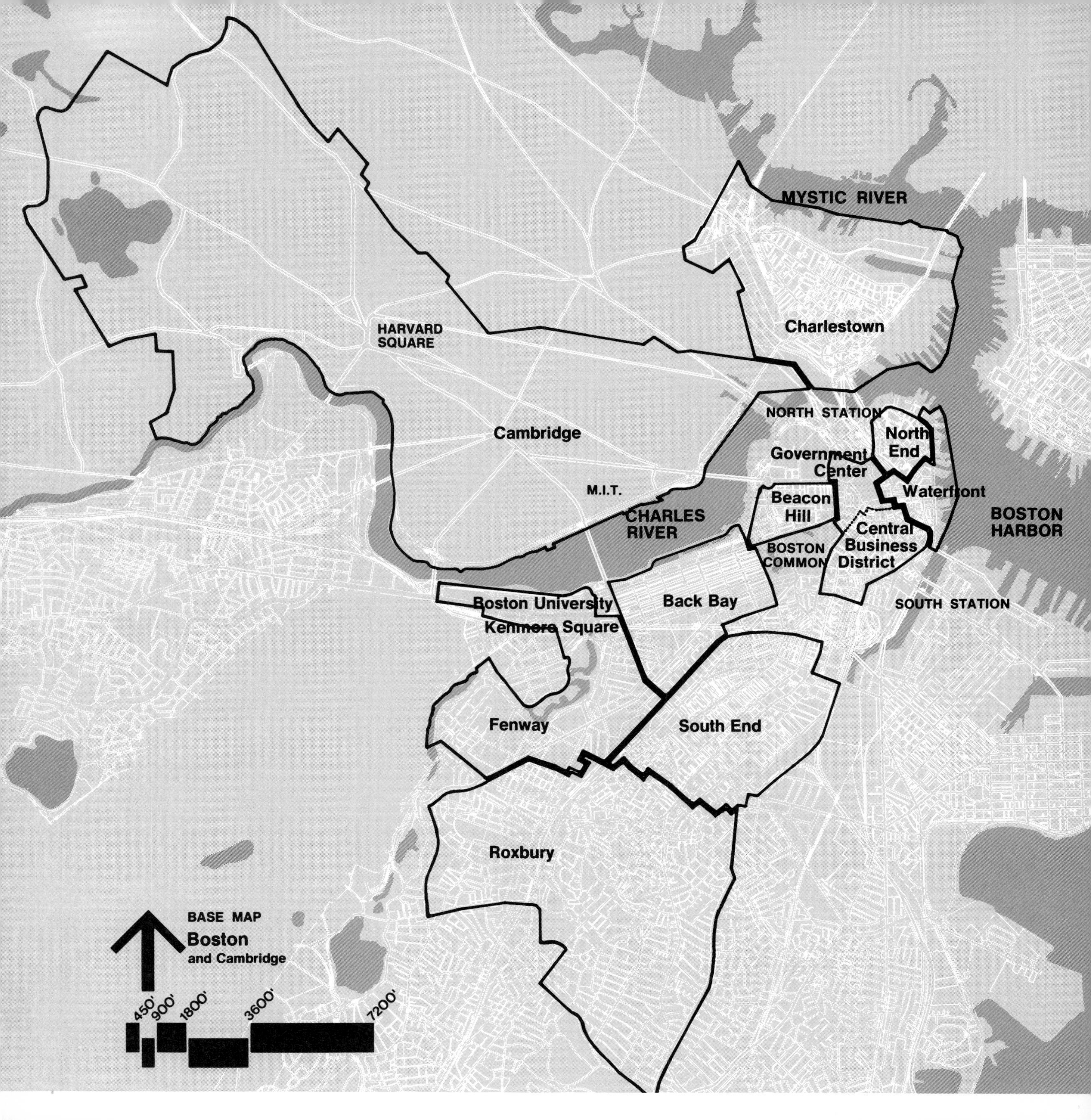
MYSTIC RIVER
Charlestown
HARVARD SQUARE
Cambridge
NORTH STATION
North End
Government Center
Waterfront
M.I.T.
Beacon Hill
CHARLES RIVER
BOSTON HARBOR
Central Business District
BOSTON COMMON
Boston University
Back Bay
SOUTH STATION
Kenmore Square
Fenway
South End
Roxbury
BASE MAP
Boston
and Cambridge
450'
900'
1800'
3600'
7200'

CONTENTS

ACKNOWLEDGMENTS

The Boston Society of Architects would like to express its gratitude to several people for their work in making this edition of *Architecture Boston* a reality.

We wish to give special thanks to Joseph Eldredge, FAIA, for his extensive historical research and his carefully prepared text. Thanks and appreciation go to William J. Geddis, FAIA, Chairman of the Architectural Book Committee, and to Pamela R. Geddis for their supervision of the production and photographic layout of the book. We would also like to thank the members of the Architectural Book Committee who contributed their time and judgment: Earl R. Flansburgh, FAIA; H. Morse Payne, FAIA; and Lowell Erickson, Executive Director of the Boston Society of Architects. We are most grateful to Mark Driscoll for his excellent graphics. We also wish to acknowledge the many architects and photographers who contributed their work.

We would like to give very special thanks to Walter Muir Whitehill for his advice, criticism, and continuous assistance. His contribution is everywhere in the book, not simply confined to his splendid introduction.

And finally, we would like to acknowledge all those citizens of Boston and Cambridge who have for over three centuries supported excellence in architecture and planning. Their efforts have really made this book possible.

George M. Notter, Jr., AIA
President
Boston Society of Architects

Aerial View of Contemporary Boston. Population: 671,000. *Photo: Aerial Photos of New England, Inc.*

INTRODUCTION

by Walter Muir Whitehill

Some inadequately informed visitors to Boston believe that they will find in the city much "beautiful Colonial architecture." They are bound to be disappointed, for there is precious little left that was standing in the summer of 1776 when Massachusetts formally ceased to be a colony of Great Britain. The exterior of the old State House looks much as it did when the Declaration of Independence was read from its east end balcony on 18 July 1776, but Faneuil Hall, the only other public building of the colonial period, was in 1805 enlarged out of all resemblance to its original state. Two of the three eighteenth-century Anglican churches—Christ Church and King's Chapel—are still in use, although of the Congregational meetinghouses only one—the Old South—has survived, and that as an historic monument. A few private dwellings, three burying grounds, and the Common are all that remain of the colonial town. Even the landscape has been altered beyond recognition, for hills were cut down to fill in the coves, making what was once a water-ringed peninsula a part of the mainland.

Although Boston has preserved only a few scattered examples of its Colonial buildings, it offers an unrivaled view of nineteenth-century planning and architecture. Beacon Hill, which began to be transformed from upland pasture to a new residential district in the last decade of the eighteenth century, still presents a unified picture of the domestic architecture of the first half of the nineteenth century. In 1954, when the Beacon Hill Civic Association took the first measures that led to the protection of the area as an historic dis-

Acorn Street, Beacon Hill
Photo: James Douglass

▶
Eastern Airlines Terminal,
Logan Airport
Architects: Minoru
Yamasaki & Associates
with Desmond
& Lord, Inc.; 1971.
Photo: Balthazar Korab

trict, an architectural survey conducted by Henry A. Millon and Carl J. Weinhardt, Jr., found that the area was still overwhelmingly residential, with a large proportion of the houses still occupied by single families. Of these buildings, 75 percent were of Federal or Greek Revival style, built before 1850, while 13 percent were of the period 1850–1900.

The creation of new land by filling during the nineteenth century resulted in large-scale city planning projects. Through the efforts of Mayor Josiah Quincy in 1825/1826, a new two-story granite market house, 555 feet long and 50 wide, was built to the southeast of Faneuil Hall on land reclaimed from a miscellany of alleys, docks, and wharves. It was flanked by harmonious granite-faced warehouses, fronting on the newly created North and South Market streets. The whole complex, designed by Alexander Parris, was a noble achievement, for it provided Faneuil Hall with an approach from the harbor of extraordinary dignity and beauty. Thanks to the restoration by the Boston Redevelopment Authority, the interested visitor to Boston will be able better to appreciate the quality of this great effort in urban design that was completed by the city at the time of the fifteenth anniversary of the American Revolution.

The filling of the Back Bay, planned in 1856 and finished within three decades, provided a wholly new residential district which was completely built up by the end of the century. Restrictions of height and setback gave the region remarkable homogeneity. Although some changes that cannot be thought improvements have occurred, the Back Bay still presents a picture of Boston architecture in the second half of the nineteenth century that is as consistent and intelligible as that offered by Beacon Hill for the first half.

At the end of the American Revolution, Boston still resembled a small English seaport of narrow streets with numerous gabled wooden houses and overhanging second stories that suggest a continuity of the mediaeval tradition. At the Paul Revere house in North Square, the only recognizable seventeenth-century dwelling in central Boston, "folk Gothic survived into the age of Bernini," to borrow a phrase from John Coolidge. Urban elegance in the terms of London, Bath, or Edinburgh came to Boston through the work of Charles Bulfinch (1763–1844), who literally changed the face of the town. Between 1788, when he began to practice architecture, and 1818, when he moved to Washington to become architect of the Capitol, Bulfinch designed the State House, Court House, Faneuil Hall, a theatre, a concert hall, five banks, four insurance offices, three schools, two hospitals, four churches, three entire streets, and a considerable number of private houses. During much of this time he, as chairman of the Board of Selectmen, was the principal officer of government. He put his imprint upon Federalist Boston as completely as Bernini did upon Rome.

When one contemplates the list of Bulfinch's accomplishments, one appreciates the anecdote recalled by his granddaughter, when "asked if he would train up any

Health, Welfare and Education Service Center for the Commonwealth of Massachusetts, Government Center. Paul Rudolph, coordinating architect. Shepley, Bulfinch, Richardson and Abbott with Desmond & Lord; 1970. ***Photo: Robert Perron***

of his children in his own profession, he replied, with charming naïveté, that he did not think there would be much for them left to do. That States and towns were already supplied with their chief buildings, and he hardly thought a young man could make a living as an architect." Subsequently many have, because of our national enthusiasm for knocking buildings down and starting over. Bulfinch's State House still looks down upon Boston Common. His enlargement of Faneuil Hall and the first building of the Massachusetts General Hospital have survived; so have St. Stephen's Church in Hanover Street and some of his private houses. But the streets that he designed—Tontine Crescent, Franklin Place, Park Row, Colonnade Row—have vanished with his Court House and much of his most attractive work.

Indeed the process of demolition started within Bulfinch's lifetime. In 1792 he designed for his kinsman Joseph Coolidge (1747–1826) a three-story brick house that stood in large gardens near Bowdoin Square, between Temple and Bowdoin streets. This was a family affair, for Coolidge's wife was Bulfinch's second cousin, and the son of this pair, Joseph Coolidge (1773–1840), was in 1796 to marry Bulfinch's sister Elizabeth. This house, whose facade was inspired by Robert Adam's Royal Society of Arts in the Adelphi in London, introduced the current neoclassical style to Boston. Like many large houses, this one became a problem once its original occupants died. Its builder's grandson, Joseph Coolidge, Jr. (1798–1879), when leaving Boston for Canton in 1832 to recoup his fortunes in the China trade, installed his wife and children there for a time. But the house proved an expensive white elephant, and in a few years was torn down. Charles Bulfinch, who had returned from Washington to pass the last years of his life in Boston, wrote on 12 June 1843 to his son: "The alterations here surpass all you can conceive. I have this morning viewed those going on in Bowdoin Street. Mr. Coolidge's noble mansion, trees and all, are swept away, and 5 new brick houses are now building on the spot."

The row of Greek Revival brick houses that in 1843 seemed to Bulfinch so poor a substitute for "Mr. Coolidge's noble mansion" were in 1963 included in an extension of the Beacon Hill Historic District to prevent *their* demolition! Mr. and Mrs. Coolidge, when they returned from an extended period in China and Europe in the late forties, settled at 20 Louisburg Square. In 1850 they moved to a red brick house at 12 Pemberton Square (now demolished) and in the seventies to a large four-story brownstone house at 184 Beacon Street in the new Back Bay.

The constant change in the Boston scene is well illustrated by a letter that their son, J. Randolph Coolidge (1828–1925) wrote from 130 Beacon Street on 15 November 1909 to his son, John Gardner Coolidge (1863–1936), then in Europe. The view from the rear windows of Mr. Coolidge's large brownstone house at the corner of Beacon and Berkeley streets had recently changed dramatically. Formerly at low tide the Charles River was a modest stream in the middle of wide mud flats. The completion of a dam that excluded the harbor tides had converted the Charles River Basin into a permanent and handsome body of fresh water, with embankments that were pleasant for walking. Moreover, many cultural institutions were moving westward out of the center of the city. The Boston Symphony Orchestra had migrated to the corner of Massachusetts

The Boston Five Cents Savings Bank and Plaza, 10 School Street. Kallmann & McKinnell; 1972. *Background:* Old South Meeting House. Joshua Blanchard; 1729. *Photo: Ezra Stoller*

City Hall Plaza at Government Center. *Photo: Cervan Robinson*

Museum of Science. East Wing, 1951; Planetarium, 1958; Tower, 1961. Perry, Dean & Stewart. West Wing, Garage, and Service Building, 1972. Johnson-Hotvedt Associates. *Photo: Steve Rosenthal*

and Huntington avenues to a new Symphony Hall that opened in 1900. In that same year the Massachusetts Horticultural Society began building the present Horticultural Hall on the opposite corner of the same intersection. The New England Conservatory of Music moved in 1902 to a new building a block farther west in Huntington Avenue. In 1908 the Boston Opera House was begun on a site diagonally across Huntington Avenue from the Conservatory. Still farther west on the same avenue, the Museum of Fine Arts began construction in 1907 of its present building, from designs of Guy Lowell. These were the events reported to Europe from 130 Beacon Street in 1909.

We are once more settled in town again for the winter. The house looks nice and fresh and natural. . . . Now we are free to look about and the most noteworthy thing at this moment is the view of the embankment from my study windows. The corner park so long an eyesore is nearly completed and with its broad granolithic walk and wide grass plots already faintly green looks decidedly attractive. The light and neat iron railing between the two bridges and the walk is completed along its entire length so that one can make the complete circuit of the Charles River Basin comfortably and enjoy the different attractive views. Your mother and I went along this side yesterday. It will not be long before the widened and improved road back of Beacon Street will also be finished. What I wish for is that the Tech [MIT] should decide to move over to the embankment beyond the river in the vicinity of West Boston bridge. It would be I think a grand site for them and their new and I hope presentable buildings would shut out the sight of the objectionable chimneys and factories of Cambridgeport beyond.

Shortly before coming to town your mother and I attended the opening performance at the new Opera House and the first reception at the new Art Museum. I am a good deal disappointed at the exterior of the former. It seems to me heavy and inartistic with its big columns and rather clumsy stone trimmings, while the body is of a rather cheap looking brick. It seems to me the elevation could have easily been made much handsomer at little or no additional cost. I think it is decidedly not a success.

On the other hand, the interior of the theatre is very good. The proscenium is well shaped and very large, perhaps the largest I have seen anywhere, and its details are simple and handsome, free from over ornamentation and in good taste. The whole effect is imposing. The stage is of course very roomy. One peculiarity is that there are two rows of boxes beneath the first balcony which is therefore rather high up and very deep. The upper balcony still more so, stretching up tier above tier almost into boundless space. I should say it must be very difficult to see or hear from the back seats. The performance of La Gioconda was good. A large number of ladies present were in full dress and jewels, and the coup d'oeil was very fine. Of course the house was crowded. After the third act the parties most active in the organization of the Opera together with the principal singers came before the curtain and at the request of the audience Mr. [Eben D.] Jordan made a short address or statement in good taste and manners on what had been accomplished and the difficulties which had been surmounted in the work.

If the interior is the best part of the Opera House, the reverse seems the case with the Art Museum. The elevation of the new building is, as you know, generally admired. It was difficult to judge of the interior and impossible to inspect the collections on the first private reception day, on account of the great crowd present. The effect was that of a fine hall and staircase, many long galleries or corridors and a number of rooms which did not seem very large, with a few inner courts, the whole colored in a low rather cold tone except the picture galleries which were tinted a sad purple, almost black. I thought the effect rather cold and dreary and giving too strong an impression that the whole was meant mainly to store and serve as a background for works of art. Perhaps with greater familiarity I may like it better.

Two-thirds of a century have passed. The Charles River Basin is still a delight, although automobiles have made it less

South Station. Shepley, Rutan & Coolidge. *Photo: Phokion Karas*

pleasant for walkers. For more than forty years J. Randolph Coolidge's house at 130 Beacon Street has been part of Emerson College. The Boston Opera House was demolished in 1958 to make way for an extension of Northeastern University, which had settled across the way in 1938.

In the last third of the nineteenth century Boston annexed several neighboring towns: Roxbury in 1867, Dorchester in 1869, Charlestown, Brighton, and West Roxbury in 1873. Originally these were autonomous communities, separated from Boston either by bodies of water or open country. Their history and their architecture had been quite distinct from that of the city of which they have formed a part for the past century. With the introduction of horse-drawn and electric streetcars, large elements of the population of Boston sprayed out of the original city and submerged the once rural towns in inelegant urban sprawl. Although the town of Brookline, which had been part of Boston until 1705, was greedily eyed by the expansionists, it was able to resist annexation and maintain its independence as a separate entity only because of the determination and solvency of many of its residents.

Looking down from an airplane, or from the Prudential Tower, Boston and Cambridge seem to be one city, even though they are quite distinct places, each with its own city government, institutions, and state of mind. But Cambridge—although the fourth or fifth largest place in Massachusetts, depending upon which census you believe—is really an inadvertent nineteenth-century amalgamation of three different villages. It has none of the orderly sequence of houses in symmetrical blocks, properly related to squares and public buildings, that, to lovers of classical and baroque order, are an essential ingredient of a city.

Harvard University claims to be "a living museum of architecture in America, from colonial times to the present." But not all the exhibits have a harmonious relation to one another, and as space is at a premium, it always reminds me of a nineteenth-century museum in which objects of incongruous size and disparate provenance have been tightly jammed into overcrowded cases. Among the Harvard exhibits is Le Corbusier's only building in the United States.

The Massachusetts Institute of Technology *did* move to the Cambridge shore of the Charles River Basin, as J. Randolph Coolidge hoped in 1909 that it would. It settled in 1916 near the Harvard, rather than the West Boston (or Longfellow), bridge in a classical complex designed by Welles Bosworth. The great expansion of the Institute during World War II, combined with a desire to be in the vanguard of contemporary architecture, led MIT also to become "a living museum of architecture in America," although from 1916, rather than colonial times, to the present.

King's Chapel and Burial Ground, Tremont and School streets. Peter Harrison; c. 1749. *Photo: Phokion Karas*

It now extends from the Longfellow almost to the Boston University bridge.

Thanks to these institutions of learning, and to a great amount of new construction, public and private, during the third quarter of this century, the city's architectural offerings in the styles of the twentieth century are as rich as they are for the nineteenth, and infinitely greater than for the colonial period. Simply to go outside the range of local architects, Le Corbusier, Breuer, Nervi, Saarinen, I. M. Pei, and Philip Johnson are represented in Boston, and for many years Walter Gropius *was* local. I eschew the word "modern," for modernity evaporates overnight. The Boston temperament, however, respects what is good in the past, even of the recent past. As I write, the Society for the Preservation of New England Antiquities is raising an endowment that will permit it to accept the house that Walter Gropius built for himself in Lincoln, Massachusetts, in 1937 as a gift from the architect's widow. In the *New York Times* of 18 May 1975, Ada Louise Huxtable described this effort under the heading "Transforming the Avant-Garde Into an Instant Landmark." An illustration described the building as "once radical, now *gemütlich.*" Mrs. Huxtable's gentle reflections on this event should set the stage for the account of Boston architecture that follows.

There is first, the lovely, subtle paradox of the Gropius House, that clarion call to the future, as an authenticated antiquity. How inexorably time turns the avant-garde into history! And how much delicate irony can be obtained from the fact that this house marked the conscious rejection of history in terms of emulations of past styles (indigenous tradition was a superbly rationalized substitute) and the declaration of a new esthetic and a brave new world. The new esthetic is the norm, and the brave new world grows old. The landmark takes its place as part of the history that it has spurned, and the movement that rewrote history becomes history. Always, history wins.

AERIAL PHOTOS
OF NEW
ENGLAND

Chapter 1

GOVERNMENT CENTER/CENTRAL BUSINESS DISTRICT

Aerial View of Government Center.
Photo: Aerial Photos of New England, Inc.

In 1960 Boston held a national competition for the design of a new City Hall. Its well-ordered program gave participants from far and wide a comprehensive introduction to the city they sought to enrich. A preamble announced:

> At Massachusetts Bay the land only gradually meets the sea. Two peninsulas, Winthrop on the north and Nantasket on the south, stretch toward each other to protect from the open sea the mixture of land and water that makes Boston Harbor. The very numerous small islands, peninsulas, and hills are drumlins left seemingly at random by the glaciers that retreated 10,000 years ago. . . . The harbor receives four rivers: the Charles, the Mystic, the Chelsea, and the Neponset. The first three terminate in broad estuaries, and the greatest of these is that formed by the Charles, dammed in 1910 to produce the Charles River Basin.
>
> One cluster of hills, called Shawmut by the Indians, connected to the mainland by what was originally only a narrow neck, was well placed to be selected in 1630 for settlement and to become the place where Boston grew. Almost surrounded by water, it was easily defensible against Indians and predatory animals coming from landward, while it was in close contact with the deepest and most sheltered anchorages.
>
> The fragmented character of the terrain of the region and the way the settlement was organized combined to produce over the years a group of separate towns surrounding the bay. As the population grew they ultimately coalesced to form the continuous agglomeration of Greater Boston, but they remain separate self-governing communities to this day. (Lawrence B. Anderson, *Program for Boston City Hall Competition*).

Eloquent statistics were invoked: [Subsoil] ". . . a synclinal fold . . . covered over by marine deposits and glacial wastes." [Climate] ". . . onshore winds are not uncommon, and there is an alternation of warm and cold, wet and dry, cloudy and clear, that gives an impression of high variability." [Local materials] ". . . The color range of New England waterstruck brick lies in the dark, rich reds. . . . Granite occurs through most of New England both as glacial boulders and as ledge rock. . . . Great rectangular slabs were used for paving, for steps and platforms, and for base courses supporting, for example, nearly every brick building on Beacon Hill."

Using language that anticipated the environmental impact process, the Program drew from some 250 entries a remarkable solution. In a single building, the architects Kallmann, McKinnell and Knowles created a contemporary microcosm of Boston. Rising as if a part of its broad plaza, a brick base envelops the everyday functions of city government (licenses, permits, taxes, etc.) in a daylighted system of "indoor streets." Window openings were omitted from the vertical brick surfaces to forestall comparison with the ordered facades of Faneuil Hall, the Old State House, and Sears Crescent.

High above, a new order of precast window wall sections contains the floors devoted to those technical activities required to keep the city operating. Bold forms recall nearby granite mercantile buildings, a legacy of days when Boston was the nation's window on the world.

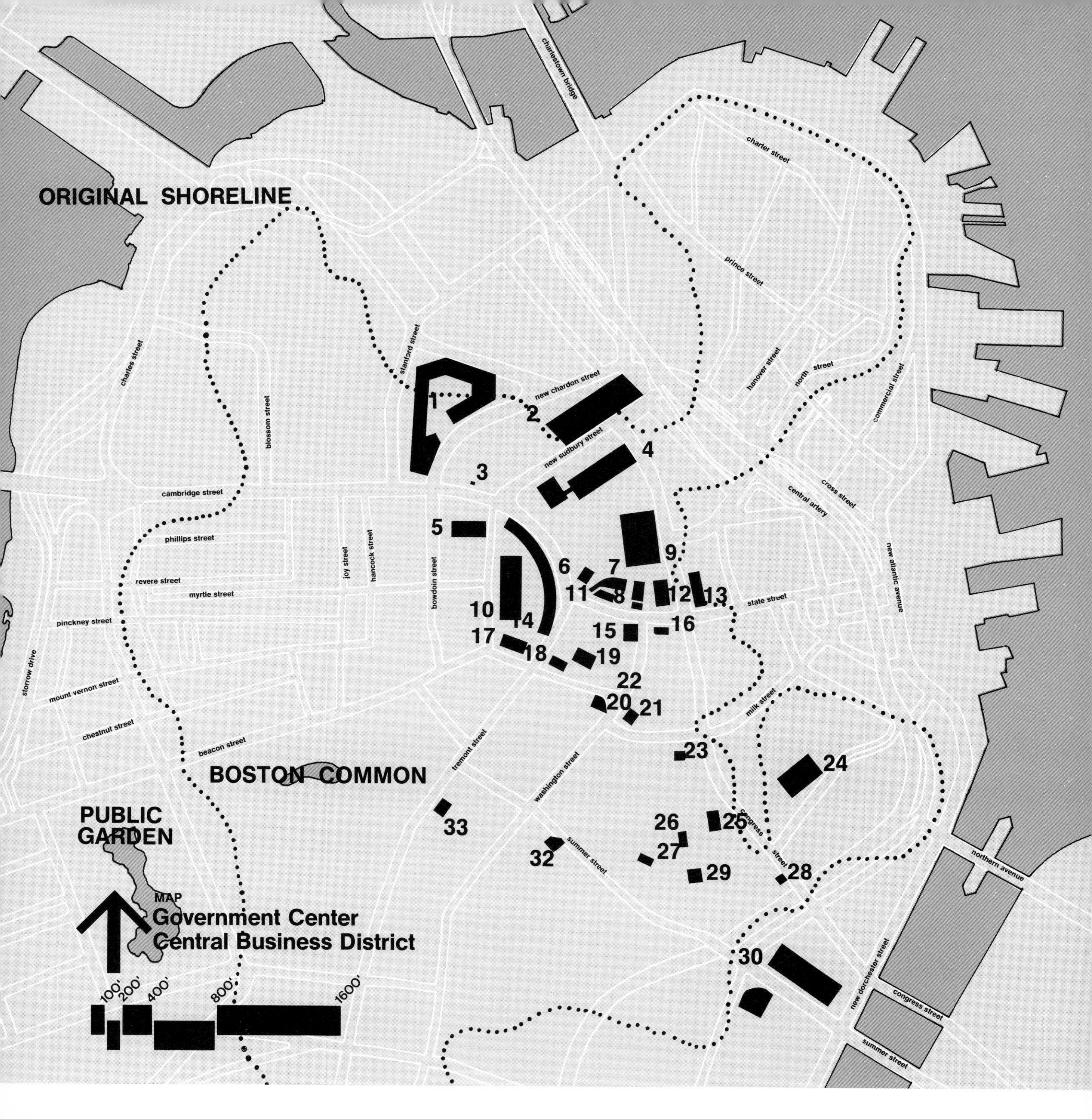
ORIGINAL SHORELINE
charlestown bridge
charter street
prince street
stanford street
new chardon street
new sudbury street
charles street
blossom street
hanover street
north street
commercial street
cambridge street
cross street
central artery
phillips street
revere street
myrtle street
joy street
hancock street
bowdoin street
new atlantic avenue
state street
pinckney street
storrow drive
mount vernon street
chestnut street
milk street
beacon street
tremont street
washington street
BOSTON COMMON
PUBLIC GARDEN
congress street
summer street
northern avenue
new dorchester street
MAP
Government Center
Central Business District
100'
200'
400'
800'
1600'
1
2
3
4
5
6
7
8
9
10
11
12
13
14
15
16
17
18
19
20
21
22
23
24
25
26
27
28
29
30
32
33

1. Health, Welfare and Education
Service Center for the Commonwealth of Massachusetts
Government Center
Paul Rudolph, coordinating architect:
Shepley, Bulfinch, Richardson and Abbott
with Desmond & Lord; 1970

2. Government Center Garage
Government Center
Samuel Glaser & Partners and
Kallmann & McKinnell; 1970

3. Bowdoin Street MBTA Station
6 Bowdoin Square
Sert, Jackson and Associates; 1968

4. John F. Kennedy Federal Building
Government Center
The Architects Collaborative with
Samuel Glaser Associates; 1966

5. Leverett Saltonstall Building
Government Center
Emery Roth & Sons; 1965

6. Government Center MBTA Station
City Hall Square
Exterior: Architects and Engineers
for the Boston City Hall; 1968
Interior: Geometrics; 1969

7. Sears Crescent Building (rehabilitation)
City Hall Square
Stull Associates; 1969

8. Ames Building
Shepley, Rutan & Coolidge; 1892

9. New City Hall
City Hall Square
Architects and Engineers for the Boston City Hall
(Kallmann, McKinnell and Knowles,
associated with Campbell, Aldrich and
Nulty, and LeMessurier Associates); 1968

10. Suffolk County Courthouse

11. City Bank & Trust
Stahl/Bennett; 1969

12. New England Merchants Bank Building
28 State Street
Edward L. Barnes and Emery Roth & Sons; 1969

13. 60 State Street
Cabot, Cabot & Forbes
Skidmore, Owings & Merrill; 1976

14. Center Plaza (office building)
Government Center
Welton Beckett & Associates; 1966-69

15. Boston Company Building
1 Boston Place
Pietro Belluschi and Emery Roth & Sons; 1970

16. Old State House
206 Washington Street
1712/13; Rebuilt: 1748
Alterations: Isaiah Rogers; 1830
Restored: George A. Clough; 1881/82

17. One Beacon Street (office building)
Employers-Commercial Union Companies
Skidmore, Owings & Merrill; 1972

18. King's Chapel
Tremont and School streets
Peter Harrison; 1750

19. Old City Hall
41-45 School Street
Gridley J. F. Bryant and Arthur Gilman; 1865
Conversion:
Anderson Notter Associates; 1970

20. Boston Five Cents Savings Bank
24 School Street
Kallmann & McKinnell; 1972

21. Old South Meeting House
Washington and Milk streets
Joshua Blanchard; 1729

22. Old Corner Bookstore
Washington and School streets
Thomas Crease; 1712

23. National Shawmut Bank
67 Milk Street
The Architects Collaborative; 1975

24. State Street Bank Building
225 Franklin Street
Pearl Street Associates (F. A. Stahl & Associates,
Hugh Stubbins and Associates, LeMessurier
Associates); 1966

25. First National Bank of Boston
100 Federal Street
Campbell, Aldrich & Nulty; 1971

26. Massachusetts Blue Cross-Blue Shield
Headquarters Office Building
133 Federal Street
Anderson, Beckwith & Haible
with Paul Rudolph; 1961

27. Conversion, Record American Building
Office Building
One Winthrop Square
Childs, Bertman, Tseckares; 1973

28. Keystone Building
High and Congress streets
Pietro Belluschi and Emery Roth & Sons; 1970

29. Union Warren Bank
formerly Blue Cross Building
Paul Rudolph/Anderson, Beckwith & Haible;
1953

30. Federal Reserve Bank
Atlantic Avenue and Summer Street
Hugh Stubbins and Associates; 1976

31. South Station
Shepley, Rutan & Coolidge

32. Charlestown Savings Bank
The Architects Collaborative; 1976

33. The Cathedral Church of St. Paul
136 Tremont Street
Alexander Parris; 1820

Interior Lobby, Boston City Hall. *Photo: Cervan Robinson*

The departments are stepped up in decreasing order of need for public access from the plaza level. Massive concrete piers supporting these upper floors define a middle space that unites the ceremonial functions with the actual seat of government: the mayor's office and city council chambers. These are dramatized in hanging or projecting forms expressive of their functions, set in a composition of open courtyard, exhibition hall, multiple level interior circulation, and concrete shafts bringing daylight from clerestory windows above. Grandeur is everywhere modulated by studied proportion and detail; brick, concrete, space, and daylight form a reassuring palette of materials in a building that does not intimidate the humblest of its two million owners.

The program asked that City Hall and its plaza unite four adjacent districts: business, government, financial, and historic-residential. In addition to materials and forms, the pedestrian pattern of the plaza is continuous with well-worn Boston pathways that wind down from the State House and through the Court House, into narrow alleys between tall buildings, and on down to the teeming marketplace. As a humanistic invention alone, City Hall takes its place among the finest public buildings of the world.

The winning design did much more than house the obscure and neglected processes of government in a visible, productive environment. It sparked an urban renewal process unequaled anywhere for the quality of its architecture. Construction of major state, federal, and city buildings was used to rescue a congested, decaying section of the older city from a nightmare of traffic problems and fragmented land ownership patterns. An urban design plan completed by I. M. Pei and Partners established criteria for use, location, size, shape, and circulation. Pedestrian malls and vistas were tied in with

Boston City Hall.
Kallmann, McKinnell & Knowles associated with Campbell, Aldrich and Nulty and with LeMessurier Associates; 1968.
Photo: Cervan Robinson

Sears Crescent Building (recycled), City Hall Plaza. Stull Associates; 1969. *Photo: Phokion Karas*

construction of new stops on three subway lines. The plan was made dependent upon the social, economic, and visual value of historic structures. To the vanished site of Scollay Square, where sailors and strippers shared an enthusiasm for irreverence, thousands of new people would come to work, shop, eat, and play.

The John F. Kennedy Federal Building, by The Architects Collaborative and Samuel Glazer, combines an office tower with a long, low-rise element containing functions requiring heavy public access. A mural by Robert Motherwell and a sculpture entitled *Philippi* by Dmitri Hadzi recall the death and life of the president for whom the building is named. Across Cambridge Street, a sweeping "horizontal skyscraper" contributes a covered arcade and a dignified precast concrete and brick facade to the plaza. The upper side of the Center Plaza Building, designed by Welton Becket and Associates, creates a forecourt for Suffolk County Courthouse. It has rendered this splendid German Renaissance pile so visible that it is now unlikely to be torn down. There are three "entries" from City Hall Plaza to this upper level serving as strong pedestrian connections to the County and State enclaves on Beacon Hill.

Beneath the plaza in front of City Hall two subway lines interconnect. The station at surface level was designed by Kallmann and McKinnell, who were retained to design the plaza, fountain, and details of the overall Government Center complex. The lower regions of the station were rearranged by Geometrics, Inc., using the vocabulary of materials, details, and supergraphics established by Cambridge Seven (Arlington Street Station) for revitalizing the "T" throughout metropolitan Boston.

Sears Crescent and the Sears Block are preserved as restaurant, commercial, and office space by the firms of Stull Associates and F.A. Stahl and Associates respectively. A hanging gold coin, a lobster, and a teapot salvaged from old Scollay Square set a high standard for commercial signs. An inscription on the steaming kettle proclaims that it contains 277 gallons, 2 quarts, 1 pint, and 3 gills. This low-rise block of older buildings is backed up by the gruff concrete lines of the City Bank & Trust Building on Court Street, also designed by the Stahl office.

The northern edge of Government Center is defined by a 2000-car precast concrete garage-transportation interchange bridging New Sudbury Street. It contains a commuter bus terminal and a double subway stop. A police station, bank, district post office, radio-television station, and city and private social service facilities are grouped between the Federal Building and the State Service Center to the west. Public art includes a listless, enigmatic steel trapezoid by Beverly Pepper (garage); a plywood and stainless steel bas-relief by Anthony Belluschi and Craig Roney (RKO Building); and a bristling, rusty ball by Alfred Duca (Post Office Arcade) commemorating the instrument that demolished the West End in Boston's early frenzy of indiscriminate "urban removal."

The planning of the State Service Center with its sculptural exo-structure and hammered concrete skin is the language of Paul Rudolph. Two sections have been completed to date: the Division of Employment Security and the Lindemann Mental Health Center, designed by Shepley, Bulfinch, Richardson & Abbott and Desmond & Lord, respectively, with both firms coordinated by Mr. Rudolph. A third element, to house health, education, and welfare functions, sorely needed to complete this ambitious concept, awaits funding and an administrative commitment to outstanding architecture. The Hurley Building has a plaster graffiti mural by Constantino Nivola in its dynamic lobby, plus an attenuated metal and wire offering by Fayette Taylor suspended in the portico opposite.

Mounting the north slope of Beacon Hill, the Saltonstall Building, by Emery Roth and Sons, and the McCormack Building, by Hoyle, Doran and Berry, contain an expanding state bureaucracy. The black glass facade of the newer McCormack Building is a better backdrop for the gold-leafed State House dome than either its earlier neighbor or the heavy-handed red granite grid of One Beacon Street. A monumental bronze sculpture, *Massachusetts Artifact,* by Alfred Duca, commands the McCormack lobby.

The original Government Center Plan preserved the State Street zoning envelope, terminating in a tall structure at the intersection of Washington Street. This has been admirably achieved in the forty stories of the New England Merchants National Bank Building, designed by Ed-

Chapel interior, Lindemann Mental Health Center. Paul Rudolph with Desmond & Lord; 1970.
Photo: Robert Perron

State Street Bank,
225 Franklin Street.
F. A. Stahl & Associates,
Hugh Stubbins and
Associates, and LeMessurier
Associates; 1966.
Photo: Phokion Karas

ward Larrabee Barnes with Emery Roth and Sons. A smooth granite skin with quietly proportioned windows demonstrates that a (small) skyscraper can become a background to lower buildings. The two-level ground floor preserves a view of Dock Square from the lobby mezzanine. The matching split-level top boasts an aerial garden, by Shurcliff and Merrill, with a breathtaking view of Boston Harbor. Alongside, Washington Mall is defined by the Old State House, the Richardsonesque Ames Building (1892) by Shepley, Rutan and Coolidge, and One Washington Mall, by Eduardo Catalano.

The buildings and spaces described above have all been designed under the architectural review process initiated by Edward J. Logue, Administrator of the Boston Redevelopment Authority (BRA) from 1960 to 1968. In return for land parcels assembled with federal funds plus the assurance of a comprehensive development program, private investors and public agencies were required to meet high architectural and planning standards. The State Street Bank Building, an early private venture that furthered the renewal plan by reinforcing the financial district, came under design review because it required zoning changes. Thirty-four stories of crisp concrete window units (with eight corner offices on each floor) are kind to the skyline and share in the view of a most visible city. The building, financed by British investors, was designed in a joint venture of F. A. Stahl, Hugh Stubbins, and William LeMessurier. With completion of the new State Street Bank Building and the Merchants, the plan to revitalize the financial district began to work. This prompted Walter Muir Whitehill, in *Boston—A Topographical History,* to laud the foresight of Logue and Pei, without which "State Street might have splattered itself all over the city"!

Tall buildings in the dense part of a

Ames Building. Shepley, Rutan & Coolidge; 1892. *Photo: Shepley, Bulfinch, Richardson & Abbott.*

First National Bank of Boston, 100 Federal Street. Campbell, Aldrich & Nulty; 1971. *Photo: Ezra Stoller*

nineteenth-century city present special problems. They need to be carefully related to street activity and to the older buildings at their base. They must also respond geometrically to the city at large in their upper parts. When the Customs House Tower was built during World War I on top of Ammi B. Young's Doric temple (1838), it was because critical materials could be obtained only for "alterations"; a case of preservation through bureaucratic semantics. It was already set in a generous square aligned with what used to be King Street, an integral part of the image of Boston. But at the other end of State Street, sheathed in dark aluminum instead of more compatible cementitious materials, the Boston Building (Emery Roth and Sons, with Pietro Belluschi) stands askew on a bleak plaza offering little to the pedestrian.

More interesting as a facet of urban design, if not architectural clarity, is the First National Bank Building, by Campbell, Aldrich and Nulty. Preempting a pivotal site at the heart of the financial district and creating a plaza supervised by a brooding bulge that can be discovered from all directions, the architects have rendered navigable a previously little-understood part of the city. The overhanging lines frame welcome vignettes of two smaller buildings. The Union-Warren Bank (formerly Blue Cross-Blue Shield) designed in 1953 by Paul Rudolph with Anderson, Beckwith and Haible, was a pioneer contemporary adventure in a tradition-minded city. A delicate precast and glass structure by Stahl-Bennett defines the corner of Congress, Federal, and Franklin streets and seems to be quietly wondering what this passion for architectural altitude is all about.

The Employers Building at the corner of Beacon and Tremont streets (Skidmore, Owings and Merrill) came under the BRA design review process. Its angled setback

Center: One Beacon Street (office building). Employers-Commercial Union Companies. Skidmore, Owings & Merrill; 1972.

Left: King's Chapel, Tremont and School streets. Peter Harrison; 1750.

Right: Old City Hall, 41-45 School Street. Gridley J. F. Bryant and Arthur Gilman; 1865. Conversion: Anderson Notter Associates; 1971.

Photo: Ezra Stoller

provides an excellent view of King's Chapel (1750; Peter Harrison) and receives the curving thrust of the Center Plaza Building. But its desolate, windswept base yawns with corporate arrogance, joining the "First" and the Boston Building in neglect of the street. From a distance, the upper volume offers no hint of alignment and, through its deeply recessed windows, provides an uncomfortable amount of irrelevant visual information.

Many of these problems have been addressed in the design of the headquarters of the National Shawmut Bank by The Architects Collaborative. A versatile system of precast panels permits the lower floors to relate to heights and conditions of neighboring buildings. Arcades and entrance penetrations are varied to meet the needs of a multiple-use structure. They are tied in to the building by outward sloping windows at the second floor that add intimacy and animation to the composition by reflecting pedestrian and street movement. A hospitable expanse of glass at the street level opposite 24 Federal Street incorporates the reflection of this fanciful Beaux Arts facade. It might otherwise have gone unnoticed; except perhaps by the wrecker's ball.

At the next level, deep recesses at irregular intervals contain planting boxes. They help to reduce the visual bulk of the base, while compensating inhabitants of the lower floors of the Shawmut and its neighbors for views otherwise curtailed by narrow streets. As the tower breaks free, the fenestration returns to a simple expression of office space not unlike that of the Merchants Bank. In its urbane agility, this design may well have been prophesied in the 1922 competition entry for the Chicago Tribune Building by Walter Gropius, a founder of The Architects Collaborative.

Continuing the policy of using public and semipublic construction to encourage private development, the Federal Reserve

National Shawmut Bank, 67 Milk Street. The Architects Collaborative; 1976. *Photo: Steve Rosenthal*

Building (Hugh Stubbins and Associates) across from South Station is planned to unite a growing central business district with a major transportation interchange. Complicated problems of circulation and security dictated the design of this aluminum-clad complex. Broad low-rise areas are required for receiving and processing functions. These are interconnected with the tower. One set of stairs and elevators serves in-house circulation while the other is for public and tenant use. The floors between are open for flexible planning. There is public access to a "money museum" (where some of the bank's operations can be observed), an auditorium, and a cafeteria.

The eyebrowlike spandrels between the windows are shaped to deflect the downdrafts that plague tall buildings, while an opening in the tall building mass is intended to equalize wind pressures well above street level. A heavily landscaped plaza with textured paving and benches has a "water wall" fountain 140 feet long.

Towering above Faneuil Hall and Dock Square, No. 60 State Street testifies to the success of success. Once the original zoning envelope had been compromised by the unanticipated height of the Boston Building, expectations for the rest of the street stimulated land costs "justifying" 650 feet for this parcel. After four architects, an environmental impact study, and turbulent hearings, a 500-foot tower designed by Skidmore, Owings and Merrill (Chicago) won the necessary approvals. A more sensitive approach, stepping back from Dock Square and resolving grade differences more informally in keeping with the character of Government Center, was lost in the process. The amorphous eleven-sided plan sidesteps the problem of aerial alignment, but all of that visual energy expanded by the vertical lattice of light granite is mocked by the effortless facade of the Merchants Bank Building.

Interior, Old City Hall, 41-45 School Street. Gridley J. F. Bryant and Arthur Gilman; 1865. Conversion: Anderson Notter Associates; 1971. *Photo: Carol Rankin*

Federal Reserve Bank, Atlantic Avenue and Summer Street. Hugh Stubbins and Associates; 1976.
Photo: Robert Harvey

Two serious questions are raised: Should the business district become a contest of architectural variations on a theme? Does that theme have to be "up"? The need for height and density is created by land values which are in turn established by expectations of even greater height and density. The City must come to terms with an inflationary trend which has yet to offer promised tax relief. While density in itself is not bad, several recent projects that have been conceived outside of the design review process show clearly that the public is the loser when too little skill, information, and insight is brought to bear. Without a firm public commitment to sound planning in a democratic framework, Boston will continue to carry the hidden cost of political expediency and short-term economics.

After several false starts, the plan for creating a shopping mall along Washington Street may become a reality by 1980. SEFRIUS, an international development firm, proposes to join with a major department store in construction of a hotel-office-retail complex that could pull together most of the loose ends in the congested central business district. The tallest building in Lafayette Place would be 410 feet, with others only slightly higher than adjacent structures. A continuous system of pedestrian ways and mini-plazas would connect hotel, offices, and a 1500-car garage with two subway stops and the shopping areas. The design is by I. M. Pei and Partners with Cossutta and Ponte.

Boston's experience with adaptive reuse has been rewarding. Besides Faneuil Hall–Quincy Market and the Sears Block and Crescent, granite mercantile structures along the waterfront are being preserved in an inventive residential-commercial format. The dowager Second Empire City Hall on School Street has been deftly converted to restaurant and office use by

Conversion, Record American Building, One Winthrop Square. Childs, Bertman, Tseckares; 1973. *Rendering: Childs, Bertman, Tseckares Associates, Inc.*

Anderson, Notter for Architectural Heritage, Inc. Designed by Gridley J. F. Bryant and Arthur Gilman in 1862, it supervises two important open spaces, making excellent company for King's Chapel and its tiny burial ground.

At the end of School Street, an addition to the Boston Five Cents Savings Bank resolves the line of a newly deflected street with a plaza created by the realignment. The appropriately energetic concrete and glass wall system complements its two venerable neighbors as well as the blunt classicism of the parent building. Old Corner Bookstore (1712), where literary lights of the mid-nineteenth century once met, was rescued in 1960; it now houses the in-town offices of the *Boston Globe.* Old South Meetinghouse (1729; Joshua Blanchard) had been saved from demolition many years before through public subscription. It has served since as a museum with a bookstore in the lower story. A short distance away in Winthrop Square, the Record American Building, designed by Fehmer and Emerson in 1873, has been restored to its Second Empire–Venetian Renaissance ebullience, also for office and commercial use. Renovations were by Child, Bertman & Tseckares for Neil St. John Raymond. The project reclaims a triangle of open space in front as a landscaped plaza.

In resonance with this hard-core preservation and/or extended use, other mature buildings have been rediscovered and transformed with paint, decent signs, and some long overdue respect. A visitor to Boston from any of the past three centuries would find familiar traces, if only in the names of streets and lanes. But few could reconstruct an image comparable to (or as relevant as) that provided by John Josselyn, a visitor from England in 1663. He wrote that

> . . . the houses are for the most part raised on the Sea-banks and wharfed out with great industry and cost, many of them standing on piles, close together on each side of the streets as in London, and furnished with many fair shops, their materials are Brick, Stone, Lime, handsomely contrived, with three meeting Houses or Churches, and a Town-house built upon pillars where the merchants may confer, in the Chambers above they keep their monthly Courts.
>
> Their streets are many and large, paved with pebble stone, and the Southside adorned with Gardens and Orchards. The town is rich and very populous, much frequented by strangers, here is the dwelling of their Governour. On the North-west and North-east two constant Fairs are kept for daily Traffick thereunto. On the South there is a small, but pleasant Common where the Gallants a little before Sun-set walk with their Marmalet-Madams, as we do in Morefields, &c till the nine a clock Bell rings them home to their respective habitations, when presently the Constables walk their rounds to see good orders kept, and to take up loose people (quoted in Walter Muir Whitehill, *Boston—A Topographical History).*

Indian River
INDIAN TREASURE
Citrus Fruit

Chapter 2
THE NORTH END

On the Bonner Map of 1722, the Shawmut Peninsula appears as an irregular shape, with what appears to be another peninsula extending from it toward the northeast. This part of Boston, long known as the North End, comes very close to the eastern tip of Charlestown. It was the logical point of departure for Paul Revere on the eighteenth of April 1775. With oars muffled by a flannel petticoat (reportedly still warm from its donor), he was rowed under the guns of H.M.S. *Somerset* to reach Charlestown and the road to Lexington and Concord. The map also explains why his friends, Captain Pulling and Robert Newman, used the lofty steeple of "Old North" Church from which to expose their signal lanterns.

By 1650, to get to the North End it was necessary to cross one of two drawbridges at Hanover and North streets. They spanned Mill Creek, a man-made channel dug through the marshes at the narrowest part of the neck to a large cove facing due north. The Mill Pond was created by filling in a strip of land on its outer rim (now Causeway Street) which was exposed at low tide. The power of Boston's high tides was sufficient to operate a gristmill, a sawmill, and a chocolate mill before 1700. Until this waterway was filled in the nineteenth century, the North End was an island. It became one again in the 1950s when the route selected for the Central Artery followed Canal and Blackstone streets, the line of the original creek.

Much of the Boston shoreline was low and subject to frequent flooding. From the beginning, settlers oriented to the sea for their livelihood and communication constructed piers and wharves in a pattern of filling and building that continued well into this century. At the northern tip of the North End, another of Boston's famous drumlins, Copp's Hill, was first named for the windmill on its summit. The present name comes from an early owner, William Copp, whose children's headstones are among the oldest in its burial ground. An ancient and irreverent name (and spelling) was "Corps Hill." Here among the neat rows of crumbling stones are the graves of Cotton and Increase Mather, Richard Newman, and Edmund Hart, the builder of the frigate *Constitution*. The grave of Prince Hall (and of his wife, Sarah Kitchery) is marked with a monument commemorating his leadership as a member of the black community. British marksmen, armed with the deadly "Brown Bess" and not without provocation, paid their respects to the monuments of Daniel Malcom and his wife. The pockmarked stones identify Malcom as "a true son of Liberty—a Friend to the Publick—an enemy to oppression and one of the foremost in opposing the Revenue Acts on America."

The present system of major streets below approximates the original land holdings. While houses were clustered near the water and along the two main ways, large gardens and estates were not uncommon. Subsequent subdivisions produced a patchwork of tiny lots, leaving us with street names such as Moon, Sun Court, Snow Hill, and Salutation. Other

Haymarket Square
Open Market
Photo: Phokion Karas

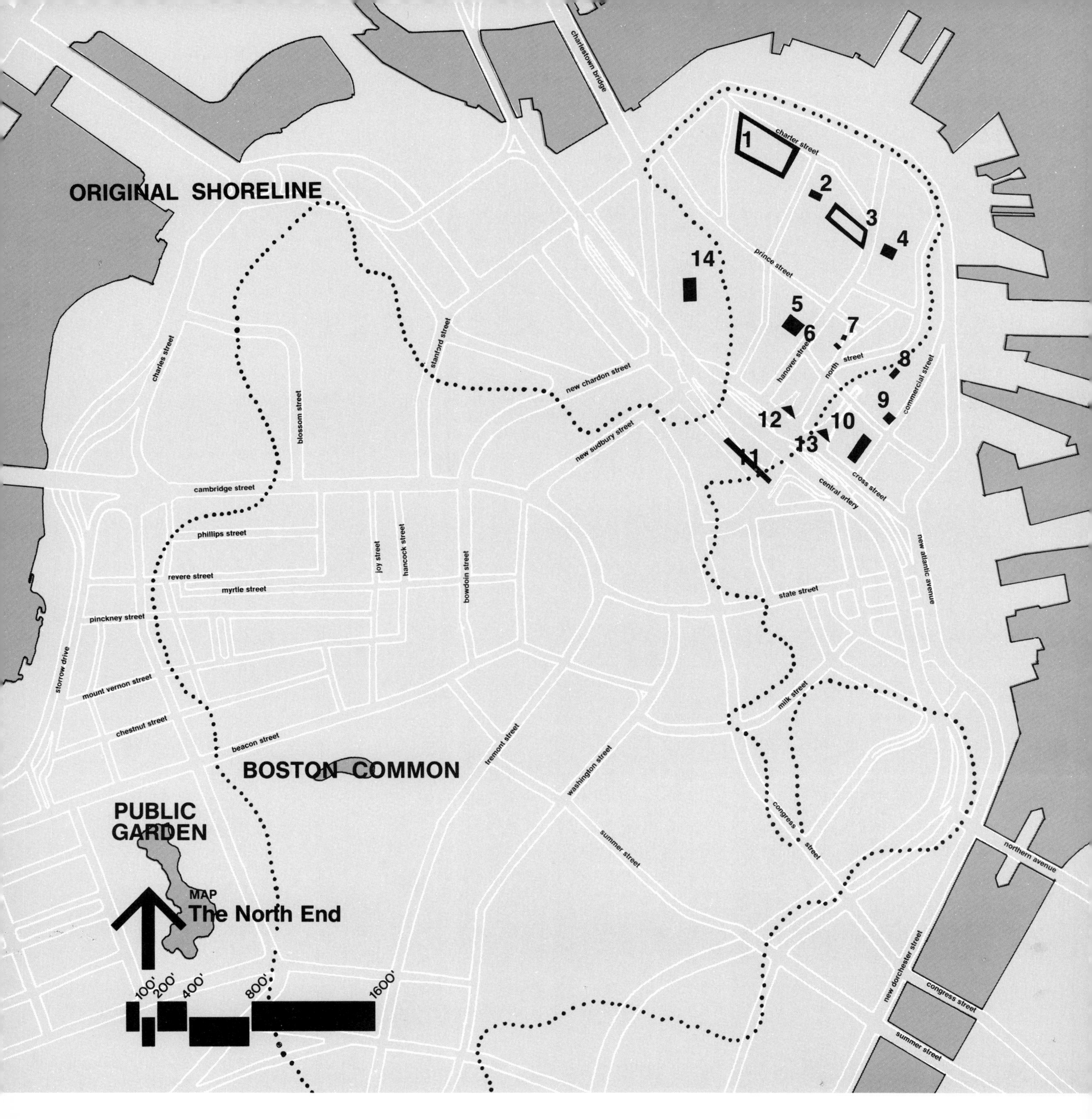

ORIGINAL SHORELINE
charlestown bridge
charter street
prince street
hanover street
north street
commercial street
1
2
3
4
5
6
7
8
9
10
11
12
13
14
stanford street
new chardon street
new sudbury street
blossom street
charles street
cambridge street
phillips street
revere street
myrtle street
joy street
hancock street
bowdoin street
pinckney street
storrow drive
mount vernon street
chestnut street
beacon street
central artery
cross street
new atlantic avenue
state street
milk street
tremont street
washington street
summer street
congress
street
northern avenue
new dorchester street
congress street
summer street
BOSTON COMMON
PUBLIC GARDEN
MAP
The North End
100'
200'
400'
800'
1600'

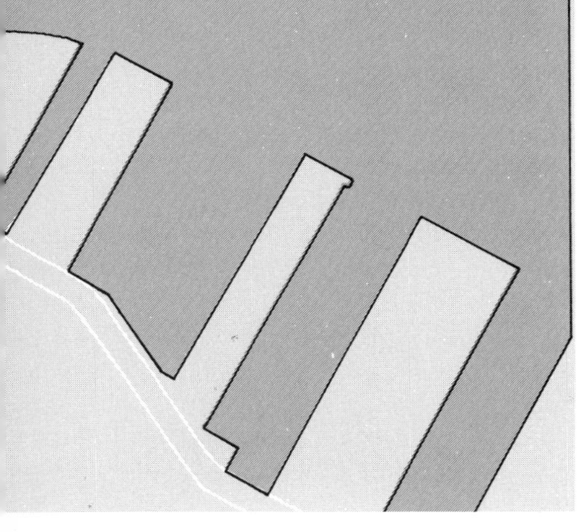

1. Copps Hill Cemetery

2. Christ Church (Old North)
   193 Salem Street
   William Price; 1723

3. Paul Revere Mall
   Hanover Street
   Planned by the City of Boston; 1933

4. St. Stephen's Church
   (originally New North Church)
   401 Hanover Street
   Charles Bulfinch; 1804

5. North End Branch Library
   25 Parmenter Street
   Carl Koch & Associates; 1965

6. Moses Pierce-Hichborn House
   North Square
   c. 1711

7. Paul Revere House
   North Square
   c. 1677

8. Cast Iron Building
   (now McLauthlin Elevator Company)
   120 Fulton Street
   Possibly Daniel Badger; c. 1850

9. Commercial Block Building
   128-42 Commercial Street
   Gridley J. F. Bryant; 1856

10. Mercantile Wharf Building
    75-117 Commercial Street
    Gridley J. F. Bryant; 1857
    Conversion to Residential:
    John Sharratt & Associates; 1976

11. Haymarket Square
    Open Market

12. Sumner Tunnel

13. Callahan Tunnel

14. St. Mary's Church
    Thatcher and Endicott streets
    P. C. Keeley; 1877

Paul Revere House, North Square, c. 1677. *Photo: Steven M. Stone*

names have been lost: Paddy's Alley, Beer Lane, Gay Alley, Black Horse Lane, Old Way, and (so narrow a drunken man could not fall either to the right or left) Back Alley. A major fire in 1676 required the selectmen to establish new street lines. But the pattern of rebuilt dwellings, shops, taverns, wharves, and meetinghouses seems not to have been greatly simplified.

North Square was only a block from the waterfront when John Jeffs built his house at No. 19 shortly after the fire. It was on the site of Increase Mather's (Second Church) parsonage. Although now enshrined as the Paul Revere house, its present appearance is closer to that of the original structure. By the time Revere moved in with his large family in 1770, it is believed that there were three stories (instead of the present two) and the windows were double-hung with rectangular panes. A 1790 census lists the house as three-story with 630 square feet and seventeen windows. It is recorded that Revere displayed some of his politically inflammatory prints (including that of the Massacre) in these windows, illuminating the oiled paper with lanterns from behind. The house was restored in 1908 by the architect Joseph E. Chandler.

The diamond-pane leaded-glass casement windows and carved pendants stimulate thoughts of what this square might have been like against a backdrop of tall masts and drying sails, infused with the smells of the sea, and accompanied by the cry of gulls and din of a busy port. Streets were lined with steep gables and overhanging second stories, fenced-in gardens, and hand-carved commercial iconography. We have lost bright representations of "Heart and Crown," "Three Nuns and a Comb," "Brazen Head," and "Tun and Bacchus." But the blue ball identifying the chandlery of Benjamin Franklin's father, Josiah, which hung at the corner of Hanover and Union streets, can still be seen in the Old State House Museum.

Boston did not remain a medieval city for long. Next door to the Revere House, the Moses Pierce–Hichborn House reflects the new affluence of the seaport town as well as a growing concern for fire. Moses Pierce, a glazier, was one of those who complied with a law passed in 1693 requiring brick or stone construction and slate or tile roofs. His house had the first hip roof recorded in Boston and one of the earliest in the colonies. Horizontal brick watercourses stepped out at the floor lines, a prim three-course running bond, and flat arch lintels over twenty-four light double-hung sashes are in the idiom of the English Renaissance. It stands in sharp contrast to its rustic neighbor. The house was literally "mined" out of a wall of five-story tenements that had closed in around it over the years and was lovingly restored inside and out by Sidney and Charles Strickland in 1953.

Nathaniel Hichborn, cousin of Paul Revere, bought the house in 1781. A shipbuilder like his father, he enjoyed with Revere the status available to the artisan class. If his house seems more elaborate than Revere's, there were two of the greatest Boston houses of the time standing in this square. One, that of Governor Hutchinson, had been built before 1700 by John Foster. It was wrecked by a mob unhappy with the Stamp Act in 1765. The other, a three-story brick house with twenty-six rooms, was built by the merchant William Clark soon after the Hichborn House.

Called Clark Square at first, North Square took its name from a wooden "North Church" which was converted into firewood by the besieged British army during the winters of '75 and '76. The other "North Church," actually Christ Church on Salem Street, was opened in 1723. Its steeple was not added until 1740. Church records show that William Price, book- and printseller, vestryman, warden, and for a time organist of the church, took an active part in its design. He had been born in England; through his business trips there and his drawings and prints he was familiar with the London of Sir Christopher Wren. While it is customary to think of much-copied Christ Church as a prototype of Colonial architecture, the 1961 Final Report of the Boston National His-

Christ Church (Old North), 193 Salem Street. William Price; 1723. *Photo: Phokion Karas*

St. Stephen's Church (originally New North Church), 401 Hanover Street. Charles Bulfinch; 1804. Restoration: Chester Wright; 1965. *Photo: Steven M. Stone*

toric Sites Commission leaves no doubt as to its stylistic origins:

> The resemblance of the interior to that of St. James in Piccadilly is recognized. . . . Less well known is its likeness to a small London Church on Queen Victoria Street near the Thames that was destroyed by blitzkrieg in World War II. The church was called "St. Andrews-by-the-Wardrobe with St. Anne, Blackfriars." . . . A retired rector of *Christ Church* on visiting St. Anne's in 1936 reported: "You enter, and practically you are in OLD NORTH—center aisle, side aisles, box pew, galleries, great east window, organ up in west gallery." Two of the original proprietors of *Christ Church,* it may be significant to note, had been parishioners of St. Anne's before emigrating to Massachusetts.

It is interesting to reflect upon the educational impact of this building on generations of colonists separated from the physical evidence of their Anglican heritage. The report notes the parallel side gallery arrangement "in sharp contrast to that of the conventional 'meeting house' from seventeenth-century New England that had a raised pulpit on one long side with galleries on both ends and the opposite side." Old North speaks with the unquestioned authority of the church of the Mathers. But Providence has dealt harshly with its steeple on the occasion of two hurricanes; one in 1804 and another in 1954. The logical, if not documented architect for the first restoration was Charles Bulfinch. His version, some fifteen feet shorter than its predecessor, was replaced with a replica of the original by Charles R. Strickland in 1955.

Steeples were built telescope fashion; the first wooden stage was passed up through the church structure (or in this case a tall brick base). Successively smaller stages, then the "lantern," and finally the spire, were built on the ground and

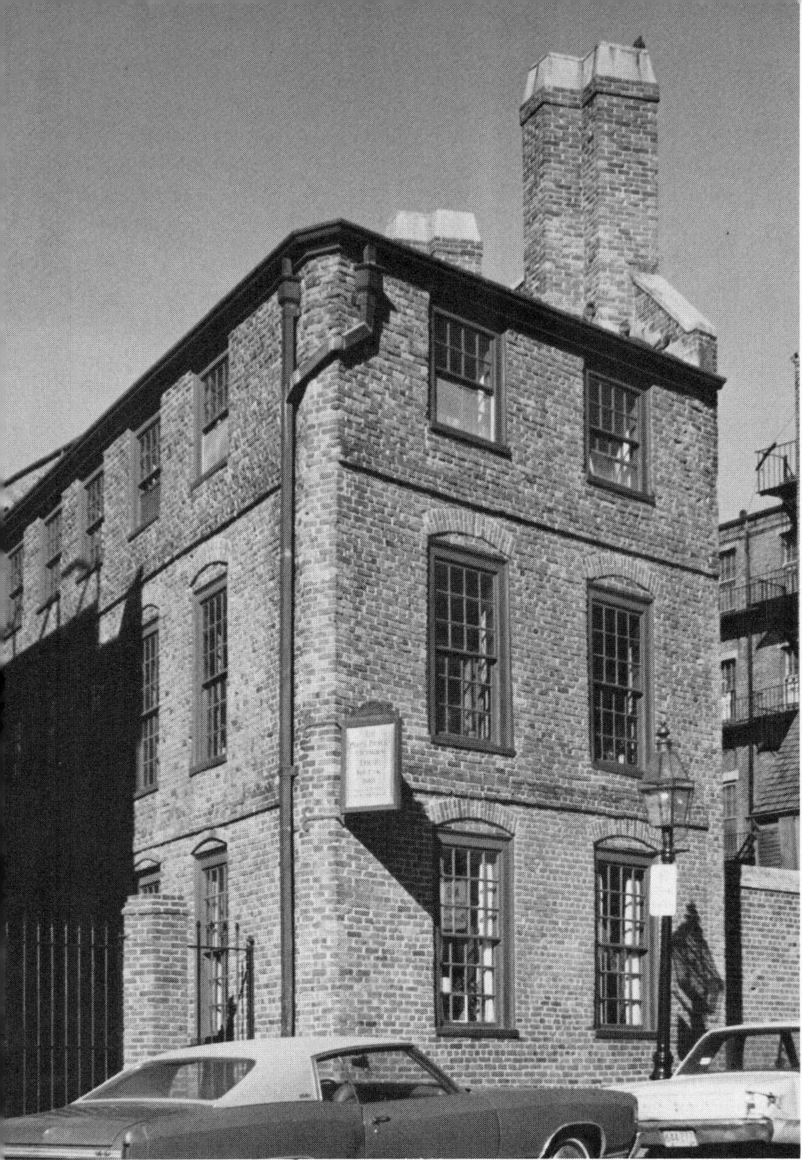

Moses Pierce-Hichborn House, North Square, c. 1711. *Photo: Phokion Karas*

Paul Revere Mall, Hanover Street. Planned by the City of Boston; 1933. *Photo: Steven M. Stone.*

pushed or pulled through into place. The vertical finials at each corner are ornamental reminders of the concealed overlapping wood framework. In 1955, however, they sent to the Portsmouth (N.H.) Navy Yard for the tallest crane in the area to finish the job. The spire is capped with its original weather vane—a flower and pot, banner, "blew" ball, and a five-pointed star.

The North End was never quite the same after the Revolution. Residents remaining loyal to the Crown had fled to Canada or England. In 1784 there were 680 houses and six meetinghouses. Although the first factory had been built in 1718, the decade prior to 1800 saw a marked increase in industry. Along the waterfront streets of the north side there were factories for brass and iron, cannon and bells, and earthenware. Families of substance moved to the latest suburb, Beacon Hill, and new Americans arrived to fill the crowded sections of the old town.

A corresponding shift in religious affiliation led to an intriguing architectural charade. In 1799 Bulfinch donated the design of the Church (later Cathedral) of the Holy Cross on Franklin Street. Soon afterward he designed, using very nearly the same plan, another in the North End on Hanover Street. This was the third in a series of churches referred to as "New North." The parishioners had already enjoyed a denominational rivalry with the Anglican ministrations of "Old North." With a shift in the Catholic population to the (new) South End in the mid-nineteenth century, a new Cathedral of the Holy Cross was built on Washington Street. The Bulfinch structure, by then in the business district, was razed; the Diocese bought its sister church, New North. Renamed St. Stephen's, it was raised a half story and moved back twelve feet when

North End Branch Library, 25 Parmenter Street. Carl Koch & Associates; 1965. *Photo: Phokion Karas*

Hanover Street was widened in 1870. The cupola and other details were altered to look like the first Holy Cross Church. Richard Cardinal Cushing had it restored to the original design (if not location) in 1965. Among the architectural artifacts recovered during reconstruction by the firm of Chester Wright were copper sheathing and nails manufactured by Paul Revere. St. Stephen's is the only Bulfinch church still standing in Boston.

With or without the canal, the North End has always maintained a separate social identity. Dr. Edward Renolds, who was seven years old in 1800 recalls the political and religious rivalry between the North and (old) South ends. For years challenging processions with effigies of the Pope, the Devil, and the Pretender had ended in street violence. This was ritualized by children, quick to adopt the prejudices of their parents: "the old feud—as old as the town itself—was the occasion of a regular battle every Thursday and Saturday afternoon—not infrequently the occasion of very serious injury to wind and limb." (Whitehill, *Boston—A Topographical History*)

After the Civil War, the large Irish and Jewish population was joined by immigrants from Italy. Today the community is predominantly Italian-American. A steady process of tenementation over the past century has complicated the already tight pattern of narrow side streets and alleys. Although one of the most densely populated urban districts in the country, the North End has suffered fewer indignities than other parts of the city. Social coherence and vitality have helped to preserve its character. For open space resourceful residents have substituted intensely cultivated side yards, roof gardens, window boxes, and fire escapes where tomatoes and *arragetta* are harvested from flowerpots. While banners of laundry fly

Cast Iron Building (now McLauthlin Elevator Company), 120 Fulton Street. Possibly Daniel Badger; c. 1850. *Photo: Steven M. Stone*

from the rooftops in Charlestown and South Boston in the North End, narrow spaces between tall walkups are converted into bright heraldic halls on washday. In 1933 enough space for a brick-paved mall was cleared between St. Stephen's and the south end of "Old North." Although formally dedicated to Paul Revere, it is nicknamed "The Prado." A border of brick tenements, historical inscriptions, indigenous graffiti, benches and trees, and a dashing equestrian statue of Revere by Cyrus Dallin all monitor the continuous movement of children at play, as well as the spirited conversation and repose of their elders.

Perhaps the price of this autonomy was progress in the form of a writhing, technically inadequate elevated highway amputating the North End from a substantial portion of its market area. The weekend pushcart market remains with the Blackstone Block and Faneuil Markets (see Chapter 3). What is left of Haymarket Square on the northern side of the Artery persists as a bustling outdoor market where it is possible to purchase an astonishing variety of foodstuffs. Most have somehow managed to escape sterile plastic packaging and, presumably, the scientific extraction of flavor and aroma. The business of the district spills down Hanover Street (the main street since before 1645) and filters back into a labyrinth of intimate side streets. Specialized shops in keeping with Old World tradition serve a knowledgeable clientele: *groceria, trattoria, patisseria, salumaria,* and a *pizzeria,* the product of which has yet to be equaled this side of the Atlantic. The fine art of dining out Italian style is further enhanced by an opportunity to take dessert in a separate shop filled with the pungent aroma of almond, the chromatic delight of traditional pastries, and the satisfying (if aggressive) gurgle of an *espresso* machine.

In late summer, under lighted arcades that span the main streets from the market to the harbor, religious fiestas bring visitors from far and wide. And of course the

Mercantile Wharf Building, 75-117 Commercial Street. Gridley J. F. Bryant; 1857. Conversion: John Sharratt & Associates; 1976. *Drawing by Paul Sun.*

Columbus Day parade terminates here in serious rejoicing of the fact that 1492 came before 1620. In her landmark work, *Life and Death of the City,* Jane Jacobs eulogized the North End as an ideal, healthy "slum" and expressed concern for its future in an age of urban renewal. Bostonians, however, had long known and admired the district as one of the safest and most hospitable parts of their city. But it is more than surface charm that holds the fierce loyalty of its residents. Overcrowding, new affluence, educational opportunities, and the automobile caused many younger families to evaporate into the suburbs after World War II. The potential for new housing together with revitalization of the Faneuil Market area and waterfront will bring many of them back. A critical lack of housing for the elderly is being met with units on Lewis, Commercial, and Richmond streets. The Boston Redevelopment Authority has sold old but solid buildings taken during renewal of the nearby waterfront to residents for rehabilitation. Local groups such as the Paul Revere Associates have redone several apartment buildings. A nineteen million dollar Galleria may soon rise from the rubble of the Quincy Market Storage Warehouse. A project of the North End Businessmen's Development Corporation, it will contain elderly housing, low- and middle-income apartments, shops, markets, parking for 450 cars, and an Italian Cultural Center and waterfront park.

Directly across from the Navy Yard berth of "Old Ironsides," an existing waterfront playground was substantially enlarged in 1971. It now has a popular indoor skating rink whose design by Zaldastani Associates (with Rich and Bennett) has shaken off the curse of that giant "Quonset hut" image so familiar to the greater Boston area. Other play spaces have begun to appear in unexpected vacant lots, and a new community garage may allow the

Copps Hill Cemetery. *Photo: Phokion Karas*

narrow sidewalks to be used once again for their intended purpose.

Starting in the 1930s, structures abutting the Old North Church have been judiciously weeded out in the interest of fire protection for this priceless national landmark. A happy by-product was the exposure and restoration of the Ebenezer Clough House, a contemporary to that of Moses Pierce. In 1955 Congress approved a study anticipating a National Historic Sites park for Boston. The *Final Report,* published in 1960, is an indispensable compendium of the conditions and events leading up to the Revolution. It made recommendations for acquisition of, or cooperative federal agreements with, the Old State House, Shirley-Eustis House (see Chapter 8), Old North Church, the houses at North Square, Faneuil Hall (and Quincy Market), Bunker Hill, and Dorchester Heights in South Boston. Creation of the National Park has now been authorized by Congress and funds have been appropriated. The concept will be expanded to include a section of the Navy Yard in Charlestown (see Chapter 8). Planning for formal agreements and interpretive programs is now in progress.

Much of the feeling of the North End has been encapsulated in its branch library, designed in 1965 by Carl Koch & Associates. An inconspicuous brick wall surrounds a top-lighted Roman atrium lined with plants, Etruscan ceramics, sculpture, a fountain, and a bas-relief of Dante. This popular landmark on Parmenter Street has a special meaning to those whose assimilation into a new land has been through language and literature, without having to abandon their own ancient cultural heritage.

Chapter 3
THE WATERFRONT

Aerial of Waterfront
Photo: Aerial Photos of New England, Inc.

From the cupola of Faneuil Hall, Deacon Shem Drowne's grasshopper weather vane has surveyed its domain for well over 230 years. Its green glass eye once saw docks, ships, and open water where the John F. Fitzgerald Expressway now commemorates the arrogance of federal highway programs. The waters of Town Cove lapped at the seawall a few feet from the eastern end of Faneuil Hall. To the right, past Fort Hill (about where the State Street Bank Building rises today), then back along Batterymarch Street toward the corner of Washington and Essex, there were wharves and open water. Griffin's, later Liverpool Wharf, where fragrant chests of Tory tea were submerged to principle, lies itself buried under the Central Artery, east of the intersection of Broad and Pearl streets. In the other direction, wharves and piers continued around the North End, some forty in all. This can be best understood while standing at the eastern edge of City Hall Plaza. On a market day, Dock Square (recently refurbished) would have been crowded with farmers' carts filled with produce brought to town across Roxbury Neck, or by boat from the surrounding countryside. Through his gift of a market house, Peter Faneuil was offering the townspeople an opportunity to compare quality and price. At the same time it would free other sections of the growing town of the nuisance and responsibility of public sanitation caused by unregulated trading centers. He decided to add a second-floor meeting hall for town affairs at the last minute. The two-and-one-half-story hall, built from a design by Jonathan Smibert (a portrait painter), followed the general plan of European markets of the period. This pattern of combining commercial and civic activities was already established. The Second Town House (now the Old State House) at the head of State (King) Street had rooms for the Governor and his Council, the House of Representatives, and the Superior and Inferior Courts on the second floor. The Secretary of the Province and County Register of Deeds were on the first floor; but the larger portion of this level was left open as a "Walk for Merchants." Here the town's important business was transacted.

The interiors of the Town House and Faneuil Hall were burned in 1747 and 1763, respectively. The fact that they were both immediately rebuilt (rather than replaced with inferior structures) suggests that such a standard is not inconceivable for today. The details of the roles that each of these great examples of Colonial architecture played in the events leading to the Revolution are so intertwined with social and personal history that the euphemism coined for Faneuil Hall, "Cradle of Liberty," cannot be amplified in less than ten thousand words. The scale of Bulfinch's enlargement of Faneuil Hall in 1805 to about three times its original size is deceptive. Smibert's hall, with its center cupola, lends a certain intimacy to the orations of Warren and Otis. While the market was being rebuilt after the fire of 1747, public meetings were held in Old South Church, to which larger space the patriots repaired

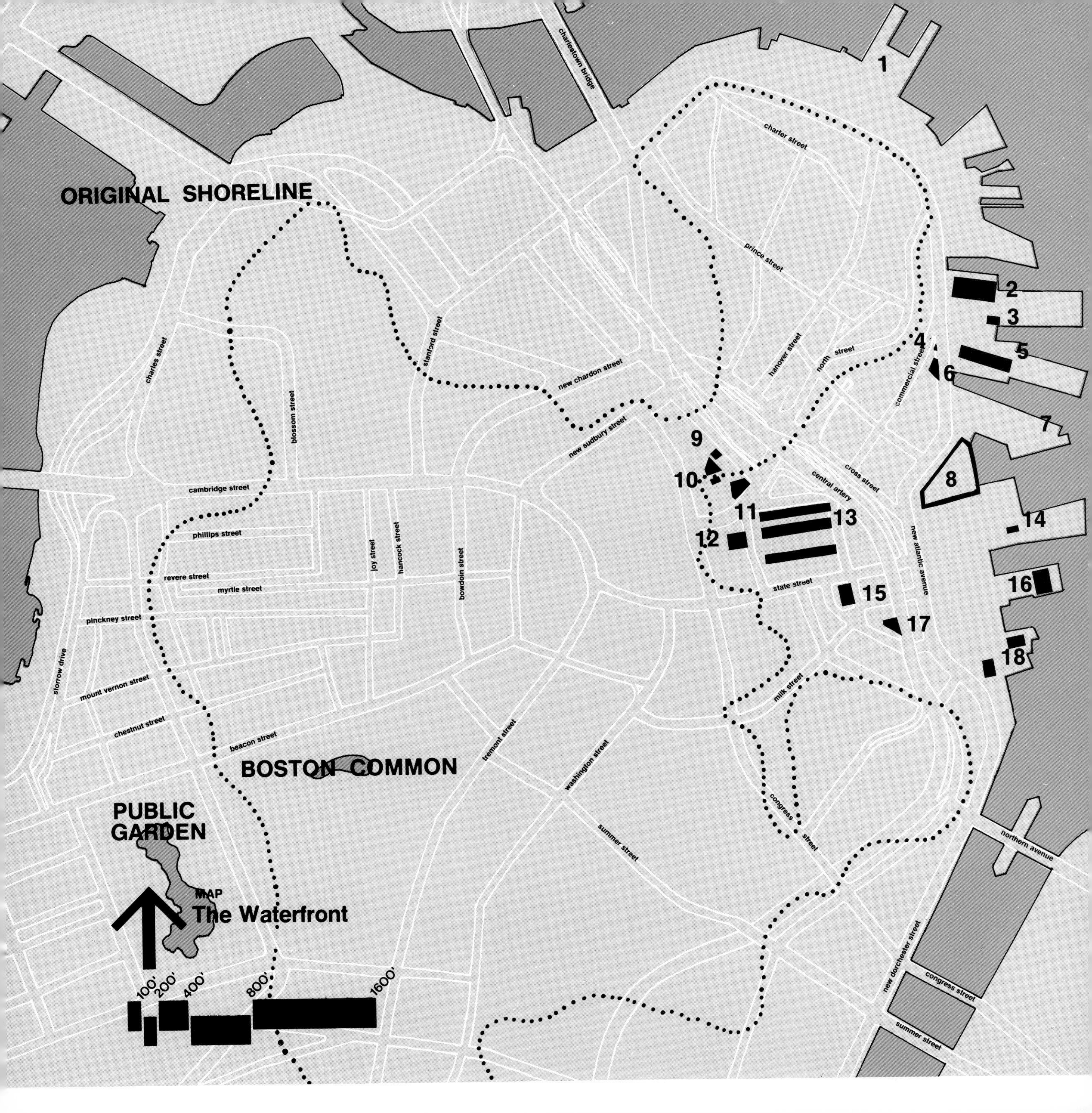

ORIGINAL SHORELINE
charlestown bridge
charter street
prince street
hanover street
north street
commercial street
stanford street
new chardon street
new sudbury street
charles street
blossom street
cambridge street
phillips street
revere street
myrtle street
pinckney street
joy street
hancock street
bowdoin street
storrow drive
mount vernon street
chestnut street
beacon street
central artery
cross street
new atlantic avenue
state street
milk street
congress street
tremont street
washington street
summer street
northern avenue
new dorchester street
congress street
summer street
BOSTON COMMON
PUBLIC GARDEN
MAP
The Waterfront
100'
200'
400'
800'
1600'
1
2
3
4
5
6
7
8
9
10
11
12
13
14
15
16
17
18

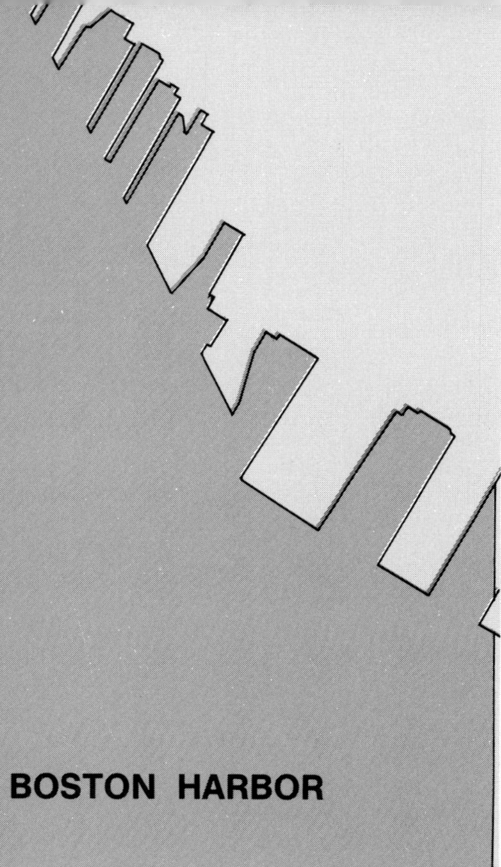

BOSTON HARBOR

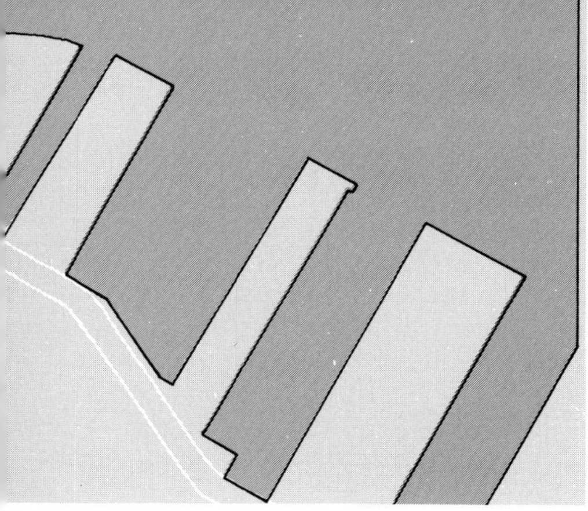

1. Coast Guard Station

2. The Galleria
Proposed Retail Complex
Gerard R. Cugini; 1977

3. Pilot House 1863
Conversion to Restaurant and Offices
Carl Koch; 1971

4. Sunoco Station
Anderson Notter Associates; 1970

5. Prince Building (conversion to apartments)
63 Atlantic Avenue
Anderson Notter Associates; 1966-69

6. Lewis Wharf Granite Buildings, c. 1836
Renovation (first phase):
Carl Koch and Associates; 1971-

7. Commercial Wharf Warehouses
Off 80 Atlantic Avenue
1826
Renovation into apartments; 1954-68

8. Francis S. Christian Memorial Park
Sasaki, Dawson, DeMay; 1976

9. Ebenezer Hancock House
Oldest extant brick building in Boston
Marshall Street
c. 1760

10. Capen House
Union Oyster House, 1714

11. Blackstone Block
Congress Street

12. Faneuil Hall
Dock Square
John Smibert; 1740-42
Reconstruction: 1762/63
Enlargement: Charles Bulfinch; 1805/6

13. Quincy Market and
North and South Market Street buildings
Alexander Parris; 1824-26
Partial restoration:
F.A. Stahl & Associates
Conversion:
Benjamin Thompson Associates; 1976

14. Chart House and Custom House Block; c. 1845
Long Wharf
Conversion to Restaurant and Offices
Anderson Notter Associates; 1974

15. Custom House
State Street and India Wharf
Ammi B. Young; 1838
Tower: Peabody and Stearns; 1913-15

16. New England Aquarium
Central Wharf
Cambridge Seven Associates; 1969

17. Grain and Flour Exchange Building
(originally Chamber of Commerce Building)
177 Milk Street
Shepley, Rutan & Coolidge; 1890-92

18. Harbor Towers (apartments)
India and Rowes wharves, Atlantic Avenue
I. M. Pei & Partners; 1973

New England Aquarium, Central Wharf. Cambridge Seven Associates; 1969. Lobby Addition/Auditorium; 1973. *Photo: Steve Rosenthal*

for major assemblies. General Burgoyne's revenge for the participation of Old South in the rebellion was to have it stripped of most of the interior finish, layer the floor with gravel, and establish a riding academy for his Dragoons. Faneuil Hall fared better as a bivouac for soldiers and a theatre for civilized performances during the occupation.

Just north of the market was Creek Square, now better known as the Blackstone Block. These isolated structures represent four centuries of Boston building. The oldest is probably the Union Oyster House, which has been used as an oyster bar continuously since 1826. But its brick watercourses, flat arch lintels, and gambrel roof date it before 1714. Here, above the dry goods establishment of Thomas Capen, the *Massachusetts Spy* was published from 1771 to 1775 by Isaiah Thomas. This "turbulently" patriotic paper, avidly read throughout the colonies, was so effective that the press had to be moved secretly to Worcester two nights before the encounter at Concord Bridge. Thomas is considered the father of the American printing and publishing business. Close by, the Ebenezer Hancock House was first owned by Ebenezer's brother, John, who inherited it from their uncle, Thomas Hancock. Ebenezer was made paymaster general of the Eastern Department of the Continental Army. While using this house he had the enviable task of caring for a pile of over two million silver crowns on loan from King Louis XVI at the behest of Benjamin Franklin. A shoe store operated continuously in the building from 1796 until very recently.

Across the street a round stone ball and trough, once used as a paint mill by Thomas Child, has been embedded in the corner of the building that replaced the painter's house. Called the "Boston Stone," it was used as a reference point to measure distances from the town. The occupations of other residents of Creek Square, according to an 1805 census, included one mariner, retailer, mantua-maker, tobacconist, conger, hauler, stone cutter, confectioner, shipwright, blacksmith, fisherman, shoemaker, housewright, tailor, coachman, glazier, tinplate worker, milliner, pilot, saddler, sailmaker, and brass founder, as well as three cordwainers, four boardinghouse owners, and ten laborers.

In addition to shards of Federal period structures, some badly "Colonialized" storefronts, and salvageable cast-iron facades, there is a tall mansard store and loft building. At the corner of Union and North streets, PARD Team has reworked the brick exteriors of two undistinguished twentieth-century buildings with sensitivity and skill. The area beyond Faneuil Hall around Town Cove had deteriorated to such an extent that in 1825 Mayor Josiah Quincy launched Boston's first urban renewal project. He tore down an intriguing triangular warehouse, filled in the cove, and built an addition to the marketplace. The cost of landfill and six new streets was paid for by sale (at public auction) of forty-seven granite-faced market buildings in two rows flanking what is now called Quincy Market. All were designed by Al-

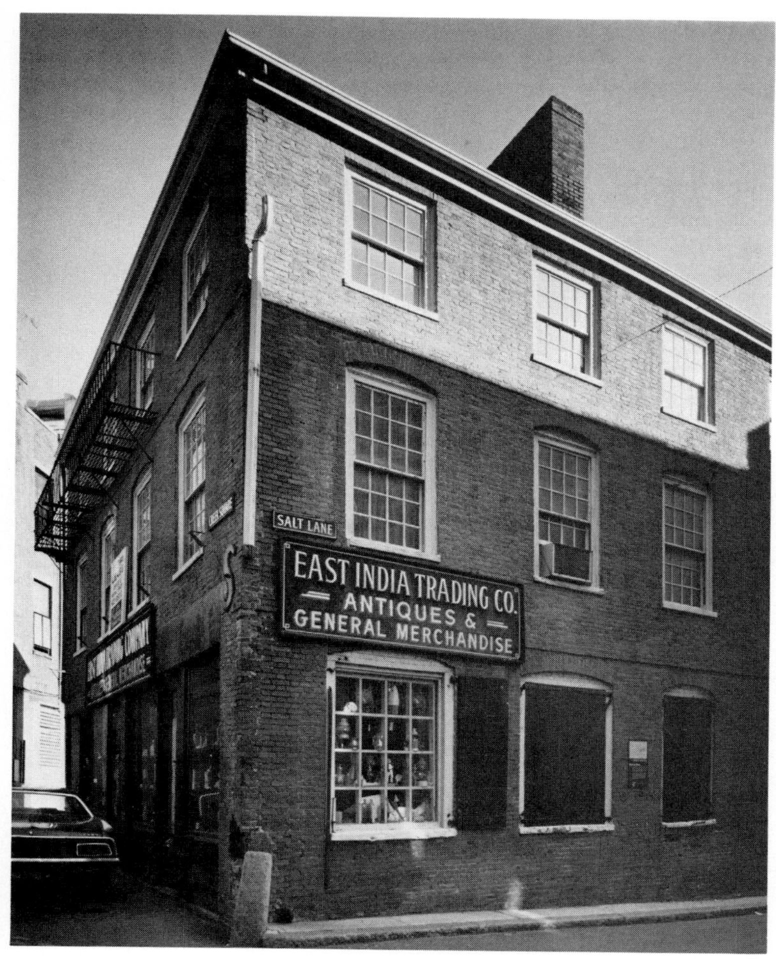

Ebenezer Hancock House, Marshall Street, c. 1760. *Photo: Phokion Karas*

Thomas Capen House, now Union Oyster House; 1714. *Photo: Phokion Karas*

exander Parris, but the units comprising North and South Market blocks were built by individual owners to Parris's design for the overall project. The policies of public acquisition of land, competitive bidding for parcels, comprehensive urban design, design controls, and deed restrictions (or zoning) were used one hundred forty years later to restore the same area.

One block to the south, King Street extended as Long Wharf from the Town House nearly two thousand feet into the harbor. To protect shipping from the Dutch and French, a Barricado was built during the 1680s. It extended from the North Battery at Fort Hill, through the midpoint of Long Wharf, to a spot near the present Lewis Wharf. Not having been needed for this purpose, the narrow fortification was allowed to deteriorate over the years. But it established a line of ownership within which the original financial backers could fill and construct more wharves. The line of the Barricado survives in the (slightly altered) path of Atlantic Avenue. Where it crossed Long Wharf, a T-shaped wharf remained until its pilings were condemned in the 1960s. Romantic loft apartments above a motley collection of shops and offices were in demand during the last decades of this soggy landmark's existence.

The number of ships arriving from foreign ports grew from about eight hundred per year in 1800 to nearly fifteen hundred in 1830, with twice again as much coastwise shipping. Samuel Eliot Morison, in *The Maritime History of Massachusetts,* states that in 1844 "fifteen vessels entered and left the harbor for every day in the year." The Broad Street Association, a group of merchants led by Uriah Cotting, and partners such as the ubiquitous Harrison Gray Otis, began to bring the waterfront to life. Starting in 1805, with Bulfinch as their architect, they built India Wharf. Half of this formidable brick block was lost when Atlantic Avenue was put through; the other half to clear a site for high-rise apartments. Morison's description of its neighbor will suffice for both:

Central Wharf, built in 1819, with fifty-four brick stores running down its center for a

Faneuil Hall, Dock Square.
John Smibert; 1742
Reconstruction; 1763
Enlargement: Charles Bulfinch; 1806
Rendering: Benjamin Thompson Associates

quarter of a mile, was a fitting companion to India Wharf. In its upper stories were three great halls for auction sales, and in its octagonal cupola the headquarters of the "Semaphore Telegraph Company," to which the approach of vessels was signalled from Telegraph Hill in Hull. Below, as on India Wharf, were warehouses, wholesale stores, and counting-rooms of leading mercantile firms. Here cargoes from all parts of the world were bought and sold and accounted for, without the aid of steam heat, clacking typewriter, and office system. An odor of tar and hemp, mingled with spicy suggestions from the merchandise stored above, pervaded everything. Respectable men clerks (*female* clerks, sir?—would you have female sailors?) on high stools were constantly writing in the calf-bound letter-books, ledgers, and waste-books, or delving in the neat wooden chests that enclosed the records of each particular vessel. Owners, some crabbed and crusty, others with the manners of a merchant prince, received you with blazing open fires of hickory or cannel coal, in rooms adorned with portraits and half-models of vessels. Through the small-paned windows one could see the firm's new ship being rigged under the owner's eye.

The Faneuil Hall Marketplace c. 1850. *Engraving: Benjamin Thompson Associates*

Commercial and Lewis wharves to the north were built of granite in the second quarter of the nineteenth century. In the Broad Street–Fort Hill section, Morison places the "proletarian quarters" where sailors' boardinghouses and dance halls could be found, as well as the homes of "longshoremen, truckmen, and Irish laborers." If Boston itself is a good place to visit, many of the sources from which this book is drawn are equally absorbing. A visit with Admiral Morison through his *One Boy's Boston* and the *Maritime History* can be a rich and unforgettable experience.

The decline of the clipper ship and coastwise trade, together with the transition to gleaming liners and sooty freighters, spelled the end of Boston's illustrious waterfront establishment. The last ferries ran to East Boston just before World War II. The fishing fleet, with marginal exceptions, moved to new facilities in South Boston. An excursion line ran to Nantasket Beach and to Provincetown, and for a while to Yarmouth, Nova Scotia. But the scene after the war was that of neglected warehouses half-filled with shops and services incidentally, if at all, related to the sea. Upper floors were tenanted by the desiccated remains of sea gulls behind a collage of broken windowpanes. Tin structures with caved-in roofs rattled on crumbling pilings. Little of the memory of a great seaport remained.

In 1962 the Boston Redevelopment Authority made a study of the waterfront-market area with financial assistance from the Greater Boston Chamber of Commerce. A plan was evolved to strengthen the area as a residential community, bolster its neighboring districts, attract new commercial interests, and reclaim the waterfront for recreational purposes. This required removal of an ancient connector railroad between North and South stations and relocation of part of Atlantic Avenue to make room for a park. Two forty-story apartment towers, with a seven-story parking garage (I. M. Pei & Partners; 1973) were built on the site of India and Rowes wharves. The New England Aquarium (Cambridge Seven; 1969) was allocated the site of Central Wharf for its impressive offering of cavorting baby seals, a five-story glass fish tank populated with representatives of temperate waters, and a floating amphitheatre, the *Discovery*. This recent addition offers daily demonstrations of the intelligence of the bottle-nosed dolphin, as amusing as they are educational.

But by far the most compelling aspect of the new waterfront is the rehabilitation of its hoard of utilitarian structures. An early conversion was that of the Prince Spaghetti Company on Commercial Street to apartments by Anderson, Notter. This firm also designed the free-form filling station to the north. Carl Koch & Associates were both developer and architect for Lewis Wharf, which has been converted into

Harbor Towers (apartments), India and Rowes wharves, Atlantic Avenue. I. M. Pei & Partners; 1973.
Photo: I. M. Pei

shops and condominiums. Next door, the Winery, also by Koch, offers a big drink of the harbor to its diners and the lucky tenants of the Pilot House office complex above. Lewis Wharf set the style for other work to follow with its authoritative idiom of stone posts, granite paving, anchors and chain, and gaff-flown flags. Impeccable sailing yachts, and some three-story power craft, animate slips that were once washed with floating garbage. An unexpected patch of lawn treats sidewalk diners to exhibitions of *bocci,* a traditional North End game of bowls.

It would be difficult to provide a complete, or even equitable, roster of new eating places that have enriched the area with opportunities for "recycling" old buildings. With the exception of Stella's, a fine local restaurant that traded its North End authenticity for an overdecorated stronghold in the arcade of Harbor Towers, these establishments offer authentic atmosphere to customers in search of new eating experiences. Outstanding examples of "sandblast research" (uncovering and cleaning of brick, stone, and timber construction details) are Dom's (Gerard Gugini) on Commercial Street, the Chart House (Anderson, Notter) on Long Wharf, and the Winery. Each invents its own vocabulary for infill, turning utilitarian obstacles into assets, and making the most of the gargantuan stone lintels and brick arches that nineteenth-century builders dared to use.

The six-story interior mall hollowed out of Gridley J. F. Bryant's (1857) Mercantile Wharf Building by John Sharatt & Associates was made feasible by a fire that all but gutted the combustible parts. Here it was necessary to reconstruct new brick arches, but undamaged older timbers and trusses were put to work in creating the vast skylighted space. Over one hundred apartments can be reached by a pair of open glass elevators, and by balconies extending

Waterfront Park. Sasaki, Dawson, DeMay; 1976. *Photo: Sasaki, Dawson, DeMay Associates*

Lewis Wharf, Granite Buildings. Renovation (first phase): Carl Koch & Associates; 1971-. *Photo: Steven M. Stone*

the full length of each floor. The mall below will have a series of shops surrounding fountains and planting.

In a city where there is a preservationist behind every fanlight and two dozen historic districts within a twenty-minute drive of the Customs House Tower, it may be surprising to learn that the fate of the Faneuil Markets has at times hung by a thin, often political thread. The buildings had been condemned for continued wholesale food market use when a survey of physical conditions was made by the Redevelopment Authority in 1964. Its administrator, Edward J. Logue, took the stand that they should be saved at all costs. The central building, named for Mayor Quincy, already belonged to the city. The BRA used federal funds to acquire the flanking buildings, with the exception of Durgin Park. This world-famous market dining room, open about 130 years, will continue its operations while cooperating in the pattern of improvements. In addition to the general waterfront program goals, there was unanimity on preserving the Market's role of "purveyor of honest beef" and other comestibles to an appreciative city; and to do justice to Alexander Parris's bold architectural concept.

The BRA advertised for developers in 1970. The solution selected, that of the architect Benjamin Thompson, addressed the needs of city people for variety, abundance, mutual exchange, personal contact, and public excitement. While retaining as many of the existing retail activities as possible, he sought a new mixture that would reinforce the market's vitality. Since the financing of nearly one-half-million square feet of commercial space took longer than expected, the City arranged to have the North and South Market blocks restored with federal preservation funds. Under the direction of F. A. Stahl & Associates, these buildings have been gutted, relieved of an accretion of unsuitable changes to roofline and facade, and now

Left: Custom House, State Street and India Wharf. Ammi B. Young; 1837-47. Tower: Peabody and Stearns; 1913-15. *Right:* Grain and Flour Exchange Building (originally Chamber of Commerce Building), 177 Milk Street. Shepley, Rutan & Coolidge; 1890-92. *Photo: Phokion Karas*

Prince Building, 63 Atlantic Avenue. Conversion to apartments: Anderson Notter Associates; 1966-69. *Photo: Hutchins Photography, Inc.*

Commercial Wharf Warehouses, off 80 Atlantic Avenue. 1826. Renovation into apartments; 1954-68. *Photo: Phokion Karas*

present a gleaming fabric of stone arches and window enframements. Working with this architectural firm were Architectural Heritage, Inc. (responsible for restoring Old City Hall) and the Society for the Preservation of New England Antiquities.

After more than a year of negotiations, the Rouse Company of Baltimore, Maryland, was selected to carry out the Thompson plan. This will invest the streets between the three long buildings with glass canopies and arcades for street vendors, flower markets, planned and impromptu entertainments, and a flea market on Sundays. The buildings themselves will contain, in addition to the Farmer's Market, restaurants, theatres, and cabarets, as well as a planned mix of retail and service establishments. What is happening here on the waterfront is encapsulated in the philosophies of Thompson and Rouse. Having built millions of square feet of conventional shopping facilities and a new town, Columbia, Maryland, Rouse now believes that America's cities will not survive indiscriminate heart transplants; that the suburbs are no place to carry on the city's business. For Ben Thompson, the marketplace is for the natural pageantry of crowds and goods, of meat, fish, and crops from the fields, of things made and things grown, all to be tasted, smelled, seen, and touched.

Bostonians, who know the weekend pushcart market and have survived a Monday sale in Filene's Basement, will identify readily with Thompson's interpretation of this resource. For the visitor, it is on the Freedom Trail, and forms a part of the "Walk-to-the-Sea." This starts at the top of Beacon Hill, passes through Pemberton Square, over or around the "mound" at City Hall, across New Sudbury Street on a bridge that *must* be built (whether by the present mayor or the next) to Dock Square, through the Marketplace and under the Artery (until present plans to have it depressed are realized) and down to the new waterfront park.

At last it is possible for the pedestrian to achieve an unfettered view of the harbor, romantically framed in cast-iron bollards and anchor chains. Brick and stone paved levels and paths surround grass and hardy seaside plantings of pine and Russian olive. A series of trellised walkways supporting roses and wisteria recalls, if not caricatures, a familiar feature seen in old prints of substantial houses when Boston was a seaside town. Two fountains, a tot-lot, and a unique dog-watering facility (three fireplugs; no waiting) complete a remarkable park dedicated to the memory of Frank Christian, whose vision and persistence got the waterfront reconstruction under way.

Chapter 4
BEACON HILL

Beacon Hill, perceived from the downtown edge of the Common, the Public Garden, Back Bay, and the Cambridge shore of the Charles River Basin, rises in an even slope of red brick, slate roofs, and chimney pots to the golden dome of the State House. Its steep and narrow streets, gas lamps, and brick sidewalks, lined with quiet town houses in ascending rows, are all zealously guarded by the residents through one of the country's oldest architectural commissions. The aggregate effect, one of social stability and architectural uniformity, leads to two misconceptions about its true character.

It all began in the last decade of the eighteenth century as a real estate venture by prominent citizens who called themselves the "Mt. Vernon Proprietors." At the end of the Revolution, the residential district stretched from an area just south of the Common, through the present business district, and into the North End. These new hillside sites had been pastureland bought up from a few owners, one of whom, loyalist John Singleton Copley, had returned to England. The developed area, today called the South Slope, lay between Pinckney Street and Beacon Street. A line of rope walks running along Myrtle Street, from Hancock to a point below Grove, separated it from the North Slope. Three distinct subdistricts had already grown up. In Bowdoin Square there were mansions, including the first Harrison Gray Otis House. The northwest slope of Mount Vernon (one of the original three hills), was popular with soldiers and seafaring men. This area, near Phillips and West Cedar streets, had earned the name of Mount Whoredom.

Along Joy Street and the other end of Phillips, a settlement of freed slaves lived in wood houses. No. 5–7 Pinckney Street was owned in 1790 by a coachman and a barber. On Smith Court, off Joy Street, this black community built the African Meeting House in 1806. When the children of its parishioners were refused admission to the public schools, a community school was founded in the basement of the Meeting House. Later, in 1820, the parish built the Abiel Smith School on the corner of Smith Court and Joy. It served until the public schools were "integrated" in 1855. The Meeting House has recently been restored by the Museum of Afro-American History.

While there are many fine examples of brick Federal houses on the North Slope (the oldest brick house on the Hill, 43 South Russell Street, was built in 1797), it developed separately from the South Slope. The wooden houses were replaced in the last third of the nineteenth century by tall brick tenements with decorated metal "bays" designed to exploit every possible inch of floor space.

After 1860, many residents left substantial houses on the South Slope for larger establishments in the Back Bay. Railroads and country estates drew other families farther afield, as did the automobile in the mid-twentieth century. A countermarch began after 1900 and another in the mid-fifties. History and fiction favor an image of old Bostonian names, deeds, and antics; the origins, incomes, ages, and occupa-

State House, Beacon and Park Streets
Charles Bulfinch; 1795-98
Rear Extension: Charles E. Brigham; 1889-95
Wings: R. Clipston Sturgis; 1916
Photo: James Douglass

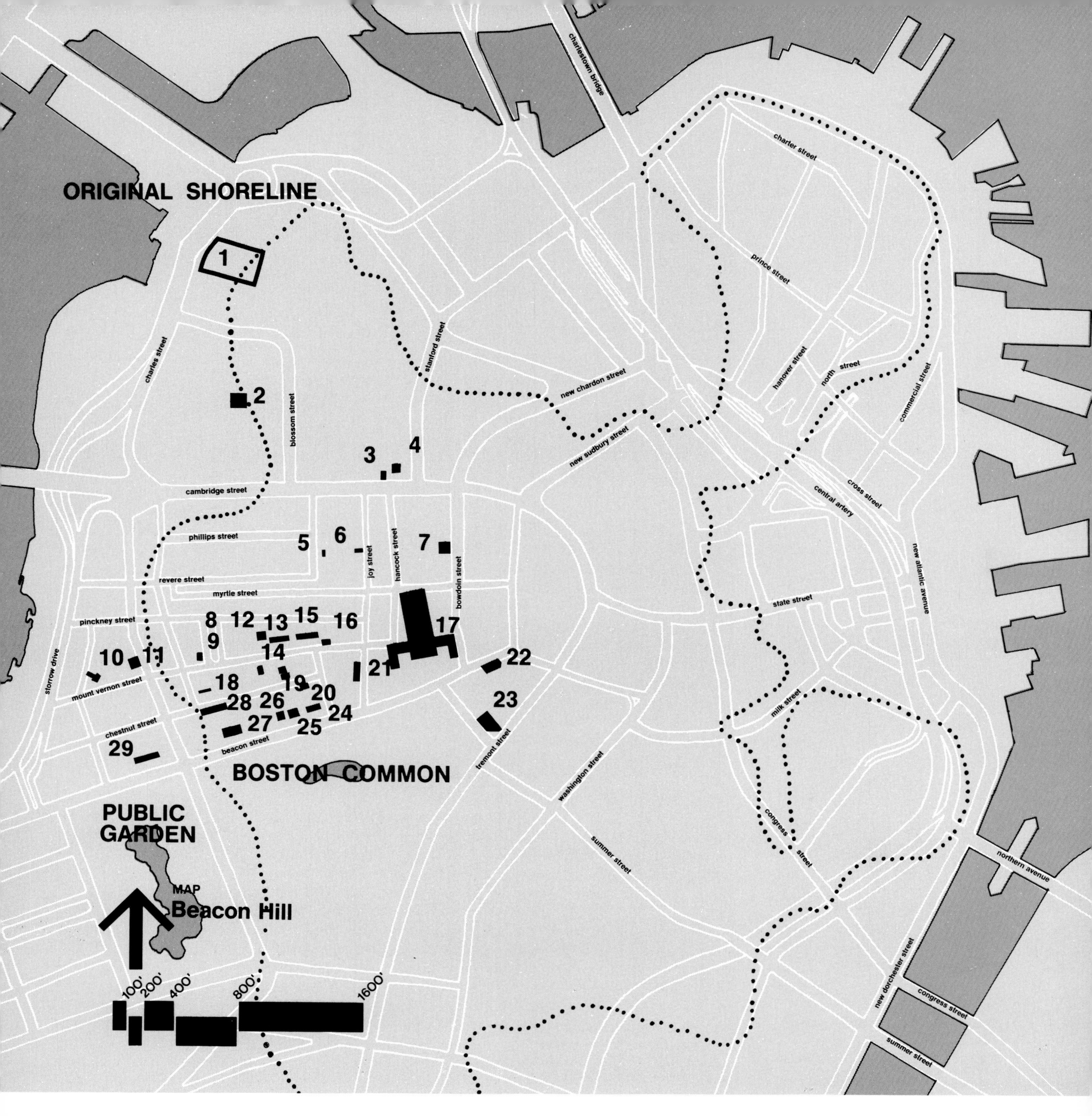

ORIGINAL SHORELINE
charlestown bridge
charter street
prince street
hanover street
north street
commercial street
stanford street
new chardon street
new sudbury street
charles street
blossom street
cambridge street
phillips street
revere street
myrtle street
pinckney street
joy street
hancock street
bowdoin street
central artery
cross street
new atlantic avenue
state street
storrow drive
mount vernon street
chestnut street
beacon street
tremont street
washington street
milk street
congress street
summer street
northern avenue
new dorchester street
BOSTON COMMON
PUBLIC GARDEN
MAP
Beacon Hill
1
2
3
4
5
6
7
8
9
10
11
12
13
14
15
16
17
18
19
20
21
22
23
24
25
26
27
28
29
100'
200'
400'
800'
1600'

1. Charles River Park
West End
Victor Gruen & Associates; 1958–

2. Bulfinch Pavilion
Massachusetts General Hospital
Charles Bulfinch; 1816/17

3. First Harrison Gray Otis House
Headquarters of the Society for the Preservation of New England Antiquities
141 Cambridge Street
Charles Bulfinch; 1796

4. Old West Church
Cambridge and Lynde streets
Asher Benjamin; 1806

5. 43 South Russell Street
Oldest house on the Hill; 1797

6. African Meeting House, 1806
Abiel Smith School, 1820
Smith Court and Joy Street

7. Saint John the Evangelist
35 Bowdoin Street
Possibly Solomon Willard; 1831

8. Louisburg Square
Mount Vernon Street to Pinckney Street
Plan: S. P. Fuller; 1826
Constructed: 1834–37

9. 2-6 Louisburg Square
Row Houses

10. Church of the Advent
30 Brimmer Street
John H. Sturgis; 1876

11. Charles Street Universalist Meeting House
70 Charles Street
Probably Asher Benjamin; 1804

12. Second Harrison Grey Otis House
85 Mount Vernon Street
Charles Bulfinch; 1800
Example of freestanding house

13. 75–83 Mount Vernon Street
Row Houses

14. 70–72 Mount Vernon Street (apartments)
(originally Thayer Brothers' double house)
Probably Richard M. Upjohn; c. 1840
Second use: Boston University School of Theology
Chestnut Street Addition: Bellows & Aldrich and James A. Holt Associates; 1917/18
Interior renovations into apartments: Bullerjahn Associates; 1965

15. 61–67 Mount Vernon Street
Row Houses, c. 1835

16. 57 Mount Vernon Street
Charles Bulfinch; pre-1807

17. State House
Beacon and Park streets
Charles Bulfinch; 1795–98
Rear extension: Charles E. Brigham; 1889–95
Wings: R. Clipston Sturgis; 1916

18. 1–5 Acorn Street
Row Houses

19. 13–17 Chestnut Street
Row Houses
Charles Bulfinch; c. 1805–10

20. 4–10 Chestnut Street
Row Houses

21. 1–5 Joy Street
Row Houses

22. Boston Athenaeum
10½ Beacon Street
Edward Cabot and George Dexter; 1847–49

23. Park Street Church
Peter Banner; 1809
Ministries Building Addition:
Stahl/Bennett; 1974

24. Women's City Club
39–40 Beacon Street
Probably Alexander Parris; 1818

25. Sears House (now Somerset Club)
42–43 Beacon Street
Alexander Parris; 1819–31

26. Third Harrison Grey Otis House
45 Beacon Street
Charles Bulfinch; 1806

27. 54–55 Beacon Street
Asher Benjamin or Peter Banner; c. 1805

28. 50–60 Chestnut Street
Row Houses

29. 70–76 Beacon Street
Granite Row Houses

African Meeting House, 1806. Smith Court and Joy Street. *Photo: Vern Patterson*

Abel Smith School, 1820. Smith Court and Joy Street. *Photo: Vern Patterson*

5 Pinckney Street. *Photo: Max Ferro*

tions of present-day residents are in fact extraordinarily varied. Growing appreciation of the architecture led to establishment of the Beacon Hill Historic District in 1955, with legal jurisdiction over changes to the exteriors of buildings on the South Slope. By 1963 there was sufficient interest to expand its control to a substantial portion of the North Slope. Community spirit has flourished in a strong Civic Association. The promise of stable property values resulting from the historic district attracted more people to Beacon Hill to participate in the great urban revival of Boston in the sixties. A few families still live in large single houses, and the supply of medium-sized properties is in constant demand. Many more, often newcomers to the city, live in a variety of apartment conversions and a few twentieth-century apartment buildings erected before 1955. Today the common denominator seems to be an appreciation of walking access to the city's resources, collective independence, and urban privacy.

The second misconception, that Beacon Hill consists of all the same "Georgian" or "Colonial" architecture, ignores the fact that Boston renounced its allegiance to King George III and its "colonial" status in July 1776, when Beacon Hill and Mt. Vernon were still open country. Its beginnings as a district coincide with the growth of postrevolutionary America. The period is properly referred to as Federal. The Greek Revival movement merged with, rather than replaced, this style, and led in turn to the "Victorian" period, made up of a succession of styles. These subtle changes, combined with alterations and renovations over the years, often make it difficult to identify the exact style of many buildings on the Hill.

Nevertheless, it is a combination of the prevailing technical and economic realities, rather than architectural style, that gives unity to the district. The freedom with which technology invests architecture today makes it difficult to equate this easy rhythm of wall and window with anything but the enlightened restraint. But

43 South Russel Street (oldest house on the Hill); 1797. *Photo: Max Ferro*

4-10 Chestnut Street. *Photo: Max Ferro*

57 Mount Vernon Street. Charles Bulfinch; pre-1807. *Photo: James Douglass*

mansion and row house alike were built with the same skills, tools, and materials, and by the same workmen. Bricks were passed up by hand to fill the thick walls required to support floors and roofs, and to provide fire separation between buildings. Instead of steel beams swung into place by cranes, stone lintels to cap window and door openings were hoisted with block and tackle. Functional limitations established a standardized opening width; when more light was needed for important rooms, the opening was made taller by adding a third sliding section. Bay windows were introduced to obtain more light as well as vistas of the street. These wood and copper projections concealed the brick wall behind as it was stepped back around the opening. Expensive arches were used sparingly for entrances and to lighten brick walls around lower windows. Walls became an exercise in enclosure: one imagines the structural forces in the walls as flowing around the windows and down to the stone foundation.

The district is unified not only by structure, but by the impact of its topography. The Proprietors' original plan was for single or double houses with gardens at the side. Economics and scarcity of land soon led to deep lots dictated by efficient layouts of steep streets; and, therefore, row houses. Some of these were first built in pairs, as at 6 and 8 Chestnut Street, with the later addition of Nos. 4 and 10 in the side yards. Across the street at Nos. 13–17, Charles Bulfinch built a row of three for the daughters of Mrs. James Swan, one of the Proprietors. Many houses were built in rows of five or more.

Although today's architect would insist that considerations of site, land value, and structure were all properly "architecture," the term was reserved in those days for the proportions, details, and ornament which such men as Bulfinch, Alexander Parris, Asher Benjamin, and Peter Banner could bring to their work. A reading of these elements will assist the curbstone archaeologist in tracing the development of

First Harrison Gray Otis House. Headquarters for the Society for the Preservation of New England Antiquities. 141 Cambridge Street. Charles Bulfinch; 1796/97. *Photo: Max Ferro*

Second Harrison Gray Otis House, 85 Mount Vernon Street. Example of Freestanding House. Charles Bulfinch; 1800. *Photo: Max Ferro*

Beacon Hill from a glacial drumlin on which the first settlers kept warning fires at the ready, to a brick Acropolis for the "Athens of America."

From a position on Mt. Vernon Street, just a few houses below the intersection of Walnut Street, it is possible to see four major periods of construction. The wide house at No. 85 (the second of three built for Proprietor Harrison Gray Otis) illustrates the freestanding house. The next houses to the west (87 & 89) still have their side yards, although No. 89 has been completely rebuilt. All three houses were set back from the street so that Jonathan Mason could see the water from his elegant mansion (demolished in 1836) which stood in a large garden above them. Mason had four more houses built for his daughters (Nos. 51–57), two of which overlooked his gardens.

All of the above buildings (including Mason's own) were designed by Charles Bulfinch in the first decade of the 1800s. They display many of the details with which he influenced the style for this period: small ground and top floor windows; tall windows on the main floor (*piano nobile*); granite lower walls; delicate wooden porticoes, cornices, and balustrades; and inset arches around windows. Some of these elements can be found in the State House, designed by Bulfinch in 1795. He also designed the other two Harrison Gray Otis houses. The first, built near Bowdoin Square in 1796, at the corner of Cambridge and Lynde streets, has survived "inelegant" uses to become the meticulously restored headquarters and museum of the Society for the Preservation of New England Antiquities. The third Otis house, at No. 45 Beacon, with its cobblestone side yard and brick stable, dates from 1806. Other good examples of this decade are the trio at 13–17 Chestnut, and a pair at 54–55 Beacon.

The latter, thought to be the work of Asher Benjamin (West Church; Charles Street Meeting House) or Peter Banner (Park Street Church), has the characteristic wooden details and "flat arch" lintels with inward slanting ends. The wide arched entrances and full-height bowfronts are unique for the period.

The War of 1812 slowed development until 1818. Buildings of the decade following show the influence, but little of the inspiration, of Bulfinch. He was then in Washington building the new Capitol. From our vantage point it is possible to identify Nos. 28–32 Mt. Vernon, above Walnut, and Nos. 44–48, below. The square-edged lintels with incised designs and windows more equal in height can also be found along the lower side of West Cedar Street, between Mt. Vernon and Chestnut; from 50 to 60 Chestnut; and in pairs at 39–40 and 56–57 Beacon. Some entrances are recessed with delicate Greek columns; others were set back under narrow brick archways with stone trim. Less elaborate are those at 1–5 Acorn Street, including examples of the triple window used to add light to a first-floor room. A granite row with a touch of Regency (70–76 Beacon) was built in this decade, as was the stone mansion at 42 Beacon, by Alexander Parris. It resembles the Mason House that stood on Mt. Vernon Street.

The row of buildings that replaced this mansion (61–67 Mt. Vernon) and those just below it are products of the thirties. While the entrances of the upper group have been tampered with, those from 75 to 83 compare favorably with the rows at 1–4 Joy Street, and on the lower side of Louisburg Square. Broad stone pilasters supporting heavy entablatures frame the entrances. Full-height bowfronts now come into their own. Rich brownstone details reveal the "Grecian" influence championed by Asher Benjamin in his

Old West Church, Cambridge and Lynde streets. Asher Benjamin; 1806. *Photo: Max Ferro*

Park Street Church. Peter Banner; 1809. Ministries Building Addition: Stahl/Bennett; 1974. *Photo: Steve Rosenthal*

Louisburg Square. Mount Vernon Street to Pinckney Street. Plan: S. P. Fuller; 1826. Constructed: 1834-37. *Photo: Phokion Karas*

(1833) handbook, *Practice of Architecture*. Number 59, with its model Ionic temple entrance, pediments over windows, inset stone panels, and carved wreaths under the cornice, reaches a high point for this style on the Hill. Smaller houses from the 1830s can be found on West Cedar Street between Mt. Vernon and Pinckney.

The remaining available sites were filled in by the forties with similar, if taller, buildings such as those at 2–6 Louisburg Square (one sounds the *s*) and several on its upper side. This genteel enclave has survived attempts by the city to take over and pave its cobblestone streets. It preserves the only statuary on the Hill in the fenced park. The figures of Columbus and Aristides the Just were brought over as ballast in a sailing ship at mid-century, the gift of a resident. Other new additions were Victorian, such as the double house at 70–72 Mt. Vernon, attributed to Richard Upjohn. It was built for the brothers Thayer, who kept bachelor quarters in the two wings while sharing the center portion for social activities. A Gothic "church" on Chestnut Street backing up to these houses was added in 1910 after the entire property was acquired by Boston University for its School of Theology. The complex narrowly escaped demolition during the 1960s in the first serious challenge to the Historic District. It now serves as spacious condominiums.

Before 1860, the water of the Back Bay came to within a few feet of Charles Street. Several of the structures still standing served as sail lofts and storehouses. By the 1870s, the land had been filled to Brimmer Street. Lower Chestnut with its stables was unofficially called "Horse-chestnut Street." A few examples of the late Greek Revival period can be found but the stylistic development of this area with its French Academic houses on Beacon Street and later twentieth-century additions, belongs to the history of the Back Bay.

St. John the Evangelist, 35 Bowdoin Street. Possibly Solomon Willard; 1831. *Photo: James Douglass*

Beacon Hill Nursery School, Hill House (formerly Joy Street Police Station), Conversion: Strickland, Brigham & Eldredge; 1968. *Photo: Max Ferro*

On the North Slope, an intriguing collection of dead end streets, often with original wood houses, offers a romantic change to the sedate South Slope. Street names recall the owners of pastures that once overlooked Charlestown and the Battle of Bunker Hill. Many of the residents have relocated from the West End community across Cambridge Street when it was demolished for high-rise apartments in the 1950s. A tiny synagogue, just off Phillips Street, has served a community with ties to Vilna, in Czechoslovakia. An Italianate police station on Joy Street serves as a community center, with a nursery school tucked away in the ground floor lockup where the night's haul from Scollay Square was once accommodated.

Botanical names for streets vie with fine specimens of linden, tulip, poplar, horse chestnut, elm, and Norway maple. Ginkgo and ailanthus brought back in the China trade have been joined by locusts and columnar maples in a vigorous street tree-planting program. Grass grows in summer between cobblestones, wooden paving blocks refuse to be obliterated by asphalt, and everywhere wrought-iron complements granite, brick, and painted wood. There are hidden gardens, and on upper Pinckney Street a hidden house. Summer brings cool shaded streets, window boxes, and a galaxy of roof decks with enviable views. While the possibilities of interior planning might seem limited, no two floor plans are ever the same. All ring the changes of invention and adaptability in the name of comfort, convenience, and necessity. Every year the curious flock to see the insides of houses and gardens on tour. At Christmastime curtains are left back to reveal festive interiors furnished with genuine antiques; carolers mob Louisburg Square; bell ringers and brass choirs resound; celebrants dwindle reluctantly, and all is finally quiet. Anyone who has ever lived on Beacon Hill finds it impossible to forget the experience.

Aerial of Back Bay
Photo: Aerial Photos of New England, Inc.

Chapter 5
THE BACK BAY

The oblong blocks and avenues of the Back Bay present an enduring framework for urban living. This framework is, in effect, a lamination of four parallel zones of use: recreational along the Charles River Esplanade; residential between Beacon and Newbury streets; local shopping mixed with residential and educational on Newbury; and general commercial, institutional, and high-rise apartments on Boylston Street. It is possible to live, shop, work, study, and play all within a few blocks in a district that Lewis Mumford called "the outstanding achievement in American urban planning for the nineteenth century."

Back Bay is also a classic American ecological blunder. The Shawmut Peninsula, on which Boston was built, was once connected to the mainland by a strip of land along the present line of Washington Street. Although by 1850 the coves at its periphery had been filled with dirt carted from the tops of Beacon and Copp's hills, land remained scarce. The first two railroads to the west and south had been built on causeways across the shallow bay. A tidal milldam built along the present line of Beacon Street further complicated the flow of sewage and drainwater from the growing city. There was pressure from the health department to fill the area. A commission was formed to plan and execute the project. From Needham, nine miles away, 145 dirt-carrying cars in trains of thirty-five cars each made twenty-five trips a day over a special railroad. One train arrived in the Back Bay every forty-five minutes, twenty-four hours a day, from the fall of 1857 until 1900.

Some of the new land was held by the original milldam owners, some was deeded to the contractors as payment for the filling work, and the rest was sold by the Commonwealth for building lots. Selected locations were set aside for institutional use. All of the land carried deed restrictions as to height, setback, and use of masonry as a building material. The natural limitations of filled land dictated pile foundations and favored row houses on the narrow twenty-six foot lots.

The history of Back Bay is punctuated with a series of narrow escapes which should be instructive to today's urban designers. As early as 1824 the City had planned for a park on the site of the Public Garden, then on the shore of the Charles River. Four times in the 1840s the City Council tried to sell off the land as building lots; it was only with the beginning of the Back Bay development that the importance of this magnificent botanical garden became generally accepted.

Visionary plans for the new land to be created included one with a "distribution railroad" and two islands; another proposed a great round lake. These are as difficult to visualize today as they must have been to the Commissioners. Luckily, such flights of fancy were avoided; men such as Arthur Gilman, architect of the Old City Hall and Arlington Street Church, concentrated on solving the functional problems of the new district. Commonwealth Avenue was laid out along the

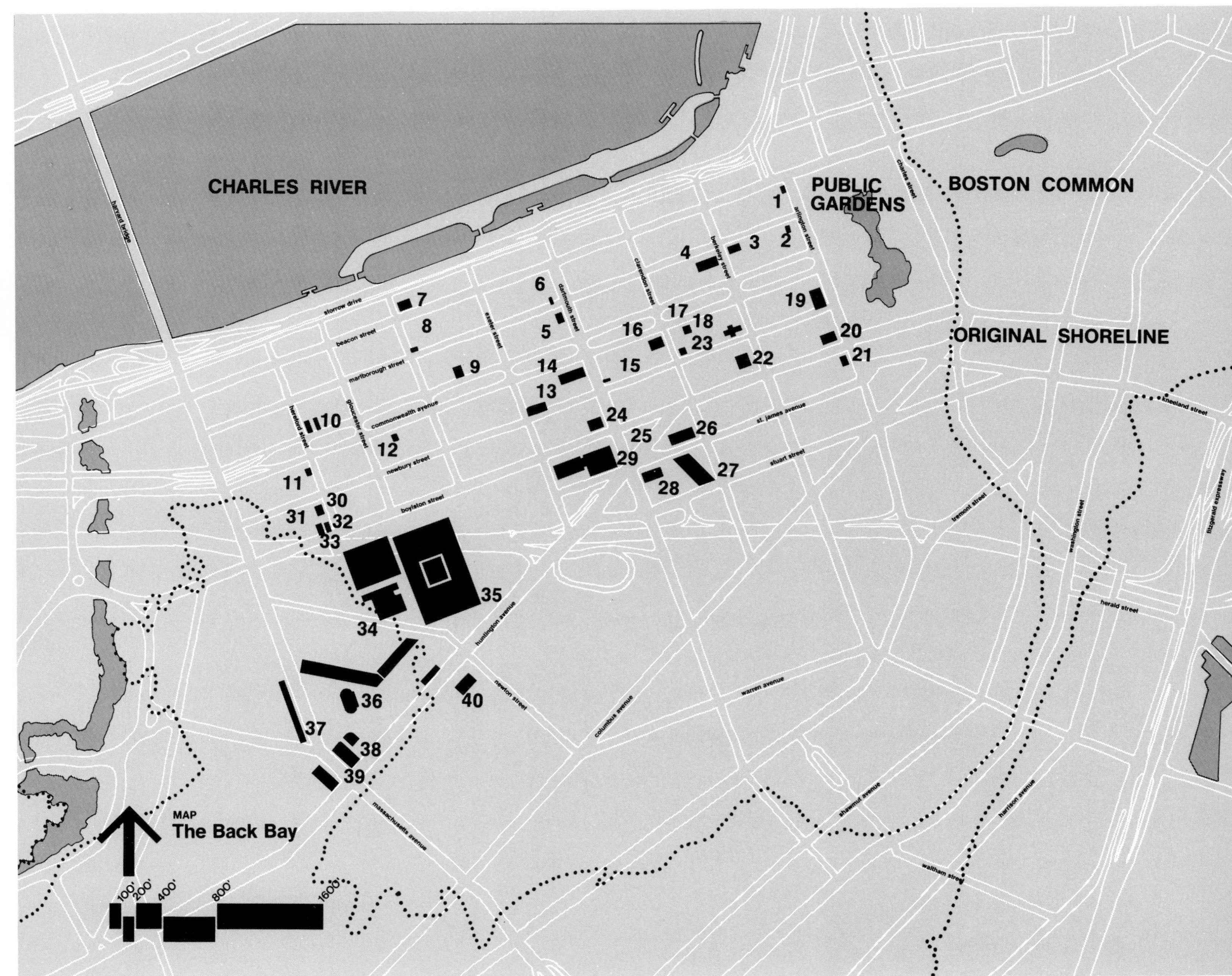
CHARLES RIVER
PUBLIC GARDENS
BOSTON COMMON
ORIGINAL SHORELINE
MAP
The Back Bay
100'
200'
400'
800'
1600'

1. 1-3 Arlington Street
French Academic Style Houses, 1861

2. 2 Marlborough Street
Panel Brick Style House, 1871

3. First Lutheran Church in Boston
299 Berkeley Street
Pietro Belluschi; 1957

4. First Church in Boston (Unitarian)
64 Marlborough Street
Ware and Van Brunt; 1867
Replacement:Paul Rudolph; 1972

5. B. W. Crowninshield House
164 Marlborough Street
H. H. Richardson; 1870

6. Cushing Endicott House
Academic Brick Style, 1870
165 Marlborough Street

7. 330 Beacon Street (apartments)
Hugh Stubbins and Associates; 1959

8. 12 Fairfield Street
Queen Anne Style; 1879

9. Algonquin Club
217-19 Commonwealth Avenue
McKim, Mead and White; 1887

10. G. A. Nickerson House
303 Commonwealth Avenue
McKim, Mead and White; 1895

11. 314 Commonwealth Avenue
Chateauesque Style; 1899

12. 264-66 Commonwealth Avenue
Academic Brownstone Style; 1882

13. Exeter Theatre
Originally Spiritualist Church
Hartwell & Richardson; 1884
Renovation: Childs, Bertman, Tseckares; 1976

14. Hotel Vendome
W. G. Preston; 1875
Conversion to apartments
Stahl-Bennett; 1975
commercial interiors Irving Salzberg; 1976

15. 277 Dartmouth Street
Ruskin Style House; 1878

16. First Baptist Church (originally New Brattle Square Church)
Clarendon Street and Commonwealth Avenue
H. H. Richardson; 1870-72

17. 76-80 Commonwealth Avenue
Brownstone Style Houses; 1872

18. Church of the Covenant
67 Newbury Street
Richard M. Upjohn; 1866

19. Ritz Carlton Hotel
Strickland, Blodgett & Law; c. 1927

20. Arlington Street Church
Arlington and Boylston streets
Arthur Gilman; 1860

21. Arlington Street Subway Station
Arlington and Boylston streets
Cambridge Seven Associates; 1968

22. Bonwit Teller
(originally Museum of Natural History)
Berkeley and Boylston streets
William G. Preston; 1862

23. Trinity Church Rectory
233 Clarendon Street
H. H. Richardson; 1879
Third story added; 1893

24. New Old South Church
Boylston and Dartmouth streets
Cummings and Sears; 1875

25. Copley Square; 1883
Redesign: Sasaki, Dawson & DeMay; 1969

26. Trinity Church
Copley Square
H. H. Richardson; 1875

27. John Hancock Tower
John Hancock Place
I. M. Pei & Partners; 1973–

28. Copley Plaza Hotel
Clarence H. Blackall; 1913

29. Boston Public Library
Copley Square
McKim, Mead and White; 1887
Addition: Philip Johnson; 1972

30. Boston Architectural Center
320 Newbury Street
Ashley Myer & Associates; 1967

31. Institute for Contemporary Art
Conversion from police station
Graham Gund; 1975

32. Fire Station
Boylston and Hereford streets
Arthur Vinal; 1884
Redesign: Arrowstreet Inc; 1972

33. John B. Hynes Civic Memorial Auditorium
Hoyle, Doran and Berry; 1970

34. Sheraton Boston Hotel
Charles Luckman & Associates; 1965-75
Addition:1976

35. Prudential Center
Charles Luckman & Associates; 1960-70

36. Christian Science Church Center
I. M. Pei and Araldo Cossutta; 1973
Mother Church
Franklin J. Welch; 1894

37. Church Park Apartments
The Architects Collaborative; 1972

38. Horticultural Hall
Huntington and Massachusetts avenues
Wheelwright and Haven; 1901

39. Symphony Hall
Huntington and Massachusetts avenues
McKim, Mead and White; 1900

40. Colonnade Hotel
Irving Salsberg; 1971

Copley Square and Trinity Church. Copley Square; 1883. Redesign: Sasaki, Dawson & DeMay; 1969. Trinity Church: H. H. Richardson; 1875.
Photo: Hutchins Photography, Inc.

lines of the French boulevard. The elegant, tree-lined streets were reserved for residents; back alleyways for delivery of goods and services by horsecart. Daily life depended upon the skills of a domestic staff. A visit to the Gibson House Museum at 137 Beacon Street will show why it took a cook, parlor maid and upstairs maid, and sometimes a butler (with one or more others who came in by day to do laundry and sewing) to run a typical household.

In his *Houses of Boston's Back Bay,* Bainbridge Bunting analyzes the eighty-year parade of styles that kept pace with the land-filling operations. The initial transition, from Federal Boston, takes place at the foot of Beacon Hill: first as Greek Revival, then French Academic. It is the latter style that dominates the beginnings of Back Bay proper. This new architecture was made by rules rather than free adaptation of classical ideas. The generation of architects that followed Bulfinch brought from studies abroad a love for the mansard roof and the Parisian ideal of a street made up of buildings designed as a unit. Outstanding examples can be found at 1, 2, and 3 Arlington Street (1861) and 22–30 Marlborough Street (1863). No. 122 Beacon Street had the first mansard roof in the Back Bay; No. 154, with its graceful center stair and three arched openings, is a successful attempt at symmetry. In narrow buildings requiring side entrances, this was no mean achievement.

Bunting employs the term "Academic Brownstone" to describe a handful of later buildings by less skilled speculative builders (1882, 264–66 Commonwealth; and 1877; 321 Marlborough). The persistent academic style, which accounted for nearly ninety percent of the buildings in the Back Bay before 1869, moderated to "Academic Brick," noted for its "inventive simplification." Two such groupings are at 59–63 Commonwealth (1874–79) and 165 Marlborough (1871) with 326 Dartmouth (1872). Next came "Panel Brick," a more conservative, if decorative, approach, full of surprises and vigorous brick corbeling (rows stepped out and/or staggered in decorative bands). There are three on Marlborough Street: No. 2 (1871), No. 63 (1875), and No. 101 (1872).

Gothic architecture, while present, is much diffused. It has been drawn from several separate European sources. Bunting divides its presence in the Back Bay into "Brownstone" and "Ruskin." Of the former there are but three "naïve—ungainly" examples: 165 Beacon (1869), 76-80 Commonwealth (1872), and 117 Marlborough (1873). The polychrome layering and "conspicuous ornamentation" of the romantic architect John Ruskin stirred his admirers in the seventies to cram *donjon* towers and complicated conical roofs into narrow sites, all in the name of the *Seven Lamps of Architecture.* Three samplings

Arlington Street Church, Arlington and Boylston streets. Arthur Gilman; 1860. *Photo: Max Ferro*

Boston Architectural Center, 320 Newbury Street. Ashley Myer & Associates; 1967. *Photo: The Boston Architectural Center*

Commonwealth Avenue. *Photo: James Douglass*

stand at 121 Commonwealth (1872), 277 Dartmouth (1878), and 191 Marlborough (1881). Charles A. Cummings, who designed the Old South Church in Copley Square, built No. 109 Newbury Street as his own residence.

In the shadow of his great churches, only two of H. H. Richardson's three Back Bay houses remain. No. 164 Marlborough was done in 1870 before he developed his characteristic style. The Rectory for Trinity Church (1879) at 233 Clarendon Street is more easily recognized. Works of imitators have captured his "gloomy robustness" if not his inventive vitality: 347 Beacon (1884), 234 Commonwealth (1889), and 21 Fairfield (1880).

The "informal—picturesque—asymmetrical—cozy" compositions collected under the name of "Queen Anne" use Renaissance details, cut and molded brick, and elaborate dormer windows to add humor and delight to the district. The old Boston Art Club at the corner of Newbury and Dartmouth streets (now a public school) is rated by Bunting as having "the handsomest Queen Anne detail in the Back Bay." No. 380 Marlborough, with its dissimilar bays, is the only "modest" double house in the district. Other examples, closer to the English model, are 178 Marlborough and 12 Fairfield, both by the same firm in 1879.

By 1885, the more imaginative development of new styles had lost much of its force. For the next fifty years architects were to spend their creative energy on revivals of the past, ending in a self-conscious rediscovery of the Federal facades with which the century had begun. Shades of the Italian Renaissance haunt 219 Commonwealth (1887) and 23 Hereford (1884), both by the New York firm of McKim, Mead and White, who had designed the Boston Public Library and were becoming the leading classical architects of America. Other works in this style are at

330 Beacon Street (apartments). Hugh Stubbins and Associates; 1959. *Photo: Hugh Stubbins and Associates*

266 and 420 Beacon Street (1886; 1892).

"Chateauesque" is the name given by Bunting to ambitious attempts to combine the "massing of the Middle Ages" with the "lavish sculptural ornamentation of the Renaissance." Nos. 426–28 Beacon (1904), 314 Commonwealth (1899), and 20 Gloucester (1886) are representative. The masquerade continues with "Plateresque" at 304 Commonwealth (1895) and "Jacobean" at 240 Commonwealth (1879).

The quieter, more dignified facades of McKim's Classical work act as a foil to the unchecked individualism of the preceding decades. In the same way that the work of Richardson leads, through Sullivan and Wright, to the "organic" aspects of the modern movement, so also does McKim loom large in the development of twentieth-century architectural ideas prior to the Bauhaus infusion of the 1930s. The firm's work in the Classical style in Boston predates comparable designs in New York and elsewhere. The house at 303 Commonwealth (1895) is by McKim; those at 246 Beacon (1886) and 479 Commonwealth (1896), by others, are nevertheless labeled "McKim Classical."

The facades of 58–60 Commonwealth (1866) with their chunky stone quoins, bowfronts, and balustrades announce the return of Georgian motifs to dominate the imagination of architect and client alike until satisfactory contemporary solutions were evolved. See also: 145–49 Bay State Road (1900). The Federal Revival examples in the Back Bay, although more elaborate than their prototypes on Beacon Hill, coincide with renewed interest in that area as a desirable place in which to live. Commonwealth Avenue has examples at 199, 413, and 415 (all 1890); Bay State Road at 49 (1893) and 57 (1890). Two buildings in a more refined Georgian Revival style named after Robert Adam, an English architect, predate the enthusiastic twentieth-century rediscovery of this graceful decoration. They can be found at 422 Beacon and 411 Commonwealth, both designed in 1899.

Since the turn of the century many buildings have been replaced or ineptly remodeled to cope with increasingly dense occupancy. In 1966 the residential section was made an architectural district, which seems to have slowed this trend. A medium-rise apartment building at 330 Beacon Street (1959; Hugh Stubbins and Associates) preserves the set-back and undulating wall rhythms of the street. A less considerate intrusion at 180 Beacon devours the space in front with an anti-social wall enclosing an area filled with largely indigestible contemporary art. Its fourteen stories exceed reason, present a rude gesture to the prospect of the river from Beacon Hill, and make a tornado out of Clarendon Street.

The ninety-foot layer of blue clay under the Back Bay fill makes foundations for buildings over six stories prohibitively expensive. It may take as many as twenty-five stories to recover the investment in deep foundations. In 1970 Back Bay had yet another narrow escape when a blue-ribbon panel recommended by a margin of one vote to retain the pattern of height limitations under which the district was first developed. For the time being the temptation to ring the district with thirty-story "aerial suburbs" has been resisted. While there are still single-family houses, most properties have been converted into apartments, rooming houses, condominiums, institutional offices, and schools. To counter this trend, zoning laws have been changed to require permits for changes to nonresidential use. As long as the intentions of zoning are upheld, housing codes enforced, and the integrity of the architectural district maintained, the future for Back Bay as a cosmopolitan inner-city residential area is secure.

The great wave of optimism that pro-

First Church in Boston (Unitarian), 64 Marlborough Street. Ware and Van Brunt; 1867. Replacement: Paul Rudolph; 1972. *Photo: Max Ferro*

Hotel Vendome. W. G. Preston; 1875. Conversion to apartments: Stahl/Bennett; 1975. Supervision: Irving Salsberg Associates. *Photo: Steve Rosenthal*

duced Back Bay is poignantly illuminated by the history of its churches. Hard hit by the flight to the suburbs in the '40s and '50s, each has struggled to preserve the relevance of its architectural presence as well as its ministry. To the Arlington Street Church (1860; Arthur Gilman; Italian-Georgian; brownstone) came Unitarians from the old Federal Street Church. A new Episcopal parish raised Emmanuel Church (1862; A. R. Estey; Gothic; Roxbury conglomerate) in the first block of Newbury Street for a popular minister who was leaving the Unitarian Church. Next door is the Leslie Lindsey Chapel (1924; Allen & Collens; Gothic; limestone) erected to the memory of a young woman who was lost on the *Lusitania*. Richard M. Upjohn, son of the architect of Trinity Church in lower Manhattan, designed the Central Congregational Church at the corner of Newbury and Berkeley streets (1866; Gothic; Roxbury conglomerate). It is now called the Church of the Covenant. The First Church of 1630 (1867; Ware and Van Brunt; Gothic; Roxbury conglomerate) moved to Marlborough and Berkeley streets, but the building was destroyed by fire in 1968. Its replacement, designed by Paul Rudolph, preserves the undamaged spire and the frame of a rose window. Textured concrete block infill avoids direct confrontation of new forms with old materials. Conceived as the locus of a contemporary ministry, it has a nursery school, space for theatrical presentations, community activities, and a stunning sanctuary that has been worked effortlessly into an informal plan.

Henry Hobson Richardson designed the powerful Romanesque church at the corner of Commonwealth Avenue and Clarendon Street (1871) for other Unitarians from Brattle Square; it later became the First Baptist Church. The frieze and trumpeting angels on the tower, by the sculptor Bartholdi, who did the Statue of Liberty, have earned the building the now fond nickname of "Church of the Holy Beanblowers." Parishioners from the Third Church (Old South Meeting House, on Washington Street) built the New Old South Church (1874; Cummings, Sears; North Italian Gothic; Roxbury conglomerate) in Copley Square.

Episcopalians from the old South End held a competition, won by H. H. Richardson, for the design of their new Trinity Church in Copley Square (1875; Romanesque; Milford Granite, Longmeadow stone trim). Its rector, Phillips Brooks, in recognizing the power, integrity, and humanity of the structure said, "The man and the work are absolutely one. The man is in the work and the work is in the man" (quoted in Henry Russell Hitchcock, *The*

Architecture of H. H. Richardson and His Times). It was Trinity more than any other of his buildings that inspired architect and client to employ the bold forms of Romanesque for schools, churches, and public buildings throughout the country well into the twentieth century.

The fate of a vacant church at Massachusetts Avenue and Beacon Street (formerly the Mt. Vernon Church, now owned by New Old South; 1891; Walker and Kimball; Gothic; Roxbury conglomerate) will depend upon the ability of the community to uphold its architectural district law in the face of expediency. There are alternatives: for many years the Spiritualist Church (1884; Hartwell and Richardson; Hybrid Romanesque; Longmeadow Freestone, Braggville Granite) at Exeter and Newbury streets maintained itself through the proceeds of its own (Exeter) theatre. It has recently been sold and is being "recycled" as a cinema, restaurant, offices, and shops. There is no more reason for destroying any of Boston's incomparable ornaments than there is for paving over the Public Garden.

Anchoring the corner of Massachusetts Avenue at Huntington, Symphony Hall (1900; McKim, Mead and White; Renaissance Revival; brick) and Horticultural Hall (1900; Wheelright & Haven; Beaux Arts; brick) are still serving the needs of their original builders. The fire station at Boylston and Hereford (1884; Arthur Vinal; Romanesque; sandstone) has been given a new lease on life with simplified fenestration and bright new interior finishes. The redesign was done in 1972 by Arrowstreet, Inc. Its next-door neighbor, a police station designed by Vinal in the same year, has been recently transformed into a new home for the Institute of Contemporary Art by Graham Gund. The old Museum of Natural History (1862; W. G. Preston; Academic; brick) has been inhabited for many years by Bonwit Teller whose merit as a

Institute of Contemporary Art. Conversion from police station: Graham Gund; 1975. *Photo: Steven M. Stone*

Boston Public Library, Copley Square. McKim, Mead and White; 1887. Addition: Philip Johnson; 1972. *Photo: Nathaniel Lieberman*

conservator almost, but not quite, atones for the profusion of window air-conditioning units, the scourge of preservation efforts everywhere!

The former Hotel Vendome at the corner of Dartmouth Street and Commonwealth Avenue has finally been rescued from disuse and several serious fires. The smaller pavilion at the corner was designed in 1875 by Wm. G. Preston; the larger portion to the west by J. F. Ober in 1881. A new roofline and pavilion to the south have been added by Stahl-Bennett in a recent renovation of the hotel as condominiums and an interior shopping galleria. (Interior work has been designed by Irving Salsberg.) It was here in French Second Empire splendor that the famous and fashionable once stayed; and where electric lighting was first installed in a public building. Another hotel, the Ritz-Carlton (Strickland, Blodgett and Law; 1927) plans a substantial addition on adjacent vacant Commonwealth Avenue lots. These elegant residences were heedlessly torn down before the area had gained the protection of an architectural district, leaving the street vulnerable to yet another high-rise intrusion.

By 1880, the Boston Public Library had already outgrown its first two locations. When land was made available in the Back Bay, McKim, Mead and White were selected to design a new one, not, however, until after a number of false starts and much official wrangling. In his memoirs, McKim recalled that it took about six months "to lose our vanity" and another six to learn that they could not be limited by foundations which had already been laid and still be able to do a building that would "go down the pages of time and be enduring." He chose a classical form to "recognize the street" and oppose "the irregular, vertical masses of Trinity." He selected a light pink Milford granite to complement "the community of dark and colored stone and brick, in which romantic characteristics prevailed" (quoted in Walter Muir Whitehill, *Boston Public Library, A Centennial History*). The final design was based on that of the *Bibliothèque St. Geneviève* in Paris. The interior is richly endowed with marble detail and the art of John Singer Sargent, Edwin Abbey, Augustus and Louis St. Gaudens, and Puvis de Chavannes. Entrance doors were cast by Daniel Chester French and the seated figures are by the sculptor Bela Pratt. One of the finest Renaissance buildings in the United States, the library has indeed "endured."

By the time Philip Johnson had been engaged to enlarge the library, in 1964, the decision had been made to build a new general library with open shelves, thus preserving the McKim building as a reference library to house special collections. Johnson and his structural engineer, William LeMessurier, divided the available building space into nine square bays, defined by sixteen square towers. These sup-

Christian Science
Church Center.
I. M. Pei & Partners;
Araldo Cossutta; 1973.
Mother Church:
Franklin J. Welch;
1894.
*Photo: Publication
Department, Christian
Science Church Center*

Church Park Apartments. The Architects Collaborative; 1972. *Photo: Wayne Soverns, Jr.*

port overhead trusses (giving a compatible shape to McKim's sloping roof) from which the upper floors are hung. The upper three levels contain stacks, while the administrative level just below can be identified by a horizontal strip of narrow, recessed windows. The graceful, inward sloping (catenary) curved second-floor windows hover above a full-width expanse of glass at the street level. They emphasize the suspended structural system which is dependent in turn upon the towers. The two buildings are unified by their size, shape, and surface material, and by the fact that each expresses its structure. The towers are used for stairways and mechanical equipment. Tall stone *stelae* shield the street level from the traffic noise and diversion. The great skylit center bay is a contemporary answer to the popular Renaissance courtyard of the older building.

The product of a decade of planning and construction, the Christian Science Church Center at Huntington and Massachusetts avenues combines religious and administrative headquarters in a spacious urban setting. Older buildings were cleared away from the granite, Romanesque Mother Church (1894; Franklin J. Welch) and its great Byzantine-Italian Renaissance limestone "domed extension" (1904; Brigham, Beman). This permitted construction of the twenty-six story administration building, a long colonnade building with offices and service functions, a 550-car garage beneath a reflecting pool, a quadrant-shaped religious education and conference building, and a plaza at Massachusetts Avenue to serve a new monumental Corinthian entrance portico. The circular fountain and the reflecting pool are part of the cooling system, but a source of delight to city-bound strollers who come to enjoy the colorful plantings, benches, and shade trees. The complex, completed in 1975, is the work of I. M. Pei

Left: Symphony Hall, Huntington and Massachusetts avenues. McKim, Mead and White; 1900. *Right:* Horticultural Hall. Wheelwright and Haven; 1901. *Photo: W. Geddis*

and Partners with Cossutta and Ponte. Carefully related to this Center through the urban renewal process are: Church Park (1972; The Architects Collaborative), combining local business in a street level arcade, a market, and a circular parking facility, with low- and moderate-income apartments above; and the Colonnade Hotel (1971; Irving Salsberg), responding sensitively to the character of the more elaborate institutional buildings on a modest budget.

None of these developments might have taken place if the Prudential Insurance Company had not launched the renewal decade in Boston by reclaiming railroad yards which had gathered weeds for years in the heart of the city. A study by the Urban Design Committee of the Boston Society of Architects had recommended that any new tall buildings in Boston be disposed along a "high spine" aligned with the railroad-turnpike access corridor leading into the downtown area. The Prudential Complex (1960–1970; Charles Luckman and Associates) combines undistinguished buildings and marginal public spaces on a site large enough to avoid impacting Boylston Street and the residential area to the north. Its observation deck at five hundred feet gave Bostonians their first good look at themselves. The drama of the great harbor whose extended arms once beckoned the China trade; the Blue Hills to the south; and the rim of Boston Basin to the west and north all became an integral part of a heightened sense of place. The layman could at last see what sensitive planners deplored: the brutalization of the city surface by the Turnpike and its access roads, and the impact of new overpasses on the entrance to the Fenway.

Not to be topped, the John Hancock Mutual Life Insurance Company, whose thirty-four-story pointed tower had been the tallest building in the city for nearly two decades, announced a sixty-story addition across the street from Trinity Church. To justify a density of three times that normally allowed by law, they promised to raze their oldest building and build another plaza. These plans were opposed by the city's official planning office and its design advisory committee of distinguished architects. In a unanimous resolve, the Boston Society of Architects asked the city to broaden the concept from a "polarized tower" and "windswept plaza" to a "building form of greater contact area—a more sheltering form that could provide colonnades and shops at ground level" and, using air rights, "make a more humane bridge between the South Cove, the Back Bay, and the city as a whole." The request was summarily rejected; a restaurant-garage complex was added over the turnpike, creating an even greater barrier against the South End. The "minimalist" detailing of a glass skin intended to reflect the sky was unable to contain the insulating glass when subjected to temperature extremes and high winds. A less reflective replacement now leaves the dream of an "invisible building"

Prudential Center. Charles Luckman & Associates; 1960-70. *Photo: Phokion Karas*

unrealized. The same city administration that accepted the "plywood tower" (named for temporary corrective measures) commissioned the poet Archibald MacLeish to write a Bicentennial poem about Boston. In it he laments "these fantasies of glass that crowd our sky and hatred like a whirling paper in the street—"; all the more relevant since the Boston Society of Architects' plea was set "in this time of urban crisis and alienation"!

Had the Hancock Tower been proposed today, it would have had to undergo an environmental impact analysis which might have saved millions of dollars, and perhaps the soul of a city in which the sky remains an indispensable asset. A proposal to develop thirty-five acres along the south side of the Public Garden and Common into a "Park Plaza" found, in 1970, the city still without an effective, democratic way to encourage *and* control urban regrowth. New environmental laws have been helpful, but mistrust and frustration on all sides, based upon blind reliance on outdated assumptions, continue to obscure the planning process.

A "Work Program" to resolve the conflicting social, economic, and environmental impacts was forged by a citizens' advisory committee, members of the Boston Society of Architects, and the Redevelopment Authority. For the first time in a legal document "design" was expressed in terms of "perceptual impacts"; environmental review, which has threatened to become a separate discipline, was reunited with the design process. At this writing the project seems to have been brought into scale with physical and economic realities. If the "Work Program" is carried out properly, the rest should be easy. The ability of Boston to resist the first wild schemes for filling Back Bay may be regained by citizens demands for equal time in the planning process.

John Hancock Tower,
John Hancock Place.
I. M. Pei & Partners; 1973.
Photo: George Cserna

PHOTOS
NEW

Chapter 6
THE FENWAY

It is difficult to assign boundaries to a district which is itself a series of smaller zones of activity strung together by a wandering parkland. The largest is a growth of hospitals and medical facilities. From the air this concentration of at least a dozen world-famous institutions appears to be a second city rising up from a plain of lower buildings. A string of small colleges and schools intersects the indefinite axis of the Fens to terminate in the largest private university in the country. Two turn-of-the-century residential districts straddle the park before its central feature, the Muddy River, attempts a rendezvous with the Charles just below Kenmore Square. That the meeting is at best clandestine can be attributed to the needs of the automobile as interpreted by highway engineers. Until this system of over- and underpasses was built, the Fenway was relatively quiet. Now, like a magnet, they draw a select group of greater Boston's most vicious rush-hour drivers who use these scenic drives as an expressway.

A map helps us to integrate the Fenway and its continuation, the Jamaicaway, with the communities which they abut. From the notes of its designer, Frederick Law Olmsted, it is clear that this great park system was meant to be experienced rather than comprehended. As the city's "Landscape Architect Advisory" he fired the imaginations of the Park Commissioners in a memorandum of 1881. It remains a landmark document in the working vocabulary of the landscape architect.

The Common, Public Garden, and Commonwealth Ave.——Turf, trees, water, and other natural objects unnaturally arranged, but not in the main unpleasingly in consideration of the stately rows of buildings and other architectural and artificial objects with which they must stand associated, and necessary thoroughfares passing among them.

Charles River Embankment.——Broad bay and river views with a rus-urban background seen from a stately promenade.

Back Bay.—[now the Fens—Ed.]——Scenery of a winding, brackish creek, within wooded banks; gaining interest from the meandering course of the water; numerous points and coves softened in their outlines by thickets and with much delicate variety in tone and color through varied and, in landscape art, novel, forms of perennial and herbaceous growths, the picturesque elements emphasized by a few necessary structures, strong but unobtrusive.

Muddy River.——The natural sequence upon slightly higher ground to the last following up a fresh-water course bordered by passages of rushy meadow and varied slopes from the adjoining upland; trees in groups, diversified by thickets and open glades.

Upper Valley of the Muddy River.——A chain of picturesque fresh-water ponds, alternating with attractive natural groves and meads, the uppermost of these ponds being——

Jamaica Pond,——a natural sheet of water, with quiet, graceful shores, rear banks of varied elevation and contour, for the most part shaded by a fine natural forest-growth to be brought out overhangingly, darkening the water's edge and favoring great beauty in reflections and flickering half-lights. At conspicuous points numerous well-grown pines, happily massed, and picturesquely disposed.

The Arboretum.——(Independently of its im-

Aerial of Fenway.
Photo: Aerial Photos of New England, Inc.

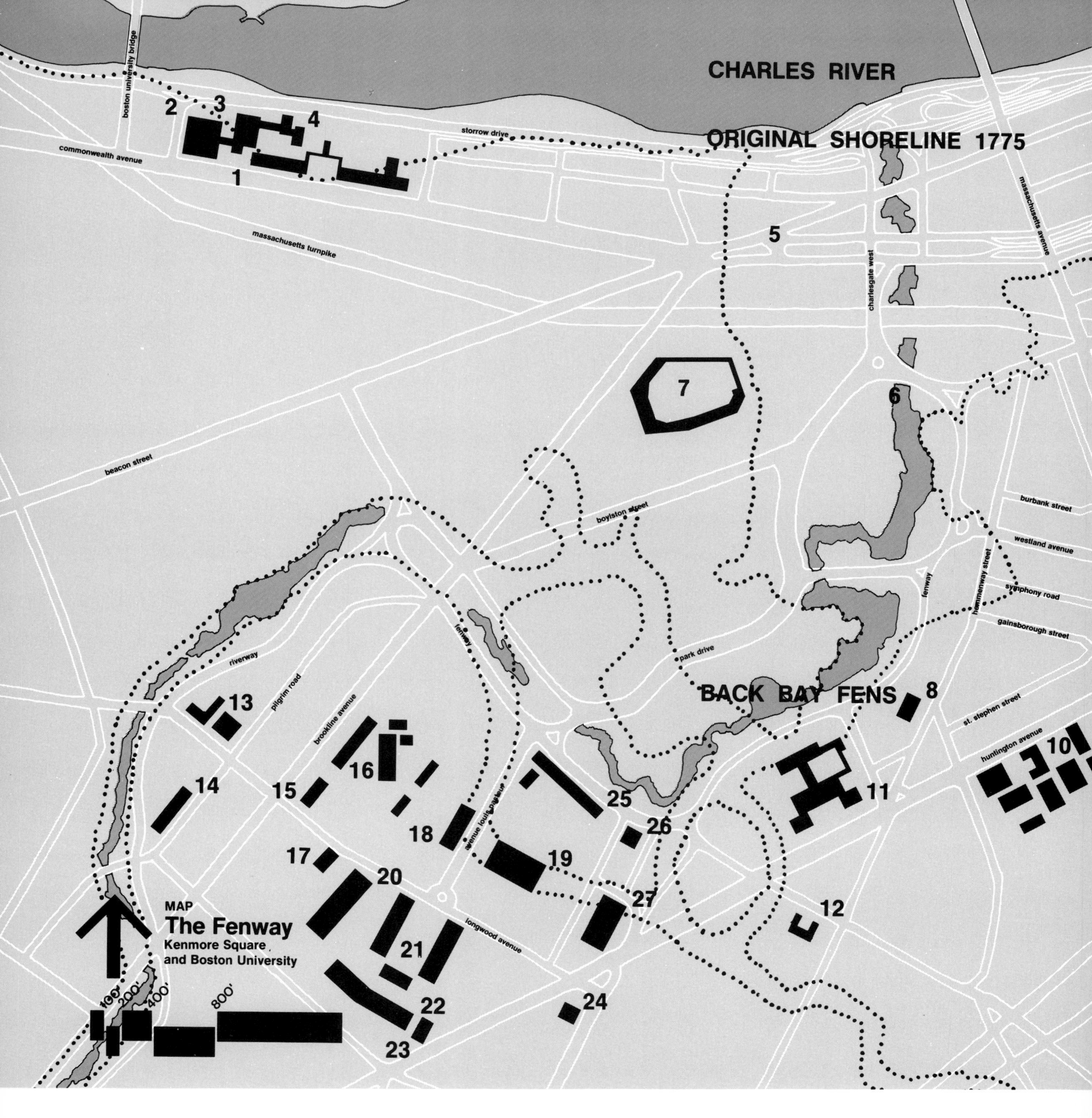
CHARLES RIVER
ORIGINAL SHORELINE 1775
boston university bridge
commonwealth avenue
storrow drive
massachusetts turnpike
charlesgate west
massachusetts avenue
beacon street
boylston street
burbank street
westland avenue
symphony road
gainsborough street
hemenway street
fenway
park drive
riverway
pilgrim road
brookline avenue
avenue louis pasteur
longwood avenue
st. stephen street
huntington avenue
BACK BAY FENS
1
2
3
4
5
6
7
8
10
11
12
13
14
15
16
17
18
19
20
21
22
23
24
25
26
27
MAP
The Fenway
Kenmore Square
and Boston University
100'
200'
400'
800'

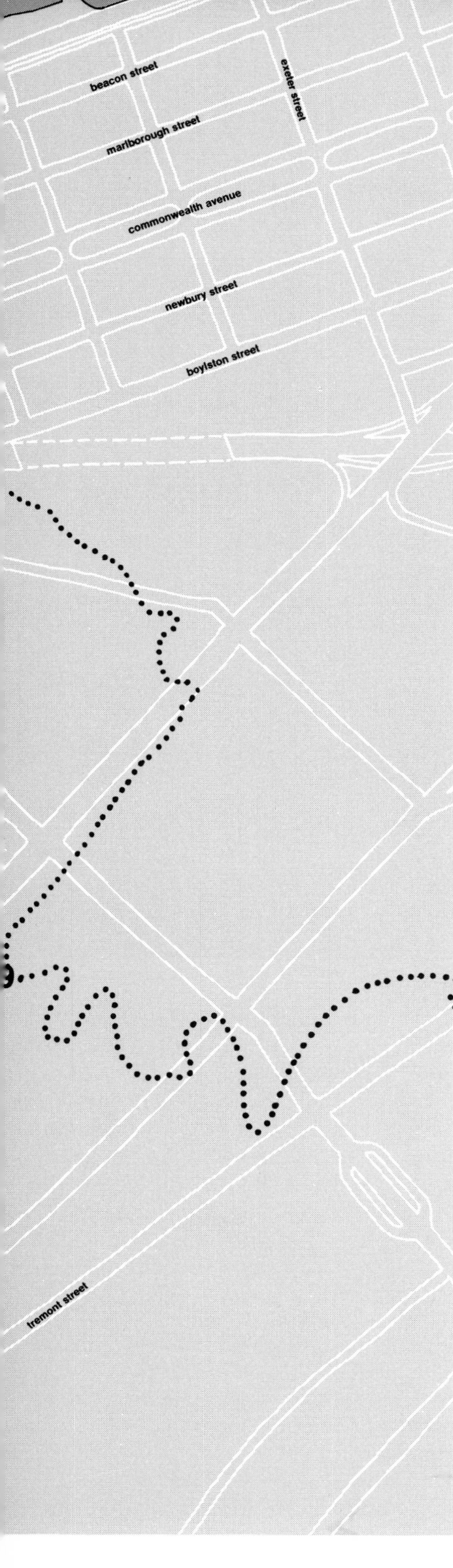

1. Boston University
Charles River Campus
Commonwealth Avenue
Original Buildings: Cram and Ferguson; 1935–50

2. Boston University
George Sherman Union
Sert, Jackson and Gourley
with Hoyle, Doran and Berry; 1963

3. Boston University
Mugar Library
Sert, Jackson and Associates
with Hoyle, Doran and Berry; 1963

4. Boston University
Schools of Law and Education Building
Sert, Jackson and Gourley
with Edwin T. Steffian; 1964

5. Kenmore Square

6. Boylston Bridge
The Fenway
H. H. Richardson; 1880

7. Fenway Park

8. Forsyth Dental Infirmary
140 Fenway
Edward T. P. Graham; 1914

9. New England Conservatory of Music
Huntington Avenue and Gainsborough, 1902

10. Northeastern University
Carl S. Ell Student Center
Shepley, Bulfinch, Richardson and Abbott; 1972

11. Museum of Fine Arts
Huntington Avenue and The Fenway
Guy Lowell; 1907–9
Additions: Hugh Stubbins and Associates; 1966–70
Foster Gallery for Contemporary Art:
The Architects Collaborative; 1976

12. Wentworth Institute

13. Temple Israel
Addition: The Architects Collaborative; 1974

14. New England Deaconess Hospital
Clinical Lab and Parking Garage
The Architects Collaborative; 1973

15. Massachusetts College of Art

16. Beth Israel Hospital
Brookline Avenue, c. 1928

17. Dana Center for Cancer Research
Bertram Goldberg; 1976

18. Boston English High School
Edward Tedesco; 1974

19. Boston Latin School
Avenue Louis Pasteur, 1933

20. Children's Hospital Medical Center Complex
Longwood Avenue
The Architects Collaborative
Master Planning, 1958–
Children's Inn, 1966–68

21. Harvard Medical School
Longwood Avenue
Shepley, Rutan & Coolidge; 1903–

22. Peter Bent Brigham Hospital
Francis Street and Brigham Circle; c. 1914

23. Countway Library of Medicine
Harvard Medical School
Hugh Stubbins and Associates; 1965

24. Charlesbank Apartments
650 Huntington Avenue
Hugh Stubbins and Associates; 1963

25. Simmons College
The Fenway
Campbell, Aldrich and Nulty
Library, 1961
Science Building, 1970

26. Isabella Stewart Gardner Museum
280 The Fenway
Edward H. Sears; 1903

27. State College at Boston
Classroom, Library, Auditorium, and Cafeteria
C. E. Maguire; 1976

Stone Bridge in Fens. *Photo: Max Ferro*

posed features.) Rocky hill-sides, partly wooded with numerous great trees, and a hanging-wood of hemlocks of great beauty. Eminences commanding distant prospects, in one direction seaward over the city, in the other across charming country-side to blue distant hills.

West Roxbury Park.—[Now Franklin Park—Ed.]——Complete escape from the town. Open country. Pastoral scenery. A lovely dale gently winding between low wooded slopes, giving a broad expanse of unbroken turf, lost in the distance under scattered trees.

Agitation for a public park that would rival New York's Central Park (also laid out by Olmsted) began as early as 1869. A Park Commission was created in 1875. It took two more years to pressure the City Council into authorizing borrowed funds for this as yet undeveloped part of the Back Bay. Advisor to an open competition for the park plan, Olmsted "improved" upon the aggregation of ideas until the plan that was approved in 1878 became his personal vision. He was aware that neat street grids help people to find their way, but he also understood the impact of the mysterious and the unexpected on the city-bound: that there must be places within great cities to which one can escape the regularity of streets and buildings. This depends upon strong land-use controls for bordering districts. A serious breach in zoning in the 1960s produced a looming apartment tower on the Jamaicaway that seems to peer into every corner of its sylvan anonymity.

It seems unlikely that Olmsted could have included in his humanistic rationale bumper-to-bumper traffic, or the impact of the elevator on land values. He took for granted Boston's most priceless asset (excepting the east wind in summer), the daily pageant of a sky not yet "improved" with architecture. That the Fenway *is* experienced becomes obvious from its perpetual garnish of broken bottles, beverage cans, windblown paper, discarded tires, and walls of parked automobiles. Olmsted professed to serve a "whole society"; perhaps in time his client will reach a level of awareness that does not require continuous vengeance upon the natural and man-made environment. And yet for those who can tolerate the noise, fumes, and litter, a walk from the State House to Franklin Park along the Emerald Necklace can be an

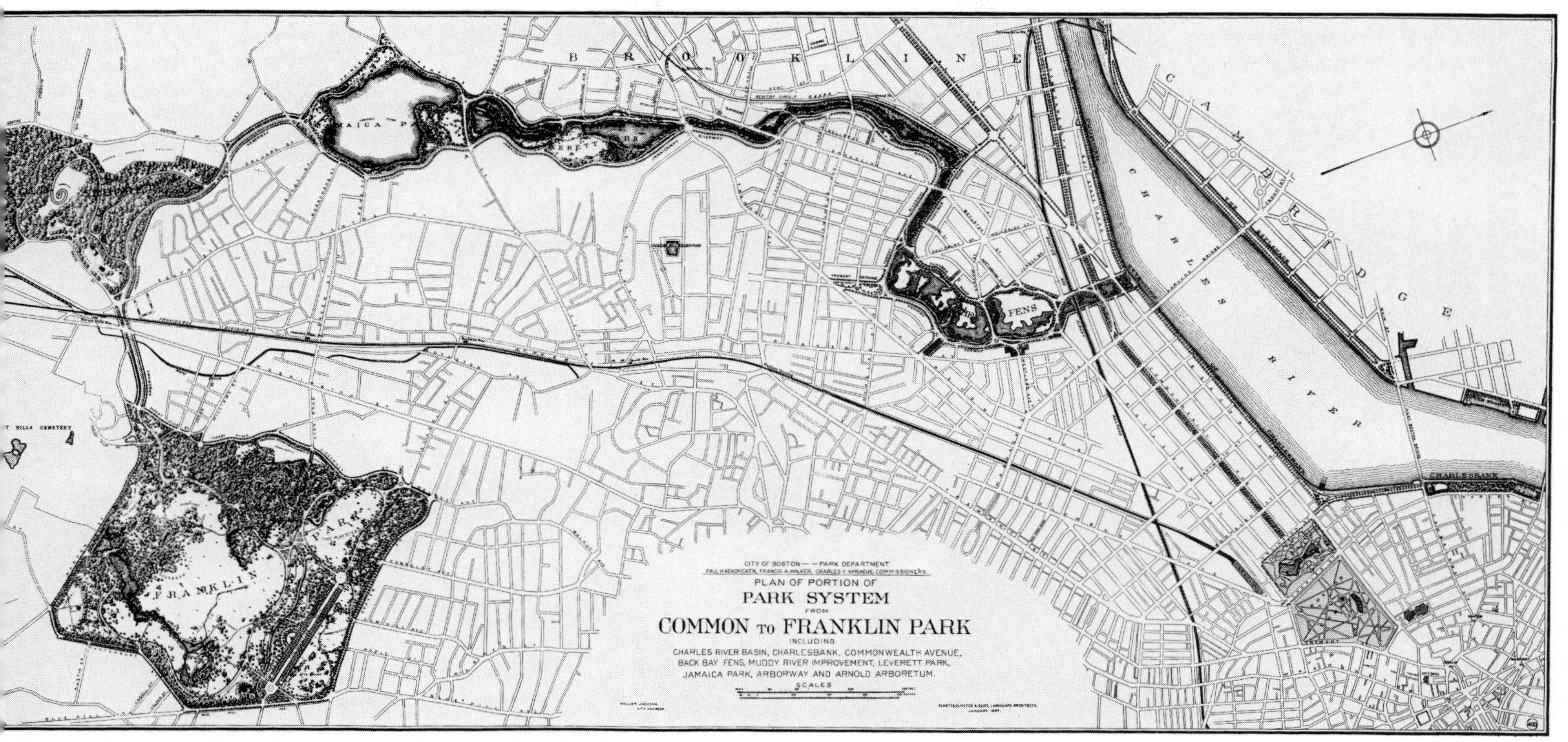

Olmsted Greenway Plan of Park System. *Photo: B. R. A. Archives*

education in urban potential. It is essential to know that these seemingly random manifestations of nature had human guidance; that slimy flats and fetid marshes were transformed by the political process under the direction of a man who believed that there was always a hyphen in the word *re-creation*.

Today over seventy percent of the land in the Fenway (which includes parts of Roxbury and Brookline) is occupied by medical, religious, or educational institutions. Fenway Park, the home of the Boston Red Sox baseball team, is a part of the mixed commercial-industrial district along the northwestern boundary. There is a low-rise apartment neighborhood to the west and a belt of schools and hospitals on the south. The eastern boundary of the Fens proper, except for the Museum of Fine Arts, is lined with buildings that are residential in scale, if largely institutional in use. It will serve little purpose to follow the precise chronology of the Fenway: the patterns of Boston's institutions have always been complex and interlocking. Nor will a stylistic analysis add clarity since the major development took place at the high point in American architectural eclecticism.

If the past decade of renewal in Boston has seemed preoccupied with construction of buildings, it is interesting to contemplate the effect of the Fenway's rapid growth upon a city which was then much smaller. The following buildings were all completed in or near the area in the decades just preceding and after the turn of the century: Museum of Fine Arts, Symphony and Horticultural halls, New England Conservatory of Music, Massachusetts Historical Society, Boston Medical Library, Harvard Medical School, Fenway Court (the Isabella Stewart Gardner Museum), Boston Opera House (now demolished), New England Deaconess Hospital, Northeastern University, Simmons and Wheelock colleges, and the Winsor School. By stretching the period a few years we can add Peter Bent Brigham and Robert Breck Brigham hospitals, Forsyth Dental Infirmary, and Emmanuel College.

Speculation took no small part in the process from the start. The City Council, hoping to kill the Fenway project, tied approval of funds to a maximum land cost

Isabella Stewart Gardner Museum, 280 The Fenway. Edward H. Sears; 1902. *Photo: James Douglass*

Museum of Fine Arts, Huntington Avenue and The Fenway. Guy Lowell; 1907-9. Additions: Hugh Stubbins and Associates; 1966-70. Foster Gallery for Contemporary Art: The Architects Collaborative; 1976. *Photo: Max Ferro*

of ten cents per square foot. As fast as Olmsted worked at "abatement of a complicated nuisance, threatening soon to be a deadly peril to the whole community as a propagating and breeding ground of pestilential epidemics," residential developers kept pace. In the East Fenway, also called the "Seven Streets" area, construction took place almost entirely between 1884 and 1912. Houses and apartments on St. Stephen's, Gainsborough, Hemenway, and Burbank streets, Symphony Road, Westland Avenue, and the Fenway itself are similar to, but less distinguished than the later buildings in the Back Bay. They represent the efforts of such architects as Arthur Vinal, F. A. Norcross, S. F. Ober, and Peabody and Stearns to work under speculative conditions. An exception is that first part of the Fenway at Boylston Street, where owners of town houses by Peabody and Stearns or Longfellow and Darrow could take advantage of the splendid park frontage.

The Seven Streets district is now inhabited by a mixture of students, professionals working at nearby institutions, and a proportion of the elderly that approaches twenty percent. The average income level is low; equivalent housing alternatives in the inner city rare. Neighborhood groups have developed skills in coping with urban renewal. Construction of Church Park was held up until about 177 federally subsidized units were made available to the poor and elderly. A resident group, the Fenway Development Corporation, was formed to rehabilitate available parcels. The neighborhood has become polarized between those who feel they do not want to see improvements that will drive the poor and elderly out and those who seek a "strong middle class" population with a reduction in the proportion of low income residents.

The situation in the residential area on the opposite side of the Fens is somewhat different. A block bounded by Park Drive, Brookline Avenue, and Boylston Street was built up by speculators in the period just before and after World War I. Although the apartment units were ample, the fill upon which the buildings were constructed was inferior to that of the South

Rose Garden in the Fens. *Photo: James Douglass*

Simmons College Library. Campbell, Aldrich and Nulty; 1961. *Photo: Phokion Karas*

End and Back Bay. So also were the construction standards. Many of the properties were bought up by a single landlord in a technique known as "pyramiding." The apartments were cut up into smaller units, inadequately maintained, and allowed to deteriorate. An unusual coalition developed between younger residents, many of them students, or recent graduates who elected to stay in the area, and the elderly who were being threatened with eviction. The result: a responsible, if aggressive counterculture movement is seeking ways to place those properties in receivership under tenant management and, if possible, ownership. Other apartments, especially those along the Drive, have remained in stable hands. With support from the courts and banks, this district with such fascinating street names as Peterborough, Queensbury, and Kilmarnock will regain a character consistent with its enviable location.

When the Museum of Fine Arts left its dark Ruskinian Gothic home in Copley Square for a fresh start in the Fenway, it seemed appropriate to house its collections from Egypt, Greece, and Rome in a neoclassic environment. This was accomplished by Guy Lowell (1907–9) without compromise. Ironically, the Oriental collections are those most closely linked with Boston's past. Starting with the China trade and continuing through the travels of scholars and wealthy patrons, Boston has acquired significant collections of the art of China, Japan, and the Middle East. For those interested in the details of life in early Boston, the decorative arts collection contains entire rooms as well as individual artifacts demonstrating the skill of early craftsmen such as George Bright, John Cogswell, and Paul Revere. The museum's exhibits of silver, china, fabrics, and furniture provide insight into the character of Bostonians of the late eighteenth and early nineteenth centuries, their reverence for beauty, and the affluence that made it

Children's Hospital
Medical Center Complex,
Longwood Avenue. The
Architects Collaborative.
Master Planning, 1958-.
Children's Inn, 1966-68.
Photo: Phokion Karas

Countway Library of Medicine, Harvard Medical School. Hugh Stubbins and Associates; 1965. *Photo: Louis Reens*

Harvard Medical School, Longwood Avenue. Shepley, Rutan & Coolidge; 1903. *Photo: Max Ferro*

New England Deaconess Hospital Parking Garage. The Architects Collaborative; 1971. *Photo: Phokion Karas*

attainable. For a fuller understanding of this period and the culture that led up to it, there are many fine examples of houses, early and late, maintained by the Society for the Preservation of New England Antiquities (first Harrison Gray Otis House on Cambridge Street) in the Boston area. Within a day's drive the Plimoth Plantation, Salem Village and Green, and Old Sturbridge Village succeed in re-creating entire historic environments. For an idea of what Boston's waterfront and early commercial growth might have been like, Newburyport and New Bedford have managed to preserve significant parts of their seagoing past.

The museum was expanded in 1915 (Guy Lowell) and again in 1928, following the same style. The firm of Saltonstall and Morton introduced contemporary ideas on the interior with a museum shop (1958) and galleries for the art of Egypt and the Near East in the 1960s. A three stage program was undertaken by Hugh Stubbins and Associates in 1966 that created a new gallery for the Forsyth Wicks Collection of European decorative arts and general remodeling of the decorative arts wing. The final stage, completed in 1970, was a service wing which created a contemporary sculpture court on the west, overlooked by an enlarged restaurant. The wing was executed in concrete using an aggregate which, when sandblasted, blended in with the older buildings. Current work at the museum includes the new Foster Gallery for Contemporary Art in the east wing and planning for improved storage and conservation facilities, all by the Architects Collaborative.

The palace that Mrs. John Lowell Gardner, Jr., built for herself at 280 The Fenway and opened to the public on New Year's Night, 1903, is a collection within a collection. Working with a vision of the Poldi Pezzoli in Milan, she and her husband collected fragments and entire sections of Italian architecture. With her architect, Edward H. Sears, she designed (and supervised every detail of construction of) a long rectangular palazzo with a tall courtyard. Loggias, stairways, columns, fireplaces, fountains, windows, balconies, floors, and ceilings were incorporated into the design as they went along. The skylight over the courtyard permits an Italian climate for year-round displays of flowers and exotic plants. These are propagated and maintained in a handsome complex of greenhouses next door, designed by James Lawrence, Jr. To this "Mrs. Jack" added the proceeds of a lifetime of collecting, advised by scholars from America, Europe, and the Far East. From 1903 until her death in 1924, she lived and entertained in an environment of great works of art from every period and from every part of the world; tapestries, paintings, prints, etchings, sculpture, furniture, books, letters, and smaller artifacts. Members of the Boston Symphony played on opening night; performances continue as a tradition today. Her guests were drawn from the world of art, letters, and society. Of those artists who were her contemporaries, many were friends to whom she gave support. Her own portrait by John Singer Sargent (after nine attempts) hangs with the works of such artists as Botticelli, Boucher, Cellini, Courbet, Degas, Giorgione, Ingres, Manet, Raphael, Rembrandt, Rubens, Tiepolo, and Titian. It is unfair to judge Fenway Court as architecture, although the carriage house is a near reproduction of a structure in Altamura. In her will, by which she gave the museum to the public, Mrs. Gardner simply refers to a collection of "pictures, statuary, works of art, bric-a-brac, furniture, books and papers." George L. Stout, director of the museum from 1955 until 1970, observed that "Fenway Court was indeed filled—without conceit or pretense—with all the things Mrs. Gardner personally loved and

Fens Scene—Muddy River. *Photo: James Douglass*

Temple Israel. Addition: The Architects Collaborative; 1974. *Photo: Phokion Karas*

nterior, Carl S. Ell Student Center, Northeastern University. Shepley, Bulfinch, Richardson and Abbott; 1972. *Photo: Shepley, Bulfinch, Richardson and Abbott*

State College at Boston. Classroom, Library, Auditorium, and Cafeteria Building. C. E. Maguire; 1976. *Photo: C E. Maguire*

wanted to collect. Scraps, small objects, and objects of small consequence stand alongside works that are famous."

The temptation to re-create a latter-day Roman Forum was given full rein in the 1906 Harvard Medical School campus (Shepley, Rutan and Coolidge) on Longwood Avenue. Its white marble formality, surrounding a generous green lawn, presented a challenge to architects that followed. For the successor firm, Coolidge & Shattuck, the obvious choice for the Boston Lying-In Hospital across the street was yellow brick Italian Renaissance. This style was later employed for a companion building, Vanderbilt Hall, to the west. The Countway Library of Medicine responds to its neoclassic environment with a direct statement of its functions. A full height, top-lighted interior court is surrounded by a ring of open stacks, outside of which a variety of study-conference alcoves can be seen as protruding from the double columns. The limestone-clad structure supports a top level of offices (for two medical journals), which in turn shelters the recessed balconies of the lounge and special functions floor. Designed by Hugh Stubbins and Associates, the clarity of its planning understates the awesome body of medical literature to which it gives effortless access.

An attempt to resolve the axis of Huntington Avenue with that of the campus determined the fanlike massing of the Harvard School of Public Health (Kessler Associates). Interior planning was "adjusted" to carry out the exterior effect, but the west facade deals responsibly with the courtyard it forms with Countway Library and the early campus. The main floor, like that of Countway, is skylighted by one of the stepped-back floors. The skin, precast concrete panels with a slight rib, is too close to the limestone in value, creating some confusion as to which material is real. A heavier corrugation of the panels might have been more comfortable.

What seems to be a caricature of the National Capitol on Longwood Avenue to the west (Shepley, Rutan and Coolidge; 1903) is the parent building of the Children's Medical Center. Once a gathering of specialized buildings and wards, the Center has grown into a massive complex. The Architects Collaborative began its master planning in 1958. The result is a community of buildings and spaces in the best tradition of urban design. A multiple-use structure at the corner of Longwood

Charlesbank Apartments, 650 Huntington Avenue.
Hugh Stubbins and Associates; 1963.
Photo: Phokion Karas

and Brookline avenues combines housing for hospital personnel, commercial and banking facilities, a garage, swimming pool, and a motel for the families of children who come for treatment in this world-renowned institution. A second tower to the east, containing laboratories, offices, and treatment facilities will be linked with the Children's Inn complex by a bridge over the intervening street. Between the Children's and Brookline Avenue are the Jimmy Fund Building (Leland & Larsen), the Shields Warren Radiation Therapy Unit (Peirce and Pierce), and the Dana Center for Cancer Research (Bertram Goldberg & Associates). With the exception of the latter, these buildings work well with the unifying cast-in-place-concrete vocabulary established by TAC, which permits a variety of infill materials: glass, masonry, or precast units. The master plan calls for the removal of a large, but obsolete, power plant to a site south of the hospital. This will permit a positive link between the Brookline Avenue buildings and the Center.

A Medical Area Service Corporation has been formed to provide and operate a "total energy" plant, providing steam, domestic hot water, cooling, incineration, and electricity for eight major institutions. Because the growth patterns of so many hospitals have become a threat to residents in the immediate neighborhood to the south, the relocation of this power plant precipitated an impasse, with the usual town-and-gown polarities. In this case the gowns were medical, but the target was Harvard. The firm of Benjamin Thompson & Associates was retained to design the plant through a community advocacy process. Some of the building will be placed belowground, higher portions stepped back. The street level will have offices and a plaza, while a covered arcade will connect the residential area with Brookline Avenue. Another community process has brought the Boston Redevelopment Authority, Harvard, and a neighborhood group, Roxbury Tenants of Harvard, together in Mission Park. Now under construction, 755 apartment units will be served by a 1,200-car garage, swimming pool, tennis courts, a playground, and community building. The design is by John Sharratt & Associates, with Glazer/deCastro/Vitols as associate architects.

Plans are in progress for the amalgamation of three other institutions, the Boston Hospital for Women and the Peter Bent and Robert Breck Brigham hospitals, in the Affiliated Hospital Center. Designed by Bertram Goldberg & Associates, it will continue the specialties of maternity and orthopedics as well as treatment of unusual diseases. Across Brookline Avenue the Joslin Diabetes Clinic has received a recent addition by Payette & Associates. The original building was designed by Shepley, Bulfinch, Richardson and Abbott in 1955. It is a part of the New England Deaconess Hospital as is the new laboratory building at the corner of Pilgrim Road and Frances Street. Here, The Architects Collaborative have used a mirrored glass wall to conceal the fact that the space between each floor and the ceiling below it is nearly high enough to stand up in. Had a conventional wall been used, the vertical distance between windows would have left the building out of scale with its older neighbors. The space between floors allows mechanical services to each laboratory to be changed to meet new requirements. Vertical air circulation is carried through stainless steel ducts running up the east facade. In addition to the flexibility and extra floor space provided, the ducts themselves have been used as a decorative element which identifies the building's function without overpowering it.

Collegiate architecture in the Fenway runs the gamut from educational Georgian and neo-Gothic to nonstop modern. Much of it is transitional, using vestiges of historic styles applied to simple structures to render them as inoffensive as possible. Almost too clean a break was made in the Simmons College Library (Campbell, Aldrich & Nulty; 1961) with a pristine limestone grid facade punctuated with stylish protruding carrels. A later science building by the same firm attempts to regain the anonymity of the original brick college facing the Fenway. Boston State College,

Fens Scene—Pedestrian Bridge. *Photo: James Douglass*

Boston University Complex from across the River. Original Buildings: Cram and Ferguson; 1935-50. *Photo: Phokion Karas*

having mushroomed its way north from the corner of Longwood and Huntington avenues through successive interpretations of Georgian, has recently exploded in a new black glass megastructure (C. E. Maguire). It appears to be an attempt to work with a small, irregular site, using broken massing and the reflective glass to minimize its presence. Northeastern University, famous for its cooperative work-study program, adopted a no-nonsense white brick with dark vertical window and spandrel elements. This consistent, if brittle, idiom has now become well established along Huntington Avenue. An inward-looking student center on the east side of the campus (Shepley, Bulfinch, Richardson and Abbott; 1968) presents an interesting break in the rhythm of their other work for the university. It must be seen from the inside to be appreciated.

While located along the Charles River, the sprawling Boston University campus can be included with the Fenway and deserves special attention. Chartered in 1869, it existed as a series of small colleges until about 1935 when it began to consolidate along the water side of Commonwealth Avenue. Early ecclesiastical beginnings and the reputation of its architect, Cram and Ferguson, dictated collegiate Gothic. By 1950 the liberal arts and theology buildings were linked by cloisters to the Marsh Chapel. In order to stand up to the longer structures, the Chapel had to be nearly all steeple. Expansion was absorbed by Bay State Road brownstones for several years until the postwar baby boom made major growth inevitable. Three large structures, all strongly influenced by José Luis Sert, the Dean of the School of Design at Harvard, set the pace for Boston University and, perhaps, for Harvard as well. The first increment was the George Sherman Union at the western end of the complex (Sert, Jackson and Gourley with Hoyle, Doran and Berry; 1963). A multipurpose structure, it houses student activities as well as dining facilities and function rooms. An early example of Sert's work in concrete, its crisp sunshades and precast panels have held up well during a period when architectural tastes have wavered between brutality and mirrored invisibility. A second building, the Law and Education Tower, makes ingenious use of a double elevator bank to provide future flexibility. Those wishing to reach the School of Education enter at one level; for the Law School, another. Elevators are assigned to each entrance level and corresponding upper floors. In the event one school or the other expands into the entire building,

Boston University. George Sherman Union. Sert, Jackson and Gourley with Hoyle, Doran and Berry; 1963.
Photo: Louis Reens

Boston University. Mugar Library. Sert, Jackson and Associates with Hoyle, Doran and Berry; 1966.
Photo: Steve Rosenthal

all elevators can be assigned to general use. The low building on the east with a series of curving shapes on the roof is the Law Library; the curves are spectacular skylights that bathe the interior with a pleasantly diffused level of illumination. The tower and library were designed by Sert, Jackson and Gourley with Edwin T. Steffian (1964). A low, stepped-back building, the Mugar Library (Sert, Jackson and Associates with Hoyle, Doran and Berry) was completed in 1966.

The significance of these buildings can be measured in at least three ways: as urban design, as architectural innovation, and as the perpetuation of an ideal. Opportunities for a single firm to design as many interrelated structures in so brief a time are rare. That they be placed so conspicuously, even rarer. By the time the tower was topped off, it was clear that these were not ordinary buildings. Strange colored slits and towering projections needed interpretation. We were asked to read a new language in which functional parts of the building (such as elevator towers and ventilating equipment) were incorporated into the overall design, rather than consigned to sheet metal boxes on the roof. But had not earlier periods of architecture been enriched by chimneys (heating equipment) and stair towers (vertical circulation)? The three buildings suggest that their parts might be interchangeable. While this might imply prefabrication (which is in fact the case), it also says that the buildings are the product of a system of construction rather than a fixed idea of what they should look like. The work of Sert is more closely related to Gothic architecture, in itself a system of construction. In fact, these buildings are more Gothic than the first buildings on the campus by Cram and Ferguson, who sought in vain for this ideal by looking backward in time. They found instead a dead "classic" image compromised by contemporary budgets and building techniques.

Caught between the Fenway and the river, and separated from the Back Bay by frantic overpasses, Kenmore Square continues its long downward slide from a fashionable residential-commercial district. Today, surrounded by colleges and proprietary schools, it is a twenty-four-hour student center supporting fast-food chains, singles bars and discotheques, and third-world specialty shops. The ground floors of once elegant Commonwealth Avenue apartments harbor pubs and dispense submarine sandwiches or instant pizza. The regional symbol is a gargantuan neon pop art visual concert—a pulsating triangle suggesting consumption of a certain brand of gasoline.

Would Mr. Olmsted approve? After some adjustment to noise and the level of air pollutants (about which he warned us in 1870), he would certainly be pleased to see so many residents at work in their Fenway garden plots. He might recognize a baseball game, but would wonder at the intensity with which young people belabor backboards with basketballs or the orderly scrimmages with footballs. He might recognize in the colorful flying Frisbies the cake-tin lids that were once a part of every Sunday school picnic. He would probably inspect the condition of H. H. Richardson's rugged stone bridges and marvel at the sophisticated play apparatus required for tot-lots. But the person who dreamed of "circumstances—favorable to a pleasureful wakefulness of the mind without stimulating exertion; and the close relation of family life, the association of children, of mothers, of lovers, or those who may be lovers, stimulate and keep alive the more tender sympathies, and give play to faculties such as may be dormant in business or on the promenade—" could not have been a stuffy man.

Boston University. Schools of Law and Education. Sert, Jackson and Gourley with Edwin T. Steffian; 1964.
Photo: Phokion Karas

Row Houses in the South End.
Photo: James Douglass

Chapter 7
THE SOUTH END/ SOUTH COVE

Before 1800 the South End of Boston was simply that part south of Union Street (near City Hall), extending between the lines of the Common and the waterfront. The waterfront followed a line close to that of Broad and Essex streets back into the Neck. Much of this area has been covered in other chapters. The early character in the seventeenth and eighteenth centuries was that of freestanding, often substantial houses, with gardens. The Boston Latin School, the first public school in America, was already established on School Street when the first King's Chapel was built in 1689. Peter Harrison's stone replacement was not built until 1749. Since there was no ledge to be found on the Shawmut Peninsula, the building material had to be brought by barge from Quincy. There were brickyards on the Neck before the Revolution. The present Old South Meetinghouse is also the second on its site. The original 1669 wooden version was destroyed in the fire of 1711. Joshua Blanchard's 1729 design provided the canopied side pulpit against which the oratory of Otis and Warren hurled the metaphors for the confusing events of the 1770s and the incentive for their resolution. It was from one such meeting, at which a reported five thousand persons were assembled, that a well-organized group of citizens shed their cloaks to reveal approximations of Indian dress, and proceeded with war whoops to Griffin's Wharf.

Near the beginning of the Neck, which was the only wooded part of the peninsula, Achmuty's Tavern was the scene of meetings held by the Sons of Liberty and a slightly more radical group, the Loyal Nine. A large elm was selected nearby, convenient for posting notices and hanging effigies of Crown officials currently in disfavor. The North End–South End rivalry had its religious overtones (Chapter 2), but they were largely based upon the degree of affiliation with the Anglican Church, unable to resolve its own relationship to Rome. On November 5, 1765, the usual Pope's Day fracas was replaced with a joint procession from the North End to the Liberty Tree at the Neck, then back to Copp's Hill. Here the traditionally rival factions celebrated in complete harmony over the repeal of the hated Stamp Act.

During the Revolution, the Neck became, in addition to the site of elaborate fortifications, a checkpoint for nearly everyone and everything entering the besieged town. After the war the pattern of expansion took on the aspect of franchises to build seawalls and new streets reaching toward Roxbury. The first of these was Front Street (Harrison Avenue) in 1804. This, and the one along the line of Shawmut Avenue, followed earlier breakwaters erected in colonial times to protect the Neck from flooding. From an area which had been regarded for over a century as fraught with danger from Indians, careless hunters, and high tides, the Neck and made land along it became the focus of new growth to the south. A part of this area, more properly referred to as the South Cove, with its neighbor, Bay Village,

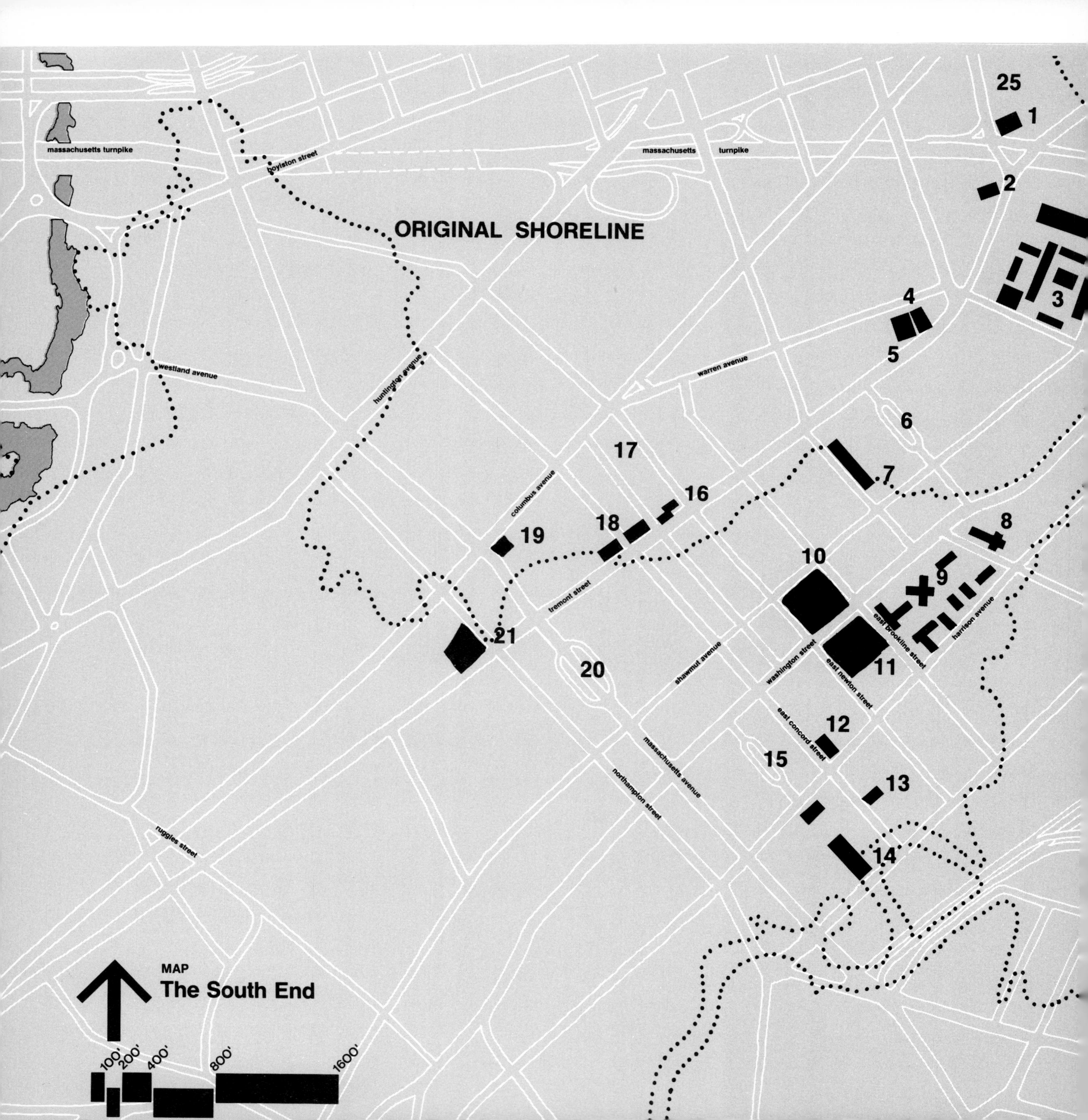

massachusetts turnpike
boylston street
massachusetts turnpike
ORIGINAL SHORELINE
westland avenue
huntington avenue
warren avenue
columbus avenue
tremont street
shawmut avenue
washington street
east brookline street
harrison avenue
east newton street
east concord street
massachusetts avenue
northampton street
ruggles street
25
1
2
3
4
5
6
7
8
9
10
11
12
13
14
15
16
17
18
19
20
21
MAP
The South End
100'
200'
400'
800'
1600'

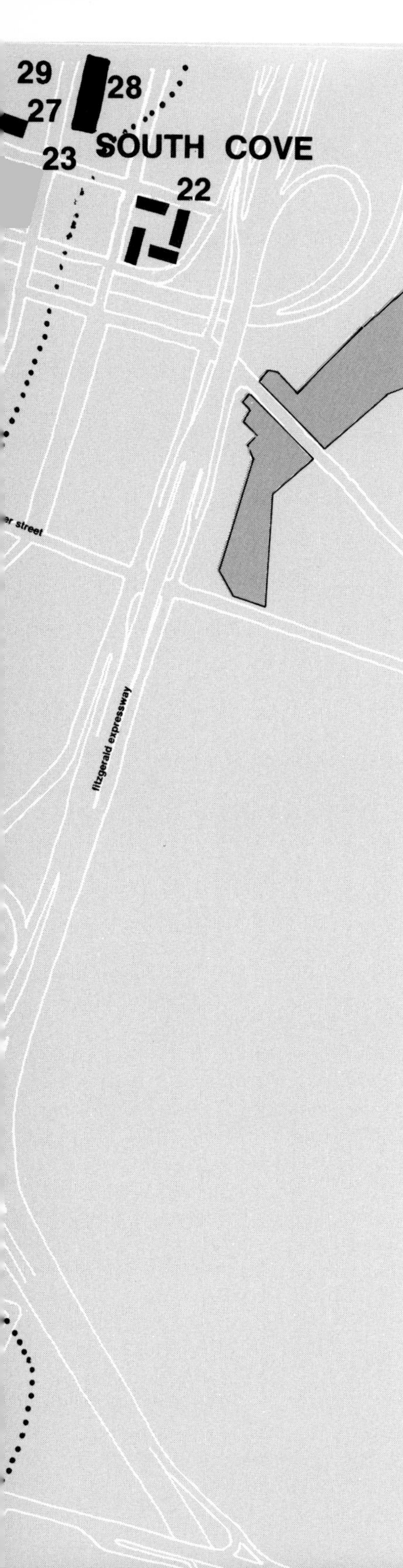

1. Goodwill Industries Rehabilitation Center
   Arlington Street and Columbus Avenue
   Perry, Dean and Stewart; 1971

2. Animal Rescue League
   10 Chandler Street
   Hugh Stubbins and Associates; 1956

3. Castle Square (housing)
   492 Tremont Street
   Samuel Glaser & Partners; 1967

4. National Theatre
   Clarence H. Blackall; 1911

5. Cyclorama—Boston Center for the Arts
   539 Tremont Street
   (Originally built to house a Cyclorama commemorating the Civil War; 1884)
   Use as a flower market; 1923–68

6. Union Park
   1851

7. Torre Unidad (elderly housing)
   80 West Dedham Street
   John Sharratt; 1974
   Addition: 1976

8. Cathedral of the Holy Cross
   P. C. Keeley; 1867–75

9. Cathedral Housing Project
   Harold Field Kellog; 1950

10. Blackstone Square; c. 1850

11. Franklin Square; c. 1850

12. Church of the Immaculate Conception
    P. C. Keeley; 1861

13. Boston University School of Medicine
    Basic Sciences Instructional Building
    80 East Concord Street
    Housman Research Building
    732 Harrison Avenue
    Shepley, Bulfinch, Richardson and Abbott; 1969 and 1968 respectively
    School of Graduate Dentistry, Albany Street
    The Architects Collaborative; 1970
    Addition: Martha & Elliot Rothman

14. Boston City Hospital
    Central Administration Building
    Gridley J. F. Bryant; 1864

15. Worcester Square
    1851

16. South End Branch Library
    Tremont Street
    Mitchell, Giurgola Associates; 1971

17. Rutland Square c. 1862

18. Tremont Homes
    Tremont Street from Rutland Square to Worcester Square
    Sert, Jackson and Associates; 1971

19. Neighborhood-built Playground
    Massachusetts and Columbus avenues, 1968

20. Chester Square
    Massachusetts Avenue between Tremont Street and Shawmut Avenue, 1850

21. Piano Craft Guild 1853
    Rehabilitated 1974
    Gelardin/Bruner/Cott, & Co. with Anderson Notter Associates; 1974

22. Tai Tung Village, Housing for the Chinese Community
    Stahl/Bennett & Co.; 1972

23. Quincy Elementary School
    The Architects Collaborative; 1976

24. Massachusetts Pike Towers
    Stahl/Bennett & Co.; 1972

25. Bay Village
    Many houses date back to 1820–30

26. Church of All Nations
    Bertram Goldberg; 1975

27. Addition to
    Don Bosco Technical High School
    Halasz & Halasz; 1975

28. Tufts-New England Medical Center
    The Architects Collaborative; 1973

29. Chinatown (North of South Cove)
    Beach to Essex Street

Rutland Square, c. 1862. *Photo: James Douglass*

will be dealt with at the end of this chapter.

The new South End is generally regarded as starting at Dover and East Berkeley streets. From this line the four main streets fan out: Harrison, Washington (the original route), Shawmut, and Tremont. They are connected by quiet side streets along which row houses face each other, often with shared service alleys at the rear. The success of the Tontine Crescent on Franklin Street (1793) plus the plans for Louisburg and Pemberton squares (1826 and 1835) had a strong effect on the South End street layout. The graceful curved street of sixteen houses, with its arch and fenced-in park, designed by Bulfinch for the old South End, had another fortuitous consequence. It led to his bankruptcy, and therefore his need to become a serious practicing architect. It would be hard to imagine Boston (or Washington, D.C.) without his presence.

As the business district encroached on the old South End (the Tontine Crescent was demolished in 1858, leaving a vestige of its curve in upper Franklin Street), Bostonians of means looked to the new South End as the logical extension of the prime residential area. Therefore, many of the South End side streets have varied versions of these delightful little parks, with grass, trees, fountains, and statuary. Tremont Street, the only one that is straight and wider in comparison to its building heights, has a scale that comes as close as any part of Boston to the popular notion of London. In a burst of enthusiasm over the railroad, many of the streets were named for the cities and towns through which the Boston and Albany passed.

Horsecars began to ply these routes by 1853, giving an impetus to development. Chester Square and East and West Chester parks, now only widenings in Massachusetts Avenue, were once a part of this general pattern before the present artery was rammed through. A comparison of the houses of this early part of the South End has been made by Bunting in *Houses of Boston's Back Bay*. He sees them as "relentlessly independent house units, each with its separate swell front, its own flight of front steps, its particular entrance porch." Unity is achieved through repetition without minimizing separateness. "Two or three stories tall above the basement, each house is three windows wide—two contained in the swelling bay and one over the entrance. To this simple scheme is added a quantity of brownstone decoration—undulating lintels, door frames with hoods supported by ponderous brackets, and a heavily rusticated basement. Although ornate, the decoration belongs to no historic style, and it has a heavy plastic quality that dominates the brick wall surface." He finds relationships with houses of Louisburg Square, Regency England,

and bracketed Italianate designs. His comparison of this rather heavy-handed detailing with the "more abstract principles of composition," "architectonic ornamentation," and more "accurate" archaeology of the Back Bay itself is academic and somewhat hard on a district that has great charm. He uses it to clarify differences between the two districts in general. Back Bay, with its clear boundaries and well-organized street layout, has unity, although the houses themselves are quite varied in design, if not in rules of composition. The South End, with at least three different street grid patterns, and elusive boundaries, breaks into subdistricts which have a "cellular quality." In recent times this has helped in two ways: by allowing small coherent neighborhood units to survive changes around them; and to discourage through traffic, the scourge of the Back Bay.

Following this residential movement came the churches, many of them enriched by sale of their original sites overrun by the business district. There were at least eighteen that relocated or started anew: Unitarian, Congregational, Presbyterian, Baptist, Lutheran, and two "colored" Baptist Societies, the Ebenezer and the Day Star—in West Concord and Appleton streets. Increased by immigration, the Roman Catholic Church was very much in evidence. The granite Renaissance Church of the Immaculate Conception (P. C. Keeley; 1861) was built by the Jesuit Order on Harrison Avenue. Two years later they founded Boston College in a red brick building next door. Keeley also designed the immense Cathedral of the Holy Cross on Washington Street, consecrated in 1875. It has the altar of the first (Bulfinch) cathedral in its crypt (Chapter 2).

Boston Latin School moved out from downtown to a double building designed to house it and English High School as well (George Clough; 1877). Both were for boys; a mansard style Girl's High had been built seven years earlier in the neighborhood. All are gone today, although the idea of separate secondary education for boys and girls held on in Boston until quite recently.

Although the Back Bay was well along by the 1860s, a section between it and the South End remained unimproved. It consisted of mud flats sloping from the newly filled land on either side of the Boston and Providence Railroad tracks. Columbus Avenue, with its attendant side streets, was conceived of as a solution. The momentum of development led to speculation, default, risky financing, and smaller lots and houses. This was collapsed by the panic of 1873, bringing the entire South End down with it. Accounts differ as to the rapidity with which new South Enders elected to move to the Back Bay or farther

Elevated Train Structure on Washington Street. *Photo: James Douglass*

Chester Square, Massachusetts Avenue between Tremont Street and Shawmut Avenue. 1850. *Photo: James Douglass*

out to the "streetcar suburbs." The father of George Apley (a Marquand hero) left immediately after seeing a man in his shirt sleeves sitting on the brownstone steps across the street. Warner, in his book *Streetcar Suburbs,* saw this move by the upper middle class as "not just a search for a new facade for row houses; rather—a mass exodus before the advance of industry, commerce, and immigrants." By 1885 the area had become a lower middle class and lodging house section. Once fashionable houses were occupied by three, four, or even more families. They were served by sanitary facilities that by today's standards were barely adequate for their original purpose, let alone multiple use. The patterns associated with immigration and overcrowding in the last part of the nineteenth century have plagued the South End ever since. Like Roxbury, it became a "zone of emergence" for some, the end of the line for others. By 1919 it was characterized as a district of people without local attachments, separated from each other by race and religion, near the city but remote from its best life.

The crowning indignity was the erection of the elevated railway down Washington Street in 1901. For half a century the district remained a mute, if accommodating resource, kept alive by the availability of inexpensive housing and proximity to jobs in the center of the city and in industries that sprouted indiscriminately along its elusive perimeter. From 1950 to 1970 the population declined by 30,000. Planning surveys found 50 percent of the buildings to be substandard. The Boston Redevelopment Authority began to cope with what was the largest urban renewal area in the country. It tried selective demolition, rerouting of through traffic, infill housing, and new schools. The answer was a concerted demand from both long-established and newly formed community groups to save as much of the existing housing stock as possible. Two developments of the late 1960s had changed the direction of growth. The effect of the physical and social bridge created when the Prudential Center spanned the old Back Bay railroad yards was just beginning to be felt. Properties along the Back Bay edge had become desirable alternatives for families who could not afford Beacon Hill and Back Bay. Many of these were the lower cost houses that had been built before and after the Columbus Avenue fiasco. They were smaller and had been used primarily as rooming houses, as opposed to being chopped up into tenements. This made them easier to convert into single family or duplex use. Those buildings with less elaborate brownstone ornament and angular, rather than curving, fronts had survived years of neglect. In 1960 a workable shell could be purchased for $5,000; today, on the right street, it might bring as much as $100,000 in rejuvenated condition.

Encouragement for this trend came from a hard core of South Enders who had discovered several of the choice tree-lined squares in previous years. They had joined with the multiethnic community in getting attention from city hall that had long been denied. This new influx led to a controversy between those who saw rebirth of the South End along the lines of a second Georgetown, and those who felt that increases in property values would drive out low- and middle-income families. The BRA is required to work through a Project Area Committee (SEPAC). Control of this group began to change. The predominantly black and Spanish-speaking population was becoming aware that in spite of court decisions eliminating "snob zoning" in the suburbs, there was still no place else to go. Cathedral Housing, a yellow brick "instant ghetto" of the 1950s, was festering in their midst. More successful housing solutions such as Castle Square (Samuel Glaser & Associates; 1967) still required wholesale demolition and federal subsidies.

The Massachusetts Housing and Finance Agency, organized to provide interest subsidies to semiprivate public housing, backed the Emergency Tenants' Council in an eighteen-story housing project for the elderly, Torre Unidad at 80 West Dedham Street (John Sharratt & Associates; 1976). To it has been added the Villa Victoria, lower rise housing with a shopping arcade. The complex includes space for health and social services as well as an intensely landscaped "sitz-park" between them. Just above Massachusetts Avenue on Tremont Street, this same agency has made it possible to rehabilitate an old piano factory. When it was built in 1853, the Chickering plant was second in size only to the United States Capitol. As the Piano Craft Guild it has been recycled into 174 studio-

Boston City Hospital, Residence Tower. Glaser/deCastro/Vitols; 1974.
Photo: Phokion Karas

Piano Craft Guild, 1853. Rehabilitated: Gelardin/Bruner/Cott & Company and Anderson Notter Associates; 1974. *Photo: Greg Heins*

residences for arts and craftspeople. The architects (Gelardin/Bruner/Cott, Inc.; with Anderson, Notter) uncovered painted brick and timbers, polished up maple floors, and created a variety of stimulating spaces for work and/or living.

The Boston Center for the Arts has been a bootstrap operation from the beginning. It inherited the Boston Flower Exchange at the intersection of Tremont and Warren streets after the BRA relocated this activity to the South Bay area. Its several buildings focus on the magnificent circular structure built in 1884 to house a cyclorama painting of *Pickett's Charge at Gettysburg* by the French painter, Paul Phillipoteaux. Nearly eighty feet in diameter and fifty feet high, the space had a viewing platform for spectators. The illusion was heightened by three-dimensional effects and uniformed actors with rifles in the foreground. After a second engagement, *Custer's Last Stand,* the Cyclorama was used for a variety of purposes, including a garage, and, in the memory of historian Samuel Eliot Morison, a training facility for those brave enough to purchase that newfangled device, a Columbia bicycle. The space is now used for exhibits, performances, spectacles, and a flea market.

The neighboring buildings house the Boston Ballet and its school, the Community Music Center, a children's art center, four theatre groups, two opera groups, and a gallery run by the Friends of the Boston Center for the Arts. This adds up to a total of twenty-five performing organizations and some sixty individual visual artists who have studio space in the complex. The city has closed off part of the street in front to make room for a park and a theatrical kiosk salvaged from an orphanage in Roxbury. The glass marquee from the old Jordan Marsh Building (torn down over the protests of preservationists) will be mounted at the entrance to the Cyclorama. This seems appropriate, for it was Eben Jordan, founder of the firm, that had Nathaniel Bradlee design the Hotel St. Cloud. This is a tall Second Empire residence hotel at the southern end of the Center complex which is to be remodeled into artists' studios. The National Theatre (Clarence Blackall; 1911) is being brought back to its original splendor as a vaudeville house for the Center's many performances. The exterior of the Cylcorama will be improved with federal preservation funds.

A few blocks up Tremont Street, a new branch of the Boston Public Library (Mitchell/Giurgola Associates; 1974) has been combined with a minipark. The colonnaded enclosure and attempt to bring light into the building are welcome. Less successful is the confusing interior space. This may be the result of a much-copied angular vocabulary which this firm seems to have introduced in their runner-up solution for Boston City Hall. Detailing in general is too light to stand up to the architecture of the area, or the rough usage the library receives as a play space.

At Columbus and Massachusetts avenues, the square brick tracery of the Harriet Tubman center (Stull Associates; 1975) announces a more positive direction for sympathetic work in the South End. Dark concrete arches, an intricate schedule of openings and solids, terraces, and bright lighting and colors at the interior make this multiple social service center a visual expression of the optimism embodied in its important work with children and the elderly. The Blackstone Square Community School, by this same firm, combines the square-faced brick with a naturally rusty steel facing and window frames in a rugged composition. Its somewhat stern aspect is transformed by the bright evidence of the activities within. The school shares community health facilities adjacent to it on Shawmut Avenue.

City Hospital got its start on Harrison Avenue in a series of mansarded brick pavilions reflecting Gridley J. F. Bryant's interest in French Academic. They surround a domed administration building. The original redevelopment strategy for the South End called for an almost linear separation of function, with industry and institutions to be kept east of Harrison Avenue. With a few exceptions, this has been a self-fulfilling prophecy. Boston University Medical Center has begun to emerge as a coherent complex from a series of older "hospital Georgian" buildings. The first encounter on Harrison Avenue is the concrete Doctors' Building (Edwin T. Steffian & Associates) with its pleasing contrast of interior round columns in the parking levels with exterior columns in the upper structure. It connects with a concrete and textured-block emergency building (The Architects Collaborative) which has its eastern wall pan-

Torres Unidad Housing, 80 West Dedham Street. John Sharratt & Associates; 1975. *Photo: Janis Reiters*

Cyclorama, Boston Center of the Arts, 539 Tremont Street; 1884. Conversion to Flower Market; 1923. Conversion to Center: Eco-Tecture; 1970-. *Photo: James Douglass*

eled to permit expansion. TAC also did the first three stories of the dental school building beyond on Albany Street, although a poor match of precast concrete panels was made when the building was expanded by Martha and Elliot Rothman. The other tall double-column concrete structure (Desmond & Lord; 1975) is a state-owned, University-staffed mental health center, completed this year. Opposite the entrance to the mental health building is a soft brick medical research and treatment building (Anderson, Beckwith, & Haible; 1971). It abuts the Boston University Medical School building (Shepley, Bulfinch, Richardson and Abbott). This is one of a pair by this firm—the former expressing concrete columns with red brick panel infill (plus some confusing precast concrete bays), while an earlier laboratory unit has contrasting glazed blue brick infill. The decorative columns near the roof signal a walkway at the top floor lounge level.

Thoughtful action by the faculty and staff may save the Talbot Building now facing an interior parking lot. This charming hybrid of Mansard, Ruskin, and panel brick will make a focal point for an otherwise confusing assembly of different buildings, performing a similar function to that of the Bulfinch Building at Massachusetts General Hospital.

Under a master plan prepared by the Hugh Stubbins–Rex Allen Partnership, City Hospital has a better chance for architectural coherence. By making a fresh start on the south side of Massachusetts Avenue, it was possible to clear out buildings between the avenue and the present nursing pavilions. The South Block, built under the direction of Glazer/de Castro/Vitols Partnership, surrounds a garage with plaza and play space on top, a nursing school on the east, a pool and gymnasium, a residence tower for single persons connected with the hospital, and a slab apartment structure for families. All are unified by a strong idiom of cast-in-place concrete. An ambulatory care unit bridges Massachusetts Avenue from the upper deck level of South Block to an inviting street level plaza opening onto Massachusetts and Harrison avenues. A joint venture between the Stubbins-Allen Partnership and Glazer/de Castro/Vitols, the bridge makes use of an interstitial floor system in which the spaces between the floors are made deep enough to permit efficient long-span structure as well as access to ductwork and piping. The interior is treated as a building within a building (expressed partly in wood) to allow for future changes in room layouts.

Tying into the north end of the bridge building is a bright yellow fiberglass aerial tunnel, reaching back between the older buildings and across Albany Street to a new power station. Here, rising as a giant window, an all glass housing displays the steam heating and cooling plant for the present and future hospital complex. High above, four cylindrical cooling towers are fed by the orange air intake louvers beneath them. The piping, painted in conformance with OSHA safety standards, places this structure in the category of pure sculpture (the Stubbins-Allen Partnership).

The city has wisely carried out many of the early urban renewal promises: streetlights, new water mains, sidewalks, and pocket parks in unexpected places. Boston has a model program called "Plantree" which assists both individual owners and entire neighborhood groups in the selection and planting of street trees. Many of the older private parks have been cleaned up through concerted action on the part of abutters. Three major parks have been built: the one at West Newton Street, between Columbus Avenue and the railroad, has been named in memory of Titus Sparrow, a beloved black resident without whose leadership many of the residents, both black and white, would have given up on the South End long ago.

South End Branch Library, Tremont Street. Mitchell/Giurgola Associates; 1971. *Photo: Harold Guida*

SOUTH COVE/BAY VILLAGE

Any natural continuity between the South Cove and the South End has long since been erased by the railroad lines seeking access to Boston over the area of the Neck. First horsecars, then electrics and railroads converged on the spot, with the Boston and Worcester coming in at a lower grade to a station at Lincoln and Beach streets. The Boston and Providence came straight across the Back Bay to a terminal in Park Square. Later, in the 1950s, the Massachusetts Turnpike followed the Boston and (by then) Albany route to its space-consuming interconnection with the Central Artery. This formidable barrier left the Chinese-American community in the South Cove crowded into an increasingly smaller area as the business district pressed into and finally infiltrated the neighborhood.

Thus the colorful streets of Chinatown are intermixed with the garment and leather district, a major medical center, the theatre district, and an adult entertainment section called the "Combat Zone." It has not been easy for successive generations of its Chinese residents, who from choice or necessity wished to stay in an area that had lost one-third of its housing from 1925 to 1950. Specialty stores and restaurants were family owned and operated. Perhaps more than with any other immigrant group, language and culture required an interdependent community life. A strong merchants group built a cultural center and headquarters in 1952

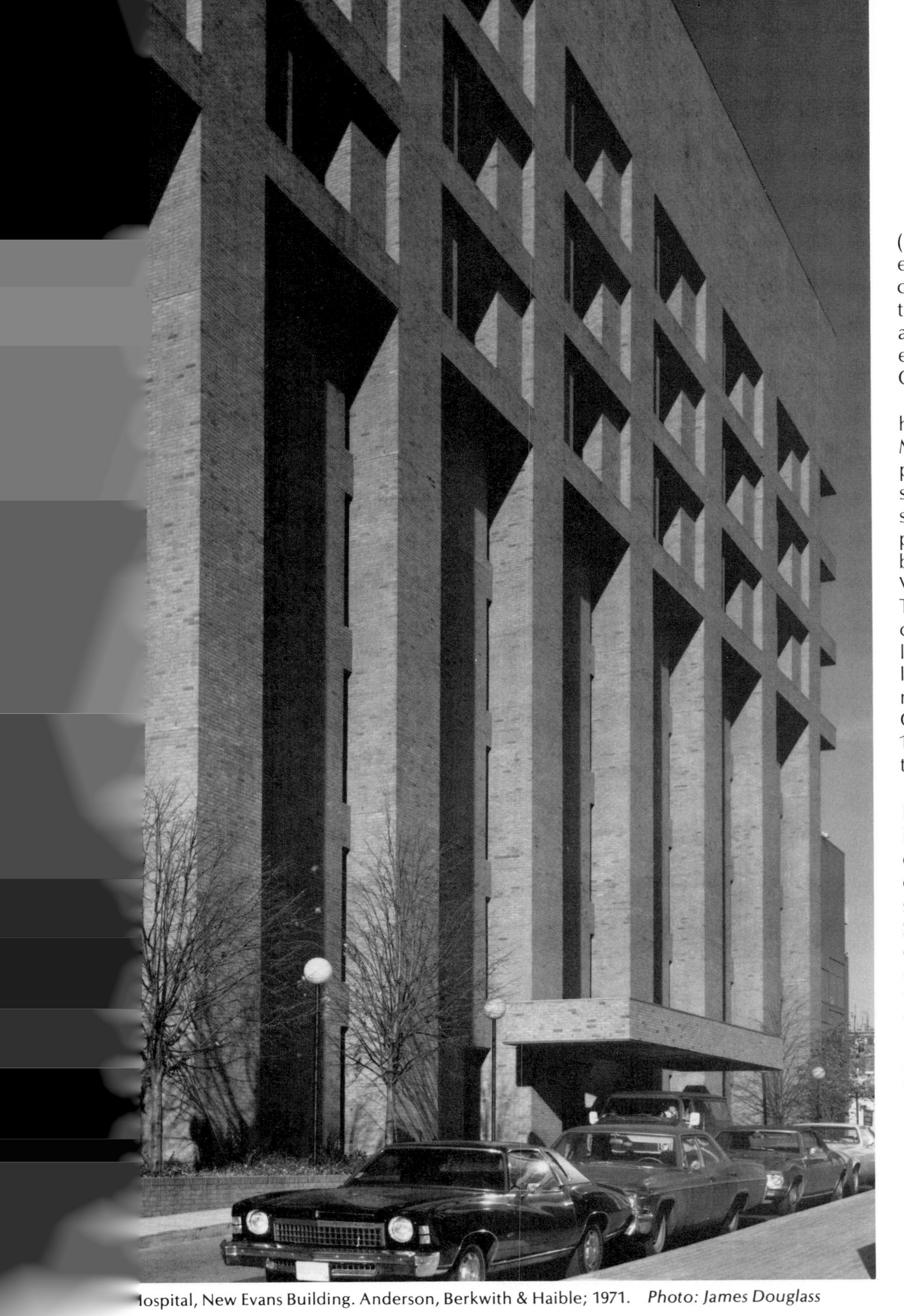

Hospital, New Evans Building. Anderson, Berkwith & Haible; 1971. *Photo: James Douglass*

(Edward Chin-Park) only to have the east end truncated by the Central Artery. Still capped by its romantic pagoda-tearoom, the Center has an interior rich with the art and tradition of China. Cast spandrel panels at its windows depict scenes from Oriental religions.

Community effort assisted by the BRA has brought obsolete housing up to date. Much of that which has survived is in pockets of Federal and Greek Revival structures dating from 1835 when this section was filled in. Two new precast panel housing complexes have tipped the balance: Mass Pike Towers and Tai Tung Village (F. A. Stahl and Associates; 1973). They used skip-stop elevators and aerial corridor bridges to effect economies that led to better unit plans. Space at the street level is provided for shops and offices. A new housing structure for the elderly, Quincy Towers (Jung/Brannen Associates; 1976), overlooks the terraced play decks of the Quincy School.

This new elementary school has established a high standard for teaching space in dense urban areas. A brick-paved indoor main street traverses the building diagonally, its open ends giving equal significance to the South End and the South Cove. This school is the first that the city has built to meet the standards for community integration set forth in a ten-year-old report that, had it been adopted, would have made all the fuss about busing unnecessary. Inside, free spaces permit open classrooms and freedom to innovate with a variety of teaching techniques. In addition to the gymnasium and pool, there is a community medical and dental clinic. The square-faced "broken-block" exterior blends well with smooth concrete. Steps and ramps gain successive access to the multiple levels of roof space ordinarily wasted in schools. At the very top, a wire enclosure identifies areas for formal sports that are a part of the in-school program.

Interior,
Renovated House,
West Brookline Street.
Photo: Greg Heins

Castle Square (housing),
492 Tremont Street.
Samuel Glaser & Partners;
1967. Sculpture: Alfred Duca.
Photo: Phokion Karas

The whole complex is lit up by delightful metal panels drawn from original children's drawings made for the purpose. The school is the result of the collaboration of three neighborhood groups, the city's Public Facilities Department, and The Architects Collaborative.

Across the street, Don Bosco Technical High School has added classroom space to an older post-neo-Georgian building, and a gymnasium and pool under a public plaza. This piece of concrete sleight of hand was accomplished by the firm of Halasz and Halasz. Both its terraces and those of the Quincy School opposite take advantage of pockets around stairs to install planting beds. In the park now under construction opposite Don Bosco is a dark glazed brick cylindrical church designed by Bertram Goldberg & Associates. The Church of All Nations, finished in 1976, houses a congregation founded by the Reverend Henry Morgan, among whose many good works were the Goodwill Industries (called in Boston the Morgan Memorial). The original church was taken by the Turnpike Authority in 1963. After several years in adopted sites, this multi-ethnic, full community service congregation has found a distinctive home.

While the Chinese community has now begun to expand into the new South End, it has maintained a strong posture with the city in regard to its symbiotic relationship with the entertainment district, as well as its concern for the future of Park Plaza (Chapter 5). The Redevelopment Authority has continued to encourage the present entertainment district, using the image of the intersection of Boylston and Tremont streets as the "Hinge Block." Projected demolition of two important theatres (The Wilbur and The Music Hall) to make room for the New England Medical Center has been reversed. This official policy of relating the excellent restaurants of Chinatown

Tai Tung Village (housing for the Chinese community). Stahl/Bennett, Inc.; 1972. *Photo: Gorchev and Gorchev Photography*

Tufts-New England Medical Center. The Architects Collaborative; 1972. *Photo: Phokion Karas*

to the theatre district has been shown in little ways, such as the pagoda-topped streetlights and telephone booths which enrich the colorful calligraphy of signs and stage-set storefronts.

In bringing together a number of separate medical and public health facilities, the Tufts-New England Medical Center has become a major factor in the renewal of the area. Starting with a run-of-the-mill assortment of "hospital Georgian" structures, as well as a Floating Hospital for Babies—actually a ship in Boston Harbor—the Center first expanded into adjacent commercial space. Then, in accordance with a master plan developed by the Center's staff under the leadership of Hermann Field, FAIA, The Architects Collaborative has completed the first two elements of a major urban medical center. Streets have been realigned, a portion of the rapid transit placed underground, and a garage has been built on the south side of Washington Street to which future elements of the Center will bridge. The general plan calls for horizontal communication between a variety of health facilities above the street level, leaving this floor for commercial and administrative functions. Vertical communication will connect with a novel "courtyard" nursing unit design, and with ancillary facilities as they are developed. The two large concrete additions, one for the School of Dental Medicine, have characteristically bright TAC interiors. They are connected visually to the warren of other buildings by a color-coded system of locational graphics, supported by frequent maps, indoors and out, needed to orient staff as well as visitors.

Bay Village

A visual inspection of the Federal and Greek Revival houses in the area just to the west of the South Cove, bounded by the Turnpike and Columbus Avenue, equates its period of construction to that of Beacon Hill. In fact, many of the artisans working on the Hill lived in and even built their own homes in Bay Village. An 1827 tabulation lists housewrights, painters, tailors, tinplate workers, toll-

Bay Village. *Photo: Steven M. Stone*

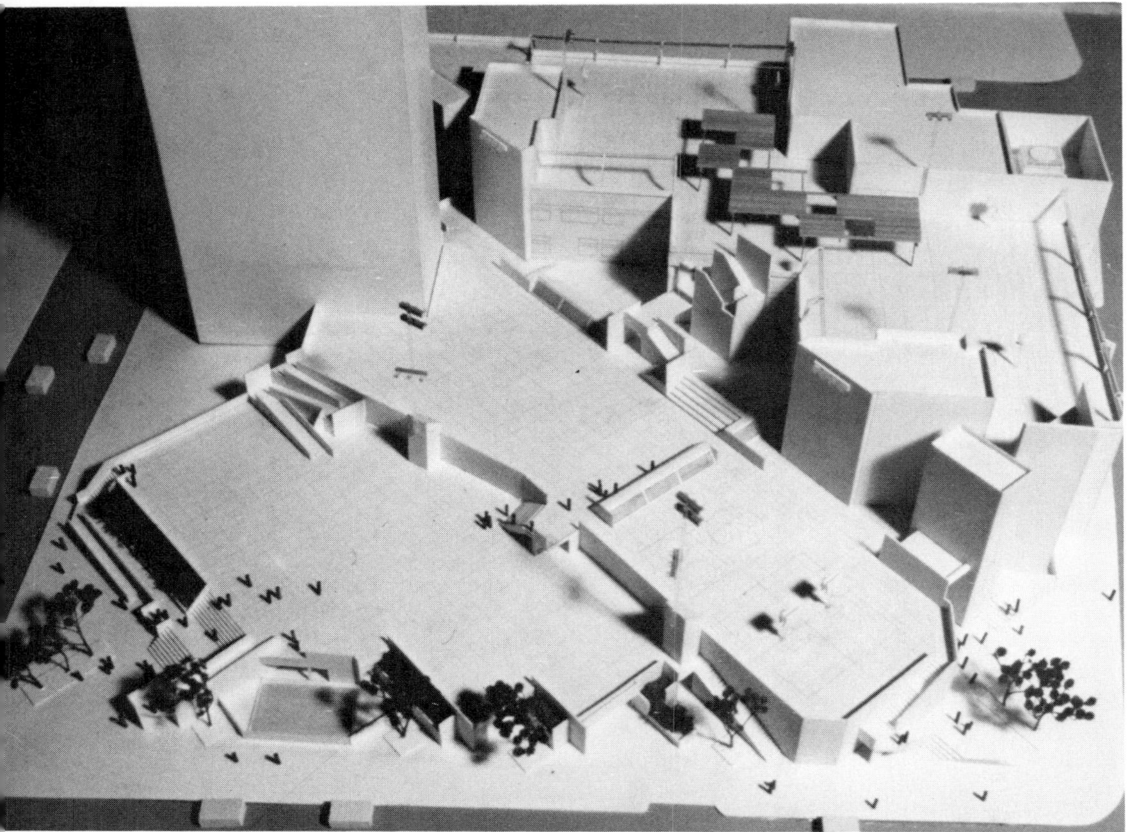
Model of Quincy Elementary School. The Architects Collaborative; 1976. *Photo: The Architects Collaborative*

gatherers, cabinetmakers, sailmakers, paperhangers, and salt merchants. (Rights to make salt on the Neck had been granted as early as 1697.) By 1830 there were organ builders and pianoforte makers. Maids from the Back Bay bought custard pies for ten cents and loaves of rye bread for eight from a German bakery on Pleasant Street. A French Huguenot contingent is preserved today in a church, Notre Dame des Victoires, that serves its parishioners in their native language. (An Italian Romanesque basilica, St. James Church on Harrison Avenue in the South Cove, is by P. C. Keeley, who, although from New York, seemed to have a monopoly on Catholic church design in Boston.) To make things more complicated, Bay Village is a recent euphemism (suggested, it is said, by a real estate agent) for what had been called the Church Street District, named for a building called, appropriately, the Church Street Church. Built in 1827 for Presbyterian services, it was used by the Third Methodist Episcopal society in 1834 until it became the Free People's Temple on Columbus Avenue. The Church Street building then became a home for Jewish congregations (Gates of Prayer Temple, 1880–82, and Zion's Holy Prophets of Israel, Orthodox synagogue, 1883–98); then by Baptists (Morning Star Baptist, 1899–1905); and then for garage purposes before being torn down.

Bay Village's renaissance started in the late 1950s when the demand for small houses on Beacon Hill began to exceed the supply. New residents followed the usual pattern of young or retired couples in professions of middle management with the resources and/or time to restore those houses that had been allowed to fall into disrepair. An interesting comparison can be found in two newspaper advertisements 124 years apart. The *Columbian Centinel,* October 4, 1828:

Addition to Don Bosco Technical High School. Halasz & Halasz; 1975.
Photo: Halasz & Halasz

Chinese Merchants Building, Edward Chin Park. 1952. *Photo: Max Ferro*

FOR SALE
NEAR PLEASANT-STREET

Two almost new three story brick Houses, containing (each House) a good cellar, kitchen, parlor, 3 or 4 chambers, large and small closets, pump and rain water, and the usual out door conveniences, together with about 800 feet of land.—Price $4,000.

Also on Pleasant-Street, just beyond Carver-street, a genteel new three story brick house, modern, built and completely finished, and every way calculated to accommodate a genteel family.—Price $3,500.

Apply to CHARLES M'INTIER, No. 7 Congress-street.

The *Boston Globe* of March 3, 1968, carried the following advertisement:

BAY VILLAGE

An attractively restored Town House in the historic Bay Village section. Fireplaced double living room; master bedroom has small dressing area with walk-in closet, second bedroom (fireplace); up-to-date kitchen looks into landscaped private garden; dining room. $48,900. Call Agent.

These new residents found common issues in traffic and parking (aggravated by proximity to the entertainment district), street lighting, liquor licenses, and police protection. The latter became especially important as changing attitudes about the public behavior of "consenting adults" nourished a cluster of marginal bars and nightclubs for which decent curfews seemed to be the only legal answer. The efforts of Bay Village residents to maintain the quality of life in their picturesque community have often been heroic, especially in dealing with an organized power structure of license and pornography. Bay Village joined with Chinatown and the other downtown residential districts in a plan for containment of the Combat Zone. The city is now experimenting with a novel form of land-use control that will circumscribe purveyors of pornographic "literature" and exotic entertainment. The problem seems to lie in the coincident and presently illegal traffic which accompanies this implied freedom of activity. It is almost too symmetrical to point out that the crossroads of this free-swinging district centers on the sidewalk directly below the bronze tablet commemorating the original Liberty Tree.

CABLE
CROSSING

Chapter 8
CHARLESTOWN

From the top of Bunker Hill Monument it is still possible to identify Charlestown as a peninsula. Through a tangled matting of elevated highways, bridges, piers, and dams, the inner reaches of the harbor and the Charles and Mystic rivers wage a losing battle against civilization. With the help of Lieutenant Page's map (page iv) and the historical dioramas on display at the base of the monument, this hilly square mile of history begins to come alive. In the distance the golden dome of the State House on Beacon Hill is replaced by a trio of connected peaks. Farms and houses dot the northern slopes facing Charlestown. In the foreground, where railroad yards approach North Station, a broad millpond is contained within a narrow strip of land. Except in wintertime, a patch of green identifies Copp's Hill in the North End, a British cannon shot away from the town below us.

Beyond, the flat reaches of Boston Harbor invite us to escape on the frigate *Constitution,* California-bound clippers, or the tiny ships of the China trade. The narrow waterway separating us from Boston gave to the towns their aboriginal place names: *Shawmut,* "narrow water"; *Mishawum* (Charlestown), "across the narrow water." Before the first Charles River bridge was built in 1786, one of the two routes to Cambridge and the interior was by ferry to Charlestown, thence overland to a narrow neck connecting the peninsula with what is now Somerville. It then followed an Indian trail (Washington and Kirkland streets) to the old town at Harvard Square. Paul Revere was met by his friends here on the Charlestown shore, ascertained that his signal lights had been seen (they were used just in case he did not elude the British sentinels), then galloped off on a borrowed horse into the history books.

The Battle of Bunker Hill, a little over a year later, lends further insight into contemporary geography. Patriot intelligence within the besieged Town of Boston disclosed that General Gage was about to fortify Bunker Hill, the highest of Charlestown's four drumlins. After a brief period of indecision, the soldier-farmers crossed Charlestown Neck at night and dug in on Breed's Hill, some fifty feet lower and much closer to the Town. British ships at anchor in the narrows began to shell the fortifications at daylight. A shallow-draft transport was able to work itself close enough to Lechmere's Point to harass the supply line to the mainland. This complicated the matter of reinforcements which, with the acute shortage of gunpowder, determined the outcome of the battle. General Gage's miscalculation of both topography and Yankee determination is admirably described in a taped tour of the site of the redoubt and monument.

That 220-foot obelisk, designed by Solomon Willard in 1832, was built of granite quarried in Quincy. The blocks were drawn by horsepower over the first railroad in America to the banks of the Neponset River, then by boat to the Charlestown shore, where they were carried by oxcart up to the site. Completed in

Overview of Charlestown
Photo: Phokion Karas

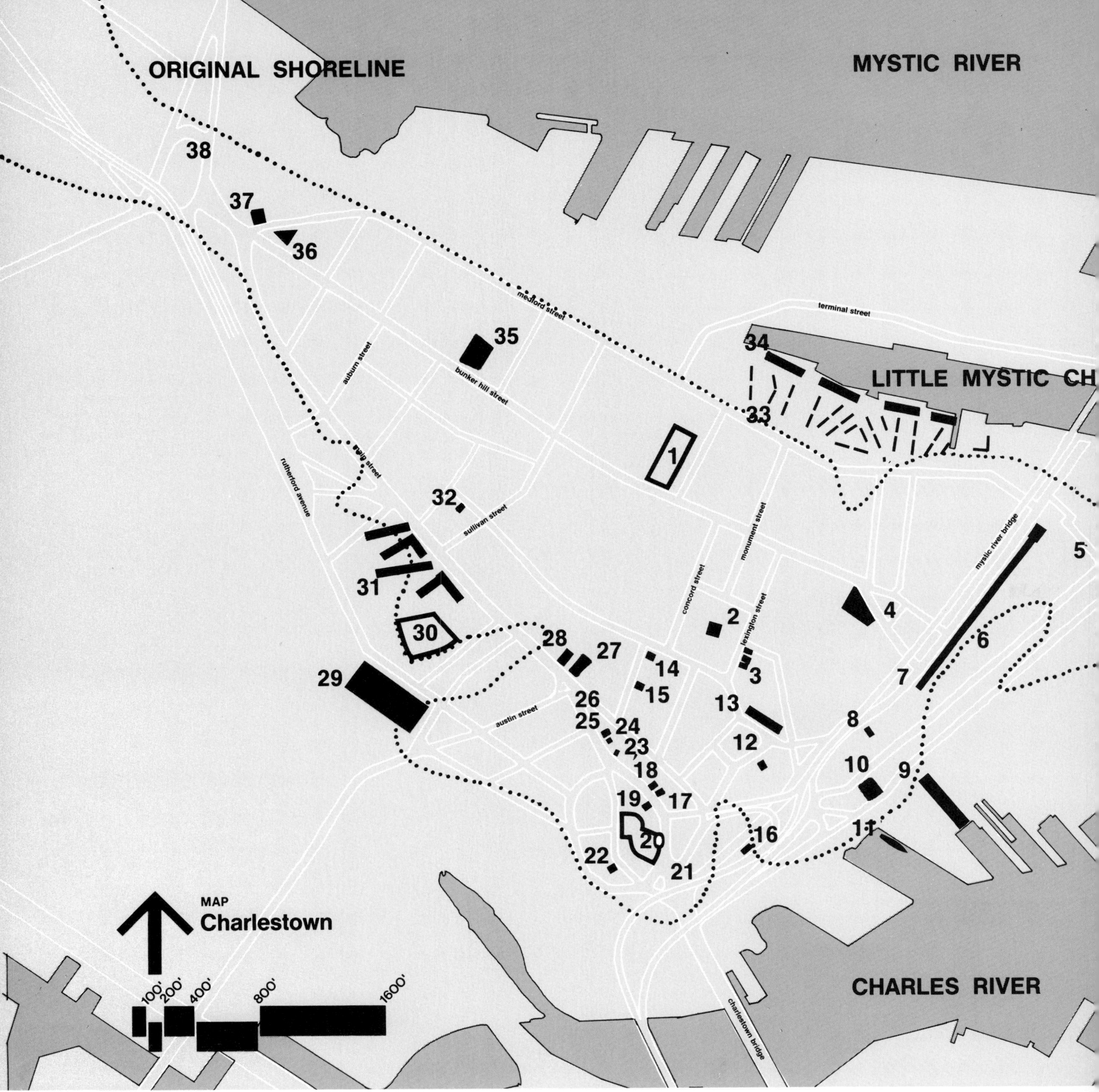

ORIGINAL SHORELINE
MYSTIC RIVER
LITTLE MYSTIC CH
CHARLES RIVER
medford street
terminal street
auburn street
bunker hill street
rutherford avenue
sullivan street
concord street
monument street
lexington street
mystic river bridge
austin street
charlestown bridge
1
2
3
4
5
6
7
8
9
10
11
12
13
14
15
16
17
18
19
20
21
22
23
24
25
26
27
28
29
30
31
32
33
34
35
36
37
38
MAP
Charlestown
100'
200'
400'
800'
1600'

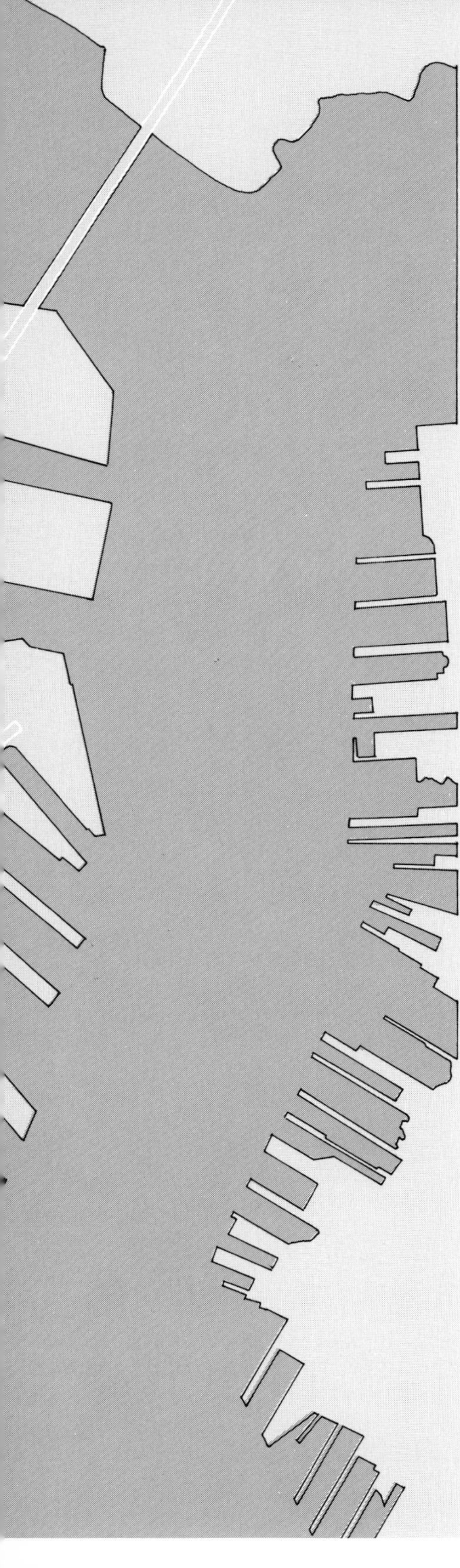

1. Bunker Hill Burial Ground 1801
2. Bunker Hill Monument
   Solomon Willard; 1825–42
   On site of battle redoubt, 17 June 1775
3. Monument Square Houses:
   No. 6. Peter Hubbel, 1847
   No. 7. George Washington Warren, 1847
   No. 8. Lynde A. Huntington, 1848
4. The William E. Kent Elementary School
   Earl R. Flansburgh Associates; 1973
5. Moultons Point
   Site of British landing, 17 June 1775
6. Navy Yard, 1800
7. Ropewalk
   Alexander Parris; 1834–36
8. Commandants House; 1809
9. Dry-Dock No. 1
   Loammi Baldwin; 1827–33
10. Officers Housing, 1833
11. U.S.S. *Constitution*
    "Old Ironsides," 1797
12. Winthrop Square, site of old training field, 1632.
13. Adams Street Row Houses, 1860
14. Swallow Mansion, 1864
    33 Cordis Street
15. Getchell House, 1802
    21 Cordis Street
16. Old Salem Turnpike Hotel, 1781
    16 Common Street
17. Larkin House, 1795
    55–61 Main Street
18. Hurd House, 1795
    65–71 Main Street
19. Austin House, 1822
    92–98 Main Street
20. Harvard Mall
    Site of fort on Town Hill, 1629
21. City Square
    Original Market Place
22. Edward Everett House, 1812
    16 Harvard Street
23. Warren Tavern, 1780
    Oldest house in Charlestown
24. "Round Corner House," 1815
    Armstrong House
    125–27 Main Street
25. Thompson Houses, 1794 and 1805
    119 Main Street
26. Thompson Square
27. Charlestown Savings Bank, 1875
    17 Thompson Square
28. Branch Library
    169–79 Main Street
    Eduardo Catalano; 1970
29. Bunker Hill Community College
    Shepley, Bulfinch, Richardson and Abbott; 1973–
30. Phipps Street Cemetery, 1630
    John Harvard buried here
31. Mishwam Park Housing
    Freeman-Hardenburgh; 1974
32. Steck House, 1790
    100 High Street
33. Bunker Hill Housing Project, 1942
34. Charles New Town Housing
    Sert, Jackson and Associates; 1971
35. St. Francis de Sales Church
    Bunker Hill Avenue
    P. C. Keeley; 1862
36. Masons Union Headquarters
    Earl R. Flansburgh Associates; 1975
37. Fire Station
    F. Frederick Bruck; 1970
38. Sullivan Square

1842, the monument's ironic function is to compound a British field report error (Bunker's for Breed's) and commemorate a lost battle that may have won a war. The swift Yankee packet that beat General Gage's official report to London told the world of the colonists' courage and intentions and told the British the price in lives required to quell the rebellion in Boston. General Howe took the war to New York the following spring.

A British promise to burn Charlestown if it was used militarily was consummated when rebels fired on the attacking grenadiers from this flank. Red hot shells from Copp's Hill reduced the town to ashes as the battle raged. This has left us with a contemporary, if lamentable, portrait. Josiah Bartlett wrote that the fire burned "the meeting house, a court house, two school houses, and a work house, with upwards of 380 dwellings and other buildings—and 2000 persons being the entire population of the peninsula were reduced from affluence and mediocracy to poverty and exile—the only objects that retained their former appearance were desolated streets and graveyards of their ancestors and relatives."

Charlestown is the second oldest town in the Massachusetts Bay Colony. In 1628 a party of ten men under Thomas Walford, a smith, came overland from Salem. A year later Governor Endecott sent one hundred more men, led by Thomas Graves, who laid out the town and built a fort on the present site of the John Harvard Mall. In 1630 John Winthrop arrived with the full complement of fifteen hundred people. They lived in cottages and tents until, beset by scurvy and a shortage of water, Winthrop and his flock crossed to the Shawmut Peninsula the following year. About fifteen families chose to remain behind. Since the meetinghouse was taken along to Boston, the ferry had to run on Sundays until Charlestown could afford to build its own church.

Bartlett described those remaining behind as "industrious, sober, and cultivate [ing] good principles." In addition to the beginnings of a thriving seaport, there were the usual craftsmen and shops; and on the hills, farms with great cornfields. Buildings were of wood and meetinghouses austere in keeping with the religious ideas they sheltered. By the time of the Revolution the Town had grown from its market (now City Square) inland as far as Phipps Burial Ground, and north to a training field at what is now Winthrop Square. During the war, Continental patrols and sporadic bombardment harassed the British (who had at last fortified the correct Bunker Hill) and completed the demolition of the Town.

After the evacuation of Boston in 1776, not more than a third of the original townspeople were able (or willing) to return. But by 1784, five hundred houses lined a new street plan laid out by John Leach. Since everything "colonial" had been burned and Massachusetts was no longer a colony, any buildings remaining from the postwar period must be classified as Federal. Some survivals have features drawn from Georgian styles, and, like a few of the houses on Beacon Hill, can be called "late Colonial." Two of these, the Larkin House (55–61 Main Street; in good condition) and the Hurd House (65–71 Main Street; endangered) have the broader proportions and heavy wooden corner quoins, although they were not built until 1795. An earlier group clustered around the recently restored Warren Tavern (105 Main; 1780) are more characteristic of Federal frugality. They include the Benjamin Thompson House next to the Tavern on Main Street, the Timothy Thompson House on Warren Street, and the somewhat later brick House (or "Round Corner House"; 1815) at 125–127 Main Street. The remains of the Old Salem Turnpike Hotel (c. 1780) at 16 Common Street and its neighbor at No. 14 lend a Federal pedigree to Winthrop Square. Some distance away at 100 High Street, the Steck House (1790) is the surviving half of an imposing Federal brick double house. Two more from this period deserve mention: the Getchell House (21 Cordis; 1802) and the Edward Everett House (1805) at 16 Harvard Street. The latter, home of the governor, United States senator, secretary of state, and president of Harvard, distinguishes itself by flared brownstone lintels and Flemish bond brickwork. Its several wings and Greek Revival portico are later additions. The lonely Austin House (1799), built of stone from Brewster Island in Boston Harbor, awaits sympathetic restoration at the corner of Main and Harvard streets.

Greek Revival houses were built along Adams, Winthrop, and Harvard streets, and Monument Avenue before 1855. The Swallow Mansion at 33 Cordis Street dates from 1864. Three ambitious bowfronts are to be found at Monument Square: the Peter Hubbell House (No. 6; 1847), the George Washington Warren House (No. 7; 1847), and the Huntington House (no. 8; 1848). The balance of the Square, with its brackets, bays, and fancy architraves is a textbook of the nonflamboyant late Victorian styles. From Greek Revival it proceeds through Italianate, French Mansard, Queen Anne, and High Victorian Gothic, finishing off with that old standby, Georgian Revival. At 58 High Street, a trim mansarded foursquare wood Academic house is a lonely example of a type that abounds in Cambridge.

Another rarity, a brick and timber stick style parish hall, nestles against St. John's Episcopal Church (1841) on Washington Street. The architect of the church, Richard

View of Bunker Hill Monument from Monument Avenue. Solomon Willard; 1825-42. *Photo: James Douglass*

Warren Tavern, 1780. Oldest house in Charlestown. *Photo: Phokion Karas.*

Phipps Street Cemetery, 1630. John Harvard buried here. *Photo: James Douglass*

Bond, concentrated his client's resources (the balance of the building is brick) in a granite Gothic Revival tribute to the façade of St. John the Evangelist on Beacon Hill. Bond was a follower of Solomon Willard, who is credited with the design of the church on Bowdoin Street. Two other churches, St. Mary's (1887) on Main Street and St. Francis de Sales (1862), both by P. C. Keeley, are high Victorian Gothic. The latter, with its carved granite, wood trim, and slender copper steeple, has an interior inspired by the Limerick Cathedral in Ireland. The Charlestown Savings Bank has wisely decided to extend the useful life of its headquarters on Warren Street. This Victorian Gothic delight (1875), now free of the shadow of the El, will become an important part of a revitalized Thompson Square.

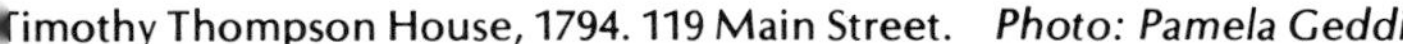

Timothy Thompson House, 1794. 119 Main Street. *Photo: Pamela Geddis*

Timothy Thompson, Jr., House, 1805. 9 Thompson Street. *Photo: Pamela Geddis*

Mud flats at Morton's (or Moulton's) Point were selected in 1800 for the site of the Boston Naval Shipyard by the man credited with design of the frigate *Constitution.* As chief naval constructor of the United States Navy, Joshua Humphreys prudently insisted upon taking Ebenezer Breed's pasture as well. Over the years the Navy Yard has come to mean much more than a place for magazines, arsenals, and nautical paraphernalia. Its unique accumulation of dockside, manufacturing, and repair facilities tells the story of the industrial revolution in America. An innovative steam-powered saw prepared the heavy timbers required for wooden ships. Dry Dock No. 1, built of great granite blocks on a pile foundation, was the first of its kind. Its initial occupant was the USS *Constitution,* now permanently berthed a few feet away. Here in Charlestown the first screw-powered steamship was built, ironclads for the Union cause, the first torpedo boat, and the first guided-missile cruiser. There was also a school for the training of naval officers before the Academy at Annapolis was founded.

Boston's architects were well represented. It is believed that Asher Benjamin designed a stately center-pavilion hospital, long since demolished. Loammi Baldwin engineered the dry dock and supervised Yard planning and construction almost from the beginning. His Middlesex Canal linked the Navy Yard, via the Mystic River, with Lowell and the Merrimac River. He was succeeded by his assistant, Alexander Parris (Quincy Market; Somerset Club), who designed and supervised some fourteen buildings. Among them was the 1,360-foot-long ropewalk. For over a century this rough granite plant produced all of the rope used by the Navy with machinery designed by another Bostonian, Daniel Treadwell. The three-story head house on the eastern end provided Parris with an opportunity to employ some classic detail in an otherwise utilitarian structure. Subsequent buildings were accomplished under the direction of Joseph E. Billings, a civil engineer. His major contribution was the Steam Engineering building, with its ambitious paneled 239½-foot-high brick chimney. Nearly twenty feet higher than the Bunker Hill Monument, it was razed in 1903.

Commodore Samuel Nicholson, the first superintendent of the Yard, had a Federal house built for his own use. It may have been inspired, but not designed, by Bulfinch. A running correspondence between Charlestown and the secretary of the navy suggests that the house was more elaborate than it should have been, including the overblown double bowfront. An 1825 account orders the sale of "marble caps, sills, window frames & blinds &c" to pay for necessary repairs. The house commands an enviable view of the oldest part of the Yard. Nearby, a row of Greek Revival officers' houses faces the broad lawn and parade ground.

This corner of the complex is now hard pressed by the roaring approaches to the Mystic River Bridge. The "sonic barrier," once assimilated, serves to isolate the older section in time as well as space, ironically reinforcing the illusion of a visit to the past. The future of these historic structures was threatened by the precipitous closing of the Navy Yard in 1974. The combined efforts of Boston's Redevelopment Authority, its Industrial Commission, the Massachusetts Congressional delegation, and the National Park Service are transforming the twenty-four acres of the Yard surrounding the berth of the USS *Constitution* into a National Historic Park. Plans for harnessing the industrial and cultural potential of the Yard's other assets are also under way.

There is a display of eighteenth and nineteenth century Charlestown industry in a tiny museum-community resource center (formerly the branch library) at Monument Square. Occupations included those of silversmith, carpenter, cabinetmaker, pewterer, goldsmith, and potter. Before mass production of metal and glass implements began to take over in the last half of the nineteenth century, there were at least forty potters in Charlestown. Some of these went on to manufacture the clay sewer and drainpipes needed for a growing metropolis.

By the middle of the nineteenth century, Charlestown was still a part of the

"Round Corner" (Armstrong) House, 1815. 125-127 Main Street. *Photo: James Douglass*

John Harvard Mall. Site of Fort on Town Hill, 1629. *Photo: James Douglass*

Steck House, 1790. 100 High Street. *Photo: Phokion Karas*

"walking city." Sam B. Warner, Jr., in *Streetcar Suburbs* identifies a "central middle class" that by 1830 had begun to leave crowded Boston for Charlestown, South Boston, lower Roxbury, East Boston, and parts of Cambridge. It included owners of small downtown stores, successful salesmen, commercial travelers, lawyers, schoolteachers, and large contractors. They were followed by a "lower middle class" typified by small shopkeepers, skilled artisans, and the better-paid office and sales personnel. These two groups remained dependent upon ready transportation to their jobs. But Charlestown never became a stronghold for those who sought the "rural ideal."

The rest of the century saw waves of immigrants place new demands upon space within range of the center city. The northern and eastern slopes of Bunker Hill were built up. A part of the top of the hill was used to fill in tidal marshes. Here were built both single and row houses, but, increasingly, the three-decker format for multiple housing. This puzzling product of the industrial revolution provided an ungainly but socially stable environment for a growing working class over many decades. From a town of 28,000 in 1874, the year it was annexed to Boston, the population had peaked at 41,000 by 1910.

In 1901 construction of the Boston Elevated Railway over City Square, and out along Main Street to Sullivan Square, decided the character of Charlestown for the next seventy-five years. Whatever convenience it may have provided was offset by the shrieking wheels of subway trains whisking a new generation of commuters to and from the more affluent suburbs. Residents began to petition for its removal as early as 1912. This forest of rusting columns and girders has at last been leveled, uncovering a community literally reborn over the past decade.

By 1960 the depression, flight to the

Commandants' House, 1809. *Photo: James Douglass*

Ropewalk. Alexander Parris; 1834-36. *Photo: James Douglass*

suburbs (especially by young families), and the beginning of absentee ownership had left deteriorated buildings, vacant town houses, and a discouraged population of 14,000. The first order of business for the newly formed Boston Redevelopment Authority was to make the renewal of Charlestown its model achievement. Strong opposition to demolition of buildings that were clearly unsuitable for rehabilitation made bitter and vocal enemies for City Hall. But under this withering return fire from the slopes of Bunker Hill, Boston planners fared better than General Gage. They answered with carefully assembled statistics on population and building conditions, and a promise to tear down the El. A community-advised program, directed at preservation of architectural character, historic sites, and most of the housing stock, prevailed.

The nucleus of the plan was home improvement made possible through a multiservice assistance program, low interest federal loans, and assurances from City Hall that assessments would not be raised on account of improvements. Residents have invested an estimated twelve million dollars in rehabilitation. Two-thirds of them live in their own homes or rent in owner-occupied buildings. A 1968 survey disclosed that nine out of ten residents preferred to remain. Young professionals working in Boston and Cambridge as well as artists and craftspeople have been attracted by the stock of historic houses ripe for restoration. Charlestown has an active Historical Society whose annual house tours vie with those of Beacon Hill, the Back Bay, and the South End. Over the past four years, forty new single-family houses have been erected on the sites of demolished tenements.

Not all of this rehabilitation will please lovers of architecture and/or antiquity. To drab asbestos siding long used to obliterate bright clapboards have been added inept applications of artificial metal siding, usually placed without regard for the integrity of the structure. One would also wish that a certain false stone facing material had never been invented. Isolated strips of variegated row housing remain. Washington Street, nearly separated from the old town, but reinforced by new trees and lighting, is considered by its inhabitants as the "mellowest" street in town. Other groupings, often centered about cul-de-sacs, are intensively gardened by determined cityphiles, well aware of the architectural treasures they so jealously guard.

Public housing tells a story familiar to most American cities. An early standardized red brick walkup "project" hatched in the optimistic forties is today in a perpetual state of self-demolition. Across Mystic Avenue, on industrial land cleared by urban renewal, the Charles New Town project (Sert, Jackson, & Gourley; 1971) enjoys a quiet promenade along the Little Mystic River. Its T-shaped units are planned in fragile reliance on the sliding glass door "ethic." Since these openings face each other across narrow courts, they remain permanently blanked by opaque draperies. Justification of such amenities awaits new living skills not likely to emerge soon from this troubled neighborhood.

A more recent development, Mishawum Park Housing (Freeman, Hardenburgh Associates) borrows a "sidewalks in the air" format from a project in the Netherlands. Its 337 units are in effect two-story row houses stacked on top of each other. Connecting bridges economize on and simplify access stairways. Except for its overall size, the broken building lines continue the pattern of single houses on the hillside above. As if to anticipate neighboring rehabilitation, the project is endlessly sheathed in off-white aluminum siding.

U.S.S. *Constitution* ("Old Ironsides"), 1797. *Photo: James Douglass*

Edward Everett House, 1812. 16 Harvard Street. *Photo: Phokion Karas*

Monument Square No. 6: Peter Hubbel House, 1847. No. 7: George Washington Warren House, 1847. *Photo: Phokion Karas*

Other public buildings include a contemporary vernacular brick-and-concrete-band fire station near Sullivan Square, expertly executed by Frederick F. A. Bruck, and a branch library at Warren and Green streets by Eduardo Catalano. The library is an exercise in concrete (rare for Charlestown) and glass, producing extremely pleasant and functional indoor spaces. The glass was intended to define an articulated interval between the base structure and an inverted "channel" roof. Much of it has been replaced with plywood. Long-time residents of Charlestown cannot remember when the combination of a normal, healthy city youngster and an accommodating brickbat did not spell trouble for undefended surfaces of glass. In this crucible of patriotism, it is difficult to fault that overt distrust of authority which, according to the history books, was repeatedly directed at official windows by exercised colonists. For those who search for behavioral overtones in the design of the man-made environment, the fate of (and subsequent planning for) other recent buildings may have special interest.

New schools were an integral part of the renewal strategy. The Kent School on Bunker Hill Avenue (Earl R. Flansburgh and Associates; 1973) turns a sloping 2.7 acre site into a miniature version of the surrounding townscape. Brickwalled classroom clusters step smartly up the hillside, facing inward around team teaching centers. Cornice lines respect the neighboring houses, avoiding an authoritarian image. Terraced playgrounds offer recreational options. The gymnasium, locker rooms, library, and a community room are arranged so that they can be used when school is not in session. Unfortunately, young scholars, infuriated by the nearly unbreakable plastic windows, have sorely tried the otherwise durable and handsome surfaces and detailing. Is this a response to a school system whose lay leaders have

Winthrop Square. Adams Street Row Houses, 1860. *Photo: Phokion Karas*

failed them by insisting that communities can remain intact through arbitrary social delineation?

The most recent academic offering, the first stage of the new Charlestown High School (Hill, Miller, Friedlander & Hollander; 1976), rises before a backdrop of warehouses, silos, dockside cranes, and the colorful towers of a sugar refinery. This unit, consisting of a gymnasium, pool, and related athletic facilities, will be linked with a new academic wing by a bridge over Mystic Avenue. Most of the lighting comes from a sawtooth skylight; other openings are kept out of the range of ordinary projectiles. With clean brick detailing, the building rises as a friendly fortress in a time when many citadels of learning are under siege.

On the site of a state prison, built in 1805 by Bulfinch, is the new Bunker Hill Community College (Shepley, Bulfinch, Richardson and Abbott; 1973). In the shadow of a triple-decked transportation corridor, it has been conspicuously placed athwart the pedestrian route from a new rapid transit station to the town. This cannot help but have an effect on the educational horizons of those to whom it is daily exposed. Primarily a commuter college, it is accessible to students from other parts of Boston. Many would otherwise be reluctant to pass through a community, which like the North End and South Boston, has yet to accept desegregation. The buildings, executed in fluted concrete block, stand up well against the strong highway environment. Inside, durable materials and an ingenious split-level faculty-office arrangement surround interior top-lighted classrooms and laboratories.

In spite of a rash of squalid one-story commercial infill in the Thompson Square area, there are plans for a new shopping mall, more housing for the elderly and

Charlestown Savings Bank, 1875. 17 Thompson Square. *Photo: Pamela Geddis*

Branch Library, 169-179 Main Street. Eduardo Catalano; 1970. *Photo: James Douglass*

The William E. Kent Elementary School. Earl R. Flansburgh & Associates; 1973. *Photo: Steve Rosenthal*

low- and moderate-income families, refurbishing John Harvard Mall, street lighting, and improved parks and playgrounds. This suggests a brighter future for a town now reduced to a steel-and-concrete-encased square mile after once including Malden, Woburn, Stoneham, Burlington, Somerville, and parts of Cambridge, Medford, and Reading. Its immigrant stock brought vitality, intelligence, and culture, provided the physical labor for factories and construction, and reared a second and third generation of men and women who have become an integral part of Boston's cultural and economic life.

Charlestowners are as proud of this as they are of their impressive roster of historic figures. Elizabeth Foster, a native, married Isaac Vergoose, a fifty-five-year-older widower with ten children. She then had ten of her own and is generally believed to have recorded the vagaries of her status in rhyme as "Mother" Goose. Samuel F. B. Morse, whose birthplace at

Bunker Hill Community College. Shepley, Bulfinch, Richardson and Abbott; 1973. *Photo: James Douglass*

Charles New Town Housing. Sert, Jackson and Associates; 1971. *Photo: Steve Rosenthal*

195 Main Street is marked by a tablet, tied a nation together with his telegraph wire; as a pupil of Washington Allston, he enriched it with his paintings and portraits. Charlotte Cushman grew up and prepared here for a career (musical at first; then on the stage) which earned her and Boston international acclaim.

The exiled Irish patriot and poet John Boyle O'Reilly lived at No. 34 Winthrop Street while editor and part owner of the *Pilot,* Boston's first Roman Catholic weekly. Add to this three college presidents and John Harvard himself, who was buried in Phipps Burial Ground a year after he arrived in his adopted country in 1637. His brief tenure as a minister has been overwhelmed by the bequest of his library and half of his estate to the "infant seminary" which bears his name.

A quiet walk up old streets, which seem perpetually open to the sky, along High Street to the summit of Bunker Hill can be instructive to urbanist and historian alike. The unforgiving industrial perimeter of this enigmatic peninsula can also be read in terms of jobs for those who are willing or required to trade nature for necessity and community. Beside our route, flowering trees still cling to the steepest slopes, albeit fertilized by an endless supply of tin cans, litter, and broken bottles. From undistinguished windows in very ordinary houses it is possible to imbibe the longer view. A stirring panorama of vigorous growth, industry, and pride evokes that metropolis for which Samuel Adams Drake has aptly dubbed Charlestown "mother." Far beyond the spectacle of the first Hancock Tower preening itself in its new mirror, the Blue Hills record elapsed time. They seem to answer Bunker and Copp's hills whose burial grounds are unspoiled outcroppings of the past. It is as close as one can come to understanding what it must have been like in the beginning.

Monument Avenue. *Right:* row houses. *Left:* three-decker houses. *Photo: Phokion Karas*

Fort Hill Tower, Highland Park.
Fort Avenue and Beach Glen Street.
Photo: Vern Patterson

Chapter 9
ROXBURY

Between 1917 and 1941 eighteen plaques on the observation balcony of a Gothic water tower at Fort Hill in Roxbury pointed out to visitors the direction and distance of landmarks in the siege of Boston. During 1775 and part of 1776, Continental forces commanded vantage points that kept the British, under General Thomas Gage, confined to the Shawmut Peninsula. The most visible of these today are the glacial drumlins characteristic of local geology. One was a British position, Copp's Hill in the North End. Bunker and Breed's hills in Charlestown were less than four miles away. To the east, Dorchester Heights, in what is now South Boston, surveyed both the town and its harbor. British trenches on the south end of Boston Common are identified just over two miles from the tower, a fort straddling the narrow neck connecting Roxbury to Boston, and advanced British defenses spreading into Roxbury along the present lines of Canton and Dover streets.

Continental guns were placed on both sides of the Charles at Muddy River (now Brookline) and Fort Washington in Cambridgeport near MIT. From Lechmere's Point, near the present transit station, cannon dragged overland on sleds during the winter from recently captured Fort Ticonderoga were used to force the ships of the Royal Navy to anchor in the outer harbor.

It was this scene, so graphically recorded on Pelham's map of the siege, that General Washington inspected through a spyglass from a steeple on Meetinghouse Hill. He concluded that Continental defenses thrown up at Dorchester and Roxbury necks, the "Burial Ground Redoubt" at Washington and Eustis streets, a large fort near Highland and Dorr, and a fort on the site of the present observation tower, were all secure from British attack.

On April 18, 1775, William Dawes rode over Meetinghouse Hill on his way through Brighton and Cambridge to Lexington and Concord. Had His Majesty's "military advisors" chosen to go by land instead of "by sea," they would have had to march across this same neck through Roxbury under Continental gun emplacements. British guns could be heard shelling Breed's and Bunker hills in June of that year, and the smoke from burning Charlestown was seen from the windows of the Dillaway-Thomas House across the square. More cannon from Ticonderoga and two thousand men under the command of General John Thomas quietly crossed Roxbury on the night of March 4, 1776, to fortify Dorchester Heights. This move was instrumental in forcing the evacuation of Boston by the British on the following St. Patrick's Day.

Roxbury's deceptive proximity to Boston has been compromised by social and natural forces ever since. The narrow, often flooded, neck encouraged separate development of the town, the sixth established in the Commonwealth by 1630. Its first settlers were Puritans who had landed in Salem with Governor Winthrop. Their leader, William Pynchon, left to establish Springfield six years later. The Reverend

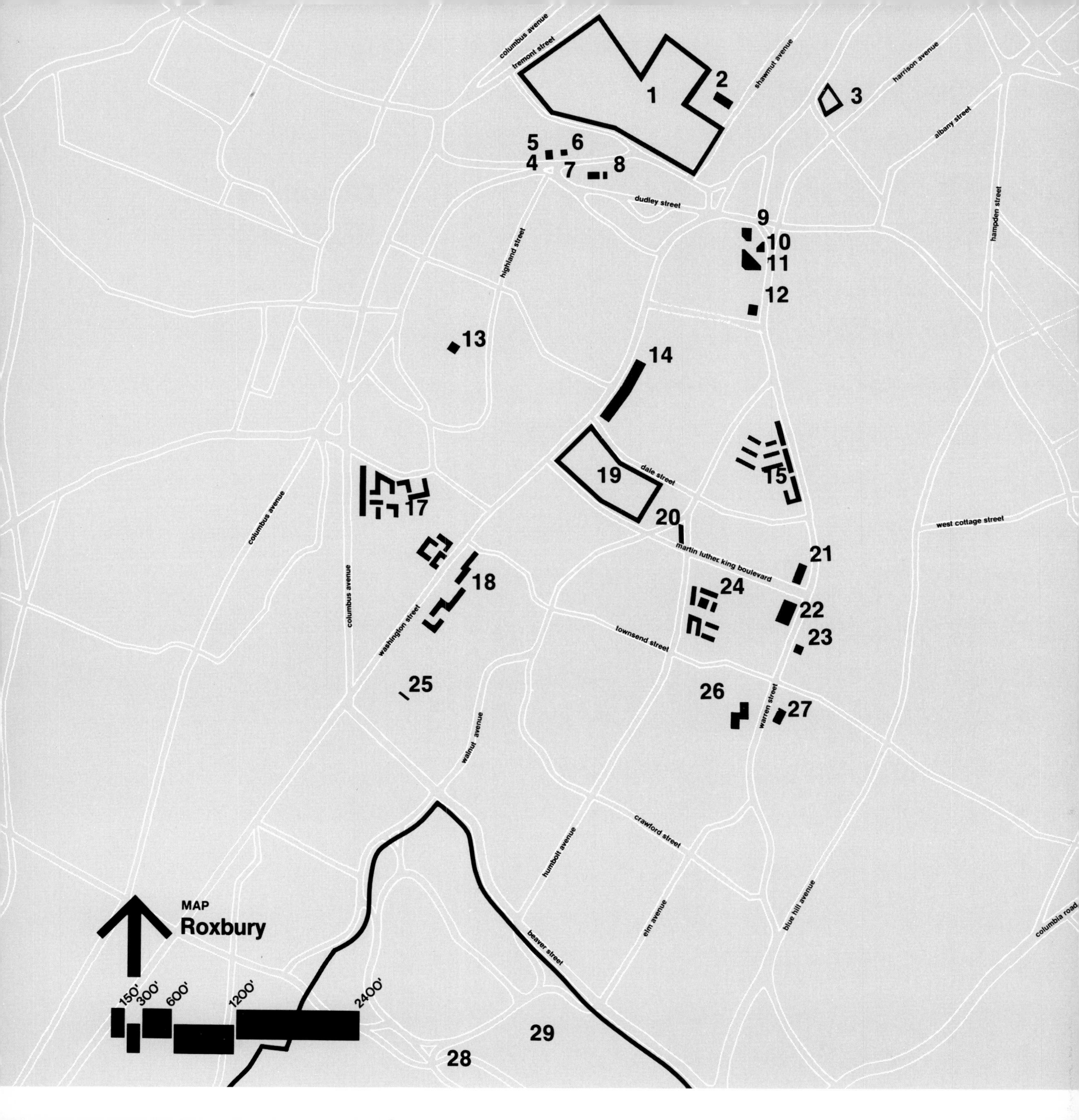

MAP
Roxbury
150'
300'
600'
1200'
2400'
columbus avenue
tremont street
shawmut avenue
harrison avenue
albany street
dudley street
hampden street
highland street
dale street
martin luther king boulevard
west cottage street
columbus avenue
columbus avenue
washington street
townsend street
warren street
walnut avenue
crawford street
humbolt avenue
elm avenue
blue hill avenue
beaver street
columbia road
1
2
3
4
5
6
7
8
9
10
11
12
13
14
15
17
18
19
20
21
22
23
24
25
26
27
28
29

1. Campus High School
   Marcel Breuer; 1976

2. Madison Park Housing
   Haynes and Smith House
   John Sharratt & Glaser/de Castro, Vitols; 1975

3. Roxbury Burial Ground, 1630

4. John Eliot Square

5. Timilty Junior High School
   205 Roxbury Avenue, 1937

6. Dillaway-Thomas House
   Built by Oliver Peabody; 1750

7. First Church of Roxbury, Unitarian
   Founded: 1632. Rebuilt; 1741, 1746, and 1804
   Oldest standing frame church in Boston

8. Putnam Hall
   Now Fellowes Athenaeum
   Free Public Library, c. 1900

9–11. Roxbury Civic Center
   Dudley and Warren streets
   Roxbury Civic Center Associates
   (Kallmann & McKinnell and Hoyle, Doran and Berry);
   9. Muncipal Court; 1975 Kallmann & McKinnell
   10. Branch Library; 1976
   11. Boston Police Station District 2; 1971

12. Boys' Club of Boston
   Warren and Cliff streets
   The Architects Collaborative; 1968

13. Fort Hill Tower (Standpipe)
   Highland Park
   Fort Avenue and Beach Glen Street; 1869

14. St. Joseph's Housing
   Feloney Associates; 1973

15. Warren Gardens Housing
   Warren Street and Walnut Avenue
   Hugh Stubbins and Associates/
   Ashley Myer & Associates; 1969

16. Shirley-Eustis House
   33 Shirley Street

17. Academy Homes I
   Columbus Avenue and Ritchie Street
   Carl Koch & Associates; 1966

18. Academy Homes II
   Washington and Dimock streets
   Carl Koch & Associates; 1968

19. Washington Park

20. Charlame II Housing
   Humboldt and Walnut avenues
   Bedar and Alpers; 1967

21. Housing for the Elderly
   Freeman, Flansburgh Associates; 1968

22. YMCA—Washington Park
   Warren Street and Washington Park Boulevard
   The Architects Collaborative; 1965

23. Unity Bank & Trust Company (renovation)
   416 Warren Street
   Stull Associates; 1968

24. Marksdale Gardens I
   Humboldt Avenue and Townsend Street
   Associated Architect and Engineer; 1964

25. Westminster Court Housing
   Carl Koch & Associates; 1960

26. Trotter Elementary School, 1973
   Humboldt Avenue

27. Taurus Apartments
   120 Humboldt Avenue
   Richard H. Walwood; 1974

28. Franklin Park
   Frederick Law Olmsted; 1886

29. Franklin Park Zoo
   New Facilities
   Huygens & Tappé; 1977

First Church of Roxbury (Unitarian). Founded 1632, rebuilt 1741, 1746, and 1804. Oldest frame church in Boston. *Photo: Max Ferro*

John Eliot preached to the Indians in their native tongue, translated the Bible for them, and was pastor of the first two meetinghouses. The present (Eliot) church, fifth on the site, is named for him. Built in 1804, with a bell cast by Paul Revere, it is the oldest wooden religious structure in Boston.

Church records identify the occupations of its parishioners: physicians, schoolteachers, lawyers; merchants of dry goods, flour, wool, cotton, the China trade; shopkeepers, tanners, farmers, master mariners, soap boilers, candlemakers, coopers, and bankers. Dr. Joseph Warren, patriot, orator, and casualty of Bunker Hill, lived in the Highlands section. So did Governor Shirley, "probably the ablest and most disinterested of all the British governors to serve in North America" (The National Historic Sites Commission's *Final Report,* 1961). His country house, which he called Shirley Place, looked out over a broad expanse of countryside, harbor, and islands. Framed of solid oak, its two-story salon and dramatic staircases were designed for entertaining in the formal, lavish fashion of the eighteenth century. Inconclusive, but likely, evidence suggests that it was designed by Peter Harrison and that George Washington visited there shortly before undertaking his own residential construction program at Mt. Vernon. Subsequent occupants included a widow with the enigmatic name of Madame Bertell de Fitzpatrick, and privateer Captain James Magee, who with Elias Haskett Derby and Thomas Handasyd Perkins, opened the China trade.

It is called the Shirley-Eustis House today in recognition of a later owner, Dr. William Eustis. A surgeon in the Revolution, he later became a member of Congress, secretary of war, minister to the Netherlands, and governor of Massachusetts. His guest list included the names of Lafayette, Aaron Burr, John

Shirley-Eustis House, Shirley Street. Remodeled: James Ballou; 1970. *Photo: W. Geddis*

Westminster Court Housing. Carl Koch & Associates; 1968. *Photo: Phokion Karas*

Quincy Adams, Henry Clay, Daniel Webster, and John C. Calhoun, indicating that he, too, made good use of this "high" Georgian-Colonial mansion.

The Dillaway-Thomas House, in John Eliot Square, was built in 1750 as a parsonage for the First Parish Church by the Reverend Oliver Peabody. Its Doric portico and pedimented dormers qualify it as "modest Georgian." It may have served temporarily as headquarters for General Thomas during the siege. For many years it has been preserved as the home of the Roxbury Historical Society. The entire Square has been placed on the National Register of Historic Places. A brick Federal mansion called Ionic Hall (1800) and the now altered Federal house (c. 1780) of Major John J. Spooner are surrounded by a public school, hotel, and other characteristic structures of the 1870s.

In Jamaica Plain, which was, with West Roxbury, a part of Roxbury until 1852, Commodore Joshua Loring built a substantial Colonial house in 1760. He led the campaign against the French on Lake George, Lake Champlain, and Lake Ontario. The house served briefly as headquarters and a hospital for General Nathanael Greene whose fellow Rhode Islanders guarded the Back Bay from Roxbury to Brookline and Cambridge.

The first street extended from the neck to the Meeting House, then by separate roads to Dorchester, Milton, Dedham, and Brookline. Farms bordered the marshes of the Back Bay and Boston Harbor. After the Revolution, traffic increased on a newly built road along the neck. By 1826 a stage shuttled back and forth every hour for a fare of nine cents each way. Beginning in 1804, the neck was widened by filling; South Cove and the balance of the land between Roxbury and Boston were completed by the end of the century. In 1835, the Boston and Providence Railroad opened a station at Roxbury Crossing, making it feasible for successful businessmen and professionals to commute from their new country villas to Boston. The first horse-drawn trolley was opened in 1856, accelerating development. By 1870, most of the lower town was subdivided. The perfection of steam power and the availability of cheap labor from new Americans and rural New Englanders stimulated industrialization. In Roxbury it was concentrated along Stony Brook and the harbor, and included foundries, textile mills, rope walks, piano works and clockmakers, and stone and lumberyards.

Crowded Boston had already generated the social pattern that dominates Roxbury to the present day. In *Streetcar Suburbs* Warner saw the same "romantic capitalism" that brought fame and prosperity to the city offered to "one third of Boston, natives and immigrants alike . . . only the tensions of too few jobs at too little pay, inhuman work conditions, wage cuts and seasonal layoffs, accidents and disease, and, at times, terrible depressions whose effects . . . led many lower class Bostonians to attack not the methods of industrialism that caused their suffering, but each other". Rich and poor, the employer and employed retreated into often violent attitudes of ethnic nationalism that distracted "attention from the problems of poverty, housing, education, and welfare which severely limited the promise of American democracy."

Before 1840 the majority of immigrants came from the British Isles, Germany, and Canada. By 1850 they were joined by refugees from famine in Ireland; the next to come were Jews. In 1880 the population was 38.9 percent foreign-born; by 1905 the percentage was nearly sixty. Rapid development of Roxbury and other "streetcar suburbs" was spurred by expanding rail transit, first as private speculation, then semi-public, as in a metropolitan utility. In lower Roxbury the housing pattern reflected the narrow options of economic and ethnic mobility, enforced by the unquestioned assumptions of an industrial democracy. Middle-class single-family houses were cut up into flats; duplexes had attic apartments added. Row houses similar but tighter than those in the South End, first in brick, then in wood, finally coagulated into the classic three-decker and jammed the streets of the lower town. In the Highlands, upper-middle-class families continued to cultivate the "rural ideal." Farms were progressively subdivided to provide new lots for houses in a succession of styles quite similar to those found in Cambridge. Grove Hall Estate, from the Federal period, is distinguished by an elaborate roof pediment flanked with fan brackets. The porticoed Gleason House, built at the height of the Greek Revival period, has an observatory cupola which once enjoyed a view of Boston Harbor. Academic (or Second Empire), Queen Anne, and Shingle Style houses are well represented; a coherent late-nineteenth-century district remains just over the Dorchester line in Ashmont. The earliest houses are more "genuine"; most later structures were built with stock plans and ornament. A rarity in New England, "Carpenter Gothic" cottages dotted the Roxbury countryside before the Civil War. A few remain near John Eliot Square and one is being preserved on the site of the Dillaway-Thomas House.

These suburban estates were reinforced by institutions consistent with the idealized image: a library, high school, lyceum, and social clubs. Roxbury Latin School, in the northeast corner, is the oldest private school in America. Perhaps the finest amenity was and still is Franklin Park. It is the principal gem in the "Emerald Necklace," a string of parklands that reaches from the Charles River Basin to the Harbor at South Boston. Practical, visionary, persistent Frederick Law Olmsted told

Madison Park Housing. Haynes and Smith House. John Sharratt & Glaser/deCastro/Vitols; 1975. *Photo: John Sharratt*

St. Joseph's Housing. Feloney Associates; 1973. *Photo: Phokion Karas*

the Boston city fathers in 1880 that "a man's eyes cannot be as much occupied as they are in large cities by artificial things, or by natural things seen under obviously artificial conditions, without a harmful effect, first on his mental and nervous system and ultimately on his entire organization" (quoted in S. B. Sutton's *Civilizing American Cities)*.

In proposing a major urban park in the Highlands as early as 1869, he had asked for a parade ground, ball "grounds," space for refined horticulture and floral displays, streams of water and "lakes with provisions for boating, skating and bathing, as well as waterside beauty." The site he was given to work with had none of these. Through his resourceful design he transformed "stony upland pasture" covered with stunted second growth and ledge into what has been called one of the best-designed parks in the country. It combined a promenade, deer park, children's play areas, a music court, and zoological garden with broad meadows and woods. A nine-hole golf course added later is all but lost in the landscape. Acutely aware of the social implications of urban growth, Olmsted prophetically created a major bastion for the survival of Roxbury and its neighboring districts.

The ledge which America's first and greatest landscape architect turned into a dramatic visual asset was Roxbury puddingstone. The technical name is Roxbury conglomerate, consisting of a gray sandstone matrix with entrapped sand, gravel, and pebbles. (Early spellings of the town name included "Rocksbury.") The stone is found in nearly all of Roxbury and Dorchester, and in parts of West Roxbury, Brookline, Brighton, Newton, Hyde Park, Milton, Hingham, Quincy, and Hull. Relatively hard but workable, it was used for Colonial foundations and retaining walls. Too rough for styles dependent upon classical features, it came into its own after 1860 in romantic Ruskin Gothic, Queen Anne, and Romanesque work. The first puddingstone church was the Tremont Street Methodist, followed by Emmanuel Church on Newbury Street.

As the city expanded, problems of water supply, sewage, and drainage were dealt with on a metropolitan scale. Fort Hill water tower was a part of the Cochituate reservoir system. Stony Brook, along which industry and the railroad had located, was buried in a culvert to prevent flooding. Ambitious public works programs were

Franklin Park Zoo. New Facilities: Huygens & Tappé; 1976. *Photo: Steve Rosenthal*

carried out on the premise that the city and its environs could not be safe as long as any one part was a threat to public health. But the basic urban assumption remained rooted in the desirability of being able to live in one place and work in another. This pattern held firm through two wars, with an intervening depression. For the increasingly impacted areas, this included absentee ownership and its universal implications of deferred maintenance and obsolescence. When conditions reaching far beyond Boston brought substantial numbers of blacks and Spanish-speaking people into Roxbury, the resources of what had been for some time a staging area for ethnic assimilation were strained to the breaking point.

Roxbury was two-thirds white in 1950; virtually all black by 1964. It became the

Academy Homes I,
Columbus Avenue
and Ritchie Street.
Carl Koch &
Associates; 1966.
Academy Homes II,
Washington and
Dimock streets.
Carl Koch &
Associates; 1968.
Photo: Phokion Karas

prime target for federal renewal programs which found that 25 percent of the housing could not be salvaged, and that all but one percent required rehabilitation. With public subsidies, the housing industry was asked to cope with inflexible bureaucratic regulations, recalcitrant building trades, fiscal priorities, obsolete codes, public apathy, and understandable community distrust—in short, to solve the problems of society itself.

Boston's urban renewal administration gambled on working through the black middle class to arrive at a workable plan. What were then innovations in design, physical planning, construction, and financing produced a grade of housing that met all available standards and received wide recognition. After nearly a decade, a discouragingly small proportion of this housing has survived the intense demands placed upon its physical limitations, design integrity, and symbolic value. The quality of life made possible by projects such as St. Joseph's Housing (1970; Paul Feloney) and Marksdale Gardens (1964; Henry Boles) reveals a new urban ideal that is only slowly becoming understood.

Public projects designed to reinforce the process of community regrowth have suffered from changes in federal policy and the politically solvent demands of other districts. A district courthouse–police station complex (1970; Kallmann and McKinnell; Hoyle, Doran and Berry), which was to have included a library, is at the geographic center of the Washington Park district. The library (1976; Kallmann and McKinnell) was delayed by public opposition until it was enlarged to include other community functions. The city is using a number of funding sources to refurbish John Eliot Square as the historic core of a residential district under rehabilitation, including a school and playground.

Nearby, the long-awaited "campus" high school (1976; Marcel Breuer) has broken ground. Conceived in the early days of redevelopment as a regional solution to racial integration, it has been delayed by the machinations of a city divided over interpretations of "educational quality." Other school sites remain empty because they cannot be integrated without busing. This impasse is the legacy of the same destructive social forces that have shaped Roxbury for one hundred years or more. A comprehensive plan developed in the mid-sixties recommended building new schools on the borderlines of districts that had become ethnic strongholds. Integration could have been accomplished as a staged, natural process, without extended busing. The plan met an ominous, silent resistance; time has now run out and the matter is in the hands of the federal courts.

While demagogues howl, Roxbury continues to embarrass its neighbors with increasing expertise in the social and environmental planning processes. Several nonprofit planning and development groups have undertaken programs of rehabilitation and new construction. A group of black architects and planners has

Boys' Club of Boston, Warren and Cliff streets. The Architects Collaborative; 1968. *Photo: Louis Reens*

been formed to develop specific criteria for their communities, and to advocate implementation. An exceptionally imaginative Model Cities program has broken through bureaucracy and apathy to assist residents with multiple-function social service centers. The community has established its own Hispano-American "Alianza" to assist Spanish-speaking members of the community in matters of education, child care, health, employment, and youth programs. Culturally, Roxbury has produced an Afro-American performing arts center of national stature. A Museum of Afro-American History is busy interpreting the town's past from the beginning. It plans to merge its efforts and exhibits with the Roxbury Historical Association in the Dillaway-Thomas House. The private sector has built a Boys' Club and family size YMCA, both by The Architects Collaborative.

With all of this progress, the community still suffers from problems that are present in all major cities: poverty and crime. There is still a long, long way to go. But it is now possible to see Roxbury as something other than a collage of urban frustration. The image has been more that of a Dorian Gray-like portrait of Boston, moldering in a closet as a record of its sins, while other parts of the city receive beauty treatments. Roxbury's history has graphically illuminated the consequences of the narrow assumptions and woefully incomplete understanding which this city, and most others, have tolerated in the name of free enterprise. To turn away from this functional ugliness is to repeat, endlessly, the inhumanity that shaped it.

An ironic consequence of a landmark study of new highway construction versus public transportation in Boston (1972) is the Southwest Corridor program. Its alignment approximates the long-buried Stony Brook which once served Roxbury's early industry. For too many years it had been assumed that the solution to a surfeit of automobiles is more roads. Land and houses had already been taken by eminent domain along the corridor, the route of the rail line to Providence and New York, when a moratorium was called on all highway construction within the Metropolitan Boston area. The study, structured for citizen participation and environmental analysis, recommended that instead of aiming eight more lanes of limited access traffic at the heart of a city designed for walking and horsecars, existing surface arteries should be improved and rapid transit service established. The air rights and previously cleared land that will now be available for community development are at issue in the planning process. Time will tell whether Roxbury, the South End, and other communities will be able to reclaim their share of this precious resource for jobs, shopping, schools, recreation, and housing on terms consistent with stated needs. But if lobbying funds extracted from the sale of gasoline, tires, automobiles, concrete, asphalt, roadbuilding equipment, and votes prevail, Boston will remain under siege.

Delightful, romantic landforms and satisfying vistas, summers tempered by prevailing sea breezes, proximity to jobs and shopping in downtown Boston, the acres of Olmsted's great park, the potential impact of the Southwest Corridor, and two hundred years of political independence remain Roxbury's basic strengths. What once was tolerated as a "zone of emergence" could be turned into a working model for embattled communities everywhere. Thus, the water tower on Fort Hill remains as a daily reminder that, as with environmental sanitation, the welfare of an entire region is dependent upon the *social and financial* health of each of its parts.

Plan of Roxbury Civic Center, Dudley and Warren streets. Police Station; 1971. Municipal Court; 1975: Kallmann & McKinnell and Hoyle, Doran & Berry. Branch Library; 1976: Kallmann & McKinnell. *Photo: Kallmann & McKinnell*

YMCA, Warren Street and Washington Park Boulevard. The Architects Collaborative; 1965. *Photo: Louis Reens*

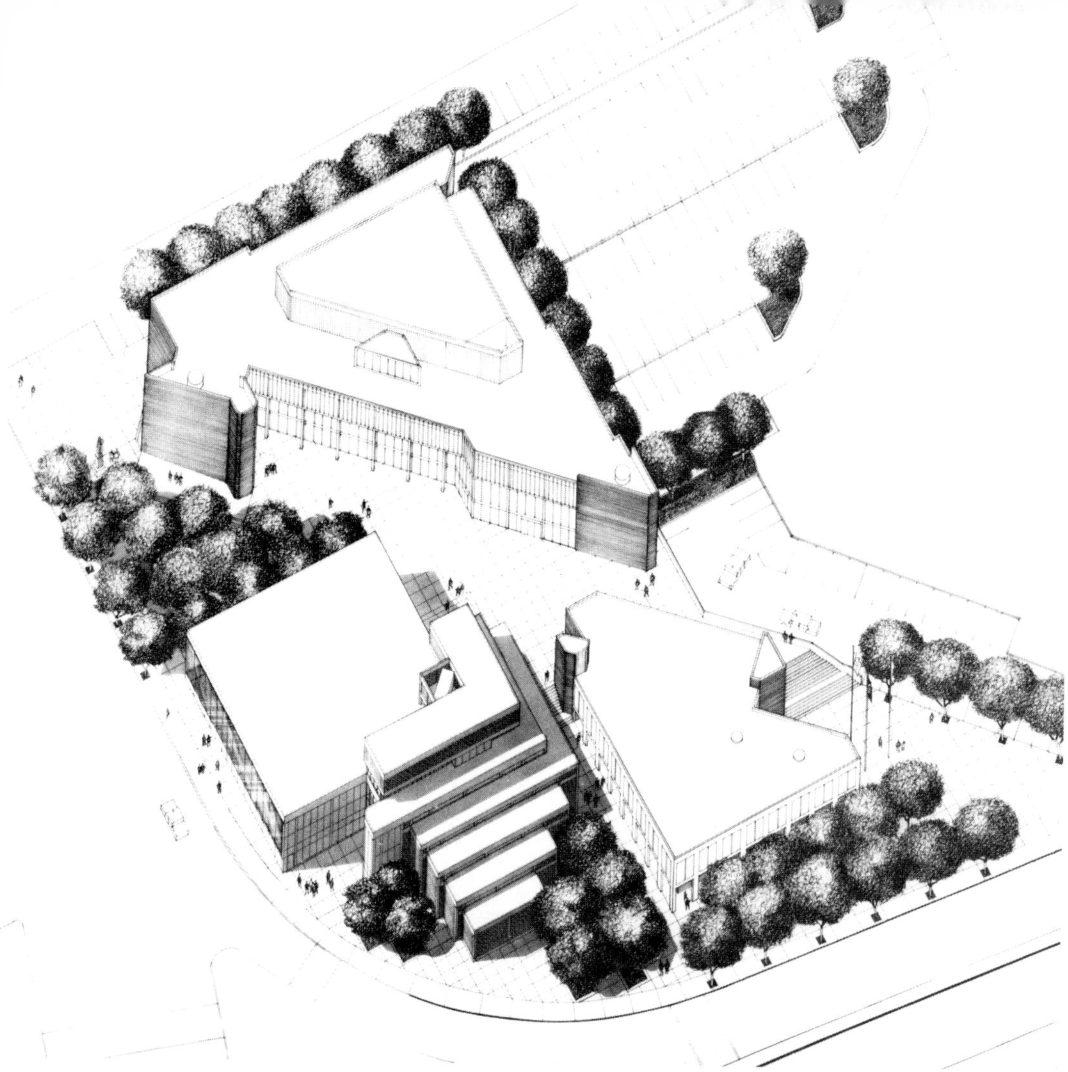

Chapter 10
CAMBRIDGE

Mather House
Cowperthwaite Street
Shepley, Bulfinch, Richardson and Abbott; 1970.
Photo: Shepley, Bulfinch, Richardson and Abbott

Nestled in the arm of the Charles River, Cambridge can be reached from Boston over any of ten bridges, including a dam, a footbridge, and another for trains. The route was once "by sea" to Charlestown then overland; or out through what is now Brighton to a ferry near the present Larz Anderson Bridge. Its other boundaries are lost against Somerville, Arlington, Belmont, and Watertown. It was called Newtowne at the time of its settlement, and included Brighton, Newton, Lexington, Arlington, and Billerica. The country roads that once reached these outposts have long since been clogged by strip development. Major streets were once the boundaries of farms. Their often-discontinuous tree-shaded side streets lead to a collection of eighteenth-, nineteenth-, and twentieth-century houses as interesting as the larger buildings for which Cambridge has become world famous. Recognition of this fact, long overdue, owes much to a comprehensive *Survey of Architectural History in Cambridge* by the Cambridge Historical Commission, and the invaluable *Guide to Cambridge Architecture; Ten Walking Tours* by Robert Bell Rettig.

The protected upriver townsite was chosen the seat of government for the Massachusetts Bay Colony but the governor preferred Boston. This left a small farming community and a college. The college was named for John Harvard, a Charlestown minister who left it his estate; Cambridge was renamed after the English university town in 1638. The two principal activities, agriculture and education, created from the very first a "town-and-gown" atmosphere that thrived on differences in wealth, religion, ideas, and, eventually, loyalty to the English throne. Post-Revolutionary growth, the American melting pot, populist demagogues, and apparent academic indifference have kept this polarity at a healthy level ever since. In recent years, there has been an increasing tendency to cross established lines over a variety of planning, economic, and social issues. Coalitions have produced better school committees and, in a landmark effort, stopped construction of an innerbelt highway across the city.

The tight grid of streets about Harvard Square preserves the pattern of the old town center. Surrounded by farms, the Common extended to Linnean Street, filling the triangle between Massachusetts Avenue and Garden Street. As the estates and public lands were broken up over the years, houses of successive periods were built between the widely spaced early homesites. None of the remaining village houses are of the seventeenth century. The Lee-Nichols House farther out at 159 Brattle was built in the 1680s, with a third story added about 1760. On what once was the far end of the Common, now 21 Linnean Street, the Cooper-Frost-Austin-Hitchings House is the oldest complete seventeenth-century structure (c. 1691). With a steep roof, lean-to addition, wide fireplaces, and chamfered beams, it is typical of many early colonial houses

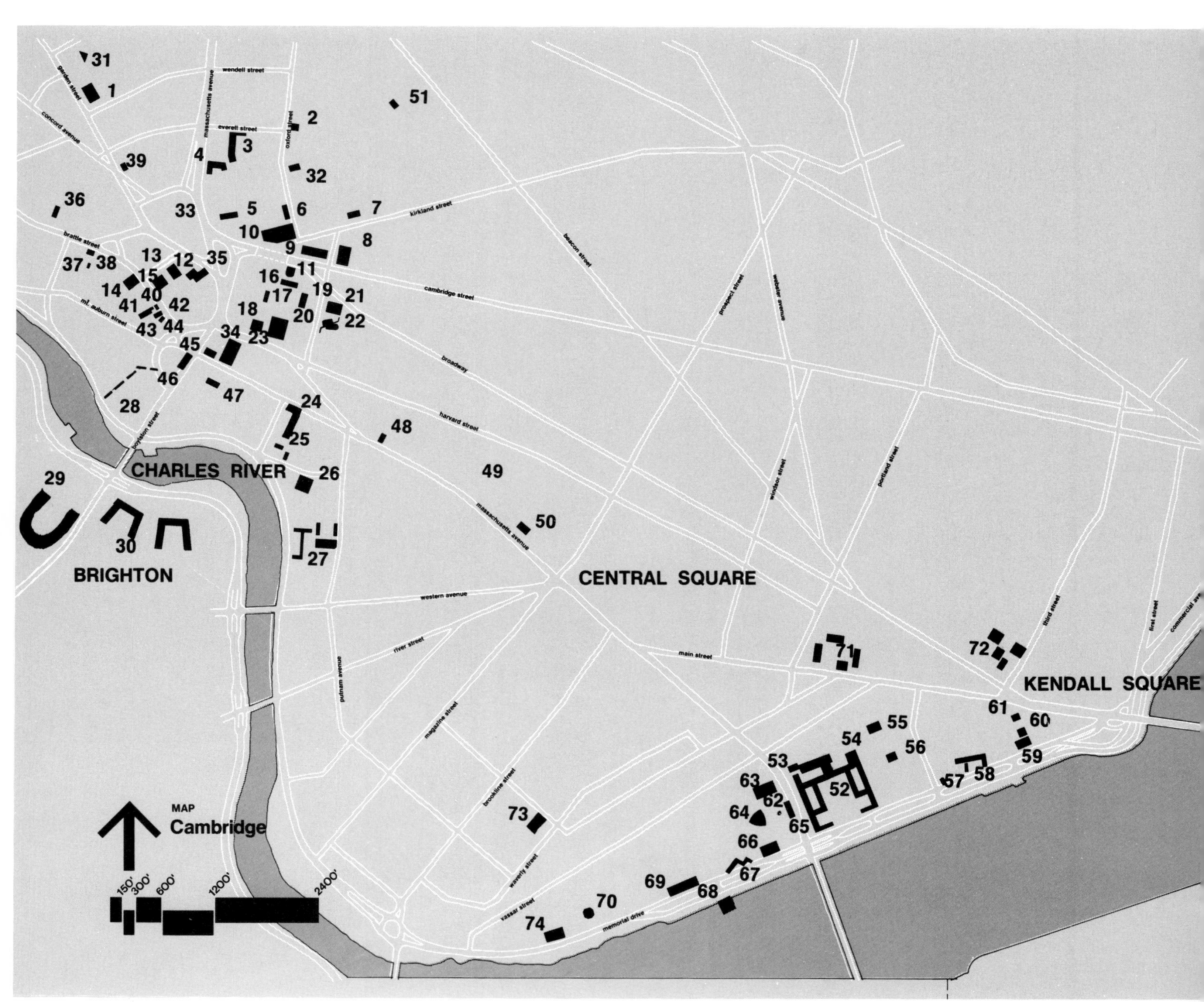

MAP
Cambridge
CHARLES RIVER
BRIGHTON
CENTRAL SQUARE
KENDALL SQUARE
garden street
concord avenue
wendell street
massachusetts avenue
everett street
oxford street
kirkland street
brattle street
mt. auburn street
cambridge street
beacon street
prospect street
webster avenue
broadway
harvard street
boylston street
windsor street
portland street
western avenue
river street
main street
putnam avenue
magazine street
brookline street
waverly street
vassar street
memorial drive
third street
first street
150'
300'
600'
1200'
2400'

1. Hilles Library, Radcliffe College
59 Shepard Street
Harrison & Abramovitz; 1965

2. Engineering Sciences Building
40 Oxford Street
Minoru Yamasaki and Associates; 1962

3. Harvard Graduate Center
14 Everett Street
The Architects Collaborative; 1949

4. Pound Building
Law School Faculty Offices
Massachusetts Avenue
Benjamin Thompson & Associates; 1970

5. Austin Hall
6 Holmes Place
H. H. Richardson; 1881

6. Gordon McKay Laboratory
9 Oxford Street
Shepley, Bulfinch, Richardson and Abbott; 1952

7. William James Hall
33 Kirkland Street
Minoru Yamasaki and Associates; 1963

8. Gund Hall (Graduate School of Design)
Quincy and Cambridge streets
John Andrews/Anderson/Baldwin; 1969

9. Memorial Hall
Cambridge and Quincy streets
Ware and Van Brunt; 1874

10. Undergraduate Science Center
Sert, Jackson and Associates; 1973

11. Canaday Hall
Ezra Ehrencrantz; 1974
(former site of Hunt Hall)
Richard Morris Hunt; 1893

12. Larsen Hall
Graduate School of Education
6 Appian Way
Caudill, Rowlett & Scott; 1965

13. Old Radcliffe Yard

14. Loeb Drama Center
64 Brattle Street
Hugh Stubbins and Associates; 1959

15. Monroe C. Gutman Library
Benjamin Thompson Associates; 1974

16. Memorial Church
Coolidge, Shepley, Bulfinch & Abbott; 1931

17. University Hall
Charles Bulfinch; 1813–15

18. Old Harvard Yard

Massachusetts Hall, 1718

Holden Chapel, 1742

Hollis Hall
Thomas Dawes; 1762

Harvard Hall
Gov. Francis Bernard and Thomas Dawes; 1764
Additions: 1842, 1870

Stoughton Hall
Charles Bulfinch, Thomas Dawes; 1804

Holworthy Hall
Loammi Baldwin; 1811

Boylston Hall
Schultze & Schoen; 1857
The Architects Collaborative; 1959

Grays Hall
N. J. Bradlee; 1862

Mathews Hall
Peabody and Stearns; 1871

Thayer Hall
Ryder & Harris; 1869

Weld Hall
Ware and Van Brunt; 1870

19. Sever Hall
Harvard Yard
H. H. Richardson; 1880

20. Widener Library
Horace Trumbauer; 1913
Nathan M. Pusey Library
Hugh Stubbins and Associates; 1976

21. Fogg Museum of Art
Coolidge, Shepley, Bulfinch & Abbott; 1925

22. Carpenter Center for the Visual Arts
19 Prescott Street
Le Corbusier with Sert, Jackson & Gourley; 1961

23. Holyoke Center
1350 Massachusetts Avenue
Sert, Jackson & Gourley; 1961–65

24. Quincy House
58 Plympton Street
Shepley, Bulfinch, Richardson and Abbott; 1968

25. Leverett House Library and Towers
Memorial Drive and De Wolfe Street
Shepley, Bulfinch, Richardson and Abbott; 1969

26. Mather House
Cowperthwaite Street
Shepley, Bulfinch, Richardson and Abbott; 1970

27. Peabody Terrace (married students' housing)
900 Memorial Drive
Sert, Jackson & Gourley; 1963

28. MBTA Car Barn Site

29. Harvard Stadium
Soldiers Field Road, Brighton; 1903
New Athletic Facilities
The Architects Collaborative; 1976—

30. Graduate School of Business Administration
Brighton, 1925—

31. Faculty Housing, Radcliffe, Linnean Street
Ronald Gourley; 1972

32. Museum of Comparative Zoology
The Architects Collaborative; 1972

33. Cambridge Common
Redesign: Mason & Fry; 1976

34. Harvard Square

35. Christ Church
Zero Garden Street
Peter Harrison; 1760

36. Vassal House (Longfellow House), 1759
105 Brattle Street

37. M. F. Stoughton House
90 Brattle Street
H. H. Richardson; 1882

38. 9 Ash Street
Philip Johnson; 1941

39. Longy School of Music
Addition:
Huygens & Tappé; 1973

40. Design Research Inc.
48 Brattle Street
Benjamin Thompson & Associates; 1969

41. The Architects Collaborative Office Buildings
46 Brattle Street and 8 Story Street
The Architects Collaborative; 1966 and 1969

42. 44 Brattle Street Office Building
Sert, Jackson and Associates; 1971

43. 14 Story Street Office Building
Earl R. Flansburgh & Associates; 1970

44. William Brattle House, c. 1727

45. The Garage
Conversion to Retail Complex
ADD Inc.; 1973

46. Crimson Galeria
Boylston Street
Childs, Bertram & Tseckares; 1975

47. University Lutheran Church
66 Winthrop Street
Arland Dirlam; 1950

48. 1033 Massachusetts Avenue
Hugh Stubbins and Associates; 1969

49. New England Gas and Electric Association
130 Austin Street
Sert, Jackson & Gourley; 1960

50. Cambridge City Hall
Longfellow, Alden & Harlow; 1889

51. José Luis Sert Residence
64 Francis Avenue
José Luis Sert; 1957

52. Cooper-Frost-Austin-Hitchings House, c. 1691
Linnean Street

53. Maclaurin Buildings
Welles Bosworth; 1913

54. Center for Advanced Engineering Studies
105 Massachusetts Avenue
Skidmore, Owings & Merrill; 1965

55. Bush Building
Center for Materials Science and Engineering
Skidmore, Owings & Merrill; 1963

56. Alumni Swimming Pool
Anderson & Beckwith; 1937

57. Green Building (earth sciences)
McDermott Court
I. M. Pei & Associates; 1964

La Grande Voile (stabile)
Alexander Calder; 1966

58 President's House
111 Memorial Drive

59. Eastgate Apartments
100 Memorial Drive
Brown, DeMars, Kennedy, Koch & Rapson; 1949

60. Sloan School for Industrial Management
Conversion:
William Hoskins Brown; 1955

61. Grover M. Hermann Building
30 Wadsworth Street
Eduardo Catalano; 1964

62. Eastgate Married Students' Housing
Wadsworth and Main streets
Eduardo Catalano; 1965

63. M.I.T. Chapel
Eero Saarinen; 1955

64. Julius Adams Stratton Building
(student union)
84 Massachusetts Avenue
Eduardo Catalano with Brannen & Shimamoto; 1963

65. Kresge Auditorium
Eero Saarinen; 1955

66. Center for Advanced Visual Studies
40 Massachusetts Avenue
Marvin E. Goody & John M. Clancy; 1962,1967

67. McCormick Hall (women's housing)
320 Memorial Drive
Anderson, Beckwith & Haible; 1962, 1967

68. Baker House (undergraduate housing)
362 Memorial Drive
Alvar Aalto with Perry, Shaw, & Hepburn; 1947

69. Boat House
Anderson, Beckwith & Haible; 1965

70. Frank S. MacGregor House
(undergraduate housing)
450 Memorial Drive
The Architects Collaborative and
Pietro Belluschi; 1974

71. Tang Residence Hall
Hugh Stubbins and Associates; 1962

Other Buildings:

72. Technology Square
Main Street
Cabot, Cabot & Forbes; 1963/64
Pietro Belluschi and Eduardo Catalano; 1965/66

73. Department of Transportation
formerly NASA facilities
Tower: Edward Durrell Stone; 1970
Optics and Guidance Laboratories:
The Architects Collaborative; 1970

74. Housing for the Elderly
Erie, Clarendon & Gore streets
Benjamin Thompson Associates; 1973

75. Hyatt House Hotel
Graham Gund; 1976

found throughout New England. Few remain so well preserved within the larger cities.

Continental troops drilled in view of another farmhouse at 7 Waterhouse Street (1753) which still faces the Common. Kirkland House now uses the colonial vernacular house of John Hicks (1762; 64 Boylston Street) as a library. Georgian-Colonial Wadsworth House (1726) clings bravely to Massachusetts Avenue near the intersection of Holyoke Street. For a short time it served as Washington's headquarters and until 1849, as a residence for the president of Harvard College.

The area to the west of present Harvard Square was divided into small lots dotted with a number of houses by 1635. These were bought up by a handful of families whose wealth came from West Indian plantations, shipping, or revenues derived from the Crown. By 1770, Brattle Street wound past seven large estates and was called "Tory Row." The street was named for William Brattle, who lived in the gambrel-roofed house at No. 42, near the corner of Church Street. When the widow of loyalist Henry Vassall left her house at 94 Brattle for the safety of England, it was commandeered as medical headquarters for Washington's army. Recently restored, this house had undergone several changes before it reached its present "country" Georgian state.

Washington's new GHQ was in the pilastered Georgian mansion across the street. It was built in 1759 by John Vassall, whose lands extended from Garden Street to the Charles River. Something of this original scope is preserved in Longfellow Park, opposite the house. Its memorial to the poet (who lived in the house from 1837 until his death in 1882) was designed by the landscape architect Charles Eliot in 1914. The sculpture is by Daniel Chester French, with the architect Henry Bacon. The house of patriot Thomas Fayerweather

Wadsworth House. *Photo: Cambridge Historical Commission*

Cooper-Frost-Austin House. *Photo: Ken Conant*

William Brattle House. *Photo: Bertram Adams*

(c. 1764; 175 Brattle) had been owned by the Ruggles family, from Jamaica. It was used as a hospital after the Battle of Bunker Hill. There are Tory mansions off Brattle Street, such as the Georgian Thomas Oliver House (1767) at 33 Elmwood Avenue. It was later owned by Elbridge Gerry, a signer of the Declaration of Independence. "Elmwood" is now the residence of the president of Harvard University.

Historians do not agree on the labeling of buildings of the colonial period. While the predominating English style was called "Georgian," it is difficult to find pure examples north of Virginia. A cumbersome, if more realistic term would be "Georgian-Colonial." This leaves a number of simpler structures which, however much influenced by a common technology, show little, if any, stylistic intention in their vernacular innocence. Two examples are the tiny gambrel-roofed house at 30 Elmwood Avenue, moved there from North Cambridge in 1965, and an authentic 1790 farmhouse moved all the way from Duxbury in 1930 to No. 20 Gray Gardens West.

Sidewalk historians should be wary of the many Colonial Revival houses found alongside the originals. Those dating from the last half of the nineteenth century are more inventive, while later efforts show a stricter interpretation of the vernacular elements. Nos. 115, 145, and 158 Brattle; No. 1 Highland; and 27 Washington Avenue were all built before 1900. Nos. 114 and 144 Brattle as well as 5 Bryant Street and 138 Irving Street were built after this date.

The preponderance of revivals were Georgian, a style which dominated academic Cambridge from the turn of the century until World War II. Its popularity can be read as a countermarch to the freedom of late nineteenth-century styles, with an opportunity to follow rules of design extracted from works of demonstrated elegance. Another explanation might be that architects, faced with the spectre of rapid industrialization, preferred the visual security of Jefferson and the "Age of Reason." Nos. 30 Holyoke and 44 Boylston were built by 1906; 72 Mt. Auburn in 1915; with 60 Boylston and 45 Dunster Street as late as 1929 and 1930.

Returning to the early part of the nine-

:eenth century, we find the simpler statements of the Federal period in greater favor today. Modest houses at 2-4 Hancock Place (1807), 35 Bowdoin (1812), 17 South (1826), and 69 Dunster (1829) are interesting to compare with more elaborate versions built within the same time span: 10 Coolidge Hill Road, 163 Brattle, 11 Hawthorn, and 19 Ash Street. The Dana-Palmer House, now on Quincy Street next to the Union, was built in 1822 on a rise of land overlooking Braintree Street (later called Harvard Street and now Massachusetts Avenue). It occupied the present site of Lamont Library. An 1803 house at 153 Brattle Street looks back to Colonial forms, as did some of the earliest Federal houses on Beacon Hill. In 1810, Ithiel Town, an architect better known for his work in New Haven and New York, designed the pilastered and balustraded house at 88 Garden Street. No. 1 Garden Street, now the Christ Church Rectory, was built by master builder William Saunders in 1820 as his own house. Federal revivals (such as those at 59 Fayerweather, 4 Gray Gardens West, and 67 Francis Avenue) enjoyed a brief popularity in the first quarter of the twentieth century.

The long summer of Greek Revival, tempered in Boston by Federal brick and Academic stone, flourished in the wooden houses of Cambridge. By this time other parts of the city were being settled. Examples of this reverence for columns, pedimented gables, pilasters, and wide cornerboards are more widespread than earlier styles: 74 Thorndike (1843); 135 Western Avenue (1846). There are out-and-out temples such as Gannett House (1838). In other houses, large and small, the Grecian formula was applied to less pretentious, if more ordered, surfaces: 1 Francis Avenue (1836), 27-29 William (1838), 78 Mt. Auburn (1839), and 112 Brattle (1846).

The innocence of these celebrations of porch and pediment gave way to a more robust indication of things to come: 9 Follen (1844) and 106-108 Inman (1845).

Pilasters grew into even wider cornerboards in the more academic Regency adaptations: 21 Kirkland (1838) and 101 Brattle (1844). A union of Gothic and Greek (7 Dana Street; 1841) seems right at home in this procession of styles. Beacon Hill and Back Bay versions are found in East Cambridge (80-82 Otis Street; 1861). This area was developed by a group including Harrison Gray Otis, a Mt. Vernon

Hugh Stubbins House. *Photo: Louis Reens*

Richardson House. *Photo: George M. Cushing*

José Luis Sert Residence,
64 Francis Avenue.
José Luis Sert; 1957.
Photo: Louis Reens

Christ Church, Zero Garden Street. Peter Harrison; 1760. *Photo: Library of Congress*

Morse School. Carl Koch & Associates; 1955. *Photo: Cambridge Historical Commission*

Proprietor, after the Craigie Bridge (now the Charles River Dam) was built.

At mid-century, Cantabrigians discovered the Italianate "bracketed" style. Featuring flat-sloping roofs with wide overhangs supported on ornate, repetitive brackets, it has been diagnosed by historians as "carpenters' frenzy." A pure and moving example can be found at 15 Berkeley (1863) together with its neighbors, Nos. 4, 5, and 6. Other examples are scattered throughout the city: 22 Putnam Avenue (1848); 79 Raymond, 26–28 Fayette, and 3 William (all 1857); and 102 River Street (1861). Their verticality and lush detail emulate English country houses, copied in turn from Italian villas. The Academic persuasion, with its tall windows, mansard roofs, and refined details, was worked out in wood rather than stone in Cambridge. An attitude toward architecture rather than a style," these intellectual investigations and their subsequent excesses account for a large portion of what we call "Victorian." Symmetrical at first, they had four-square floor plans and central entrance porches: 24 Craigie (1868), 32 Linnean (1863), and 81 Washington Avenue (1871). Two such houses, 27 Craigie (1854) and 4 Kirkland Place (1856), were designed by Henry Greenough, a leading exponent of the style and brother of Horatio Greenough, the sculptor. The second of these is a rare example in brick. One other, 1000 Massachusetts Avenue (1856) by Calvin Ryder, deserves special mention.

In the following decades more elaborate compositions evolved, with two- and sometimes three-story prism-capped entrance towers: 22 Bigelow (1870), and 1105 Massachusetts Avenue (1873), and 334 Broadway (1874). There are also tiny examples in which the second floor has been mansarded: 23 Maple (1868) and 26 Inman (1874). A few brick rows were built evoking the increasing value of land as much as

Martin Luther King, Jr., School. Sert, Jackson and Associates; 1972. *Photo: Steve Rosenthal*

Memorial Chapel, Harvard University. Coolidge, Shepley, Bulfinch and Abbott; 1931. *Photo: Shepley, Bulfinch, Richardson and Abbott*

the structured French streetscape: 357–59 Harvard (1867), 30–38 Pearl (1874), 407A–411 Broadway (1874–76), and 19–21 1/2 Inman (1875–77). While many houses were builder designed by formula, the architect began to play an increasing role in residential design during this period.

Succeeding styles grew from these roots, intermingling to produce by the century's end a recital of individual expression that embraced Richardson's romantic shingles and a succession of styles loosely grouped under the term "Queen Anne." An early development, called "Stick Style," was a wood version of Panel Brick (see Back Bay). In place of endless invocations of classic structural elements, there came a thorough exploration of edges, panels, belt courses, and trusslike diagonals: 89 Appleton (1862), 45 Highland (1872), 10 Follen (1875), and 23 Buckingham (1878).

But it is a combination of circular corner towers, variegated gables, projecting bays, brooding rooflines, and deeply recessed porches that are the hallmarks of the Queen Anne movement. It saw the "discovery of the shingle as a polite building material." No. 90 Brattle Street (1882) by H. H. Richardson, now somewhat altered, is an outstanding version of the Shingle Style. Cambridge is rich in examples of this freedom from both classic and academic clichés. They are distributed throughout the city in a kaleidoscope of stick and shingle that defies rational analysis: 35 Prentiss (1877), 44 Walker (1880), and 48 Belleview Avenue (1886). Colonial details persist in a number of the larger houses; 26 and 49 Washington Avenue (1889 and 1887), both by Hartwell and Richardson. But surface ornament is upstaged by dynamic floor plans and dreams of castles-on-the-Rhine. Henry Van Brunt (Memorial Hall) brought the style to a high point in his house at 167 Brattle Street in 1883.

A few early "Carpenter Gothic" houses (85 Brattle, 1847, and 6 Ash Street Place, 1848) were joined by late nineteenth century medieval revivals. These were more the private exercise of architect and owner than part of a movement: 71 Appleton (1876), 70 Sparks (1878), 27 Fayerweather (1896), and 128 Brattle Street, by Ralph Adams Cram (1892). The influence of Ruskin is as sparse in Cambridge as it was in the Back Bay.

In noting that the Colonial, Georgian, and Federal revivals already discussed above should now intervene in chronological order, attention should be called to the natural affinity between the energetic individualism of the Queen Anne decades and the modern movement. The presence of two great schools of architecture in Cambridge has since produced a succession of competent contemporary solutions for the few remaining residential sites. Although early examples show direct Bauhaus influence, the teachings of Wal-

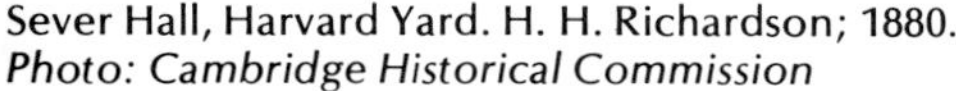

Sever Hall, Harvard Yard. H. H. Richardson; 1880.
Photo: Cambridge Historical Commission

Memorial Hall, Harvard University, Cambridge and Quincy streets.
Ware and Van Brunt; 1874. *Photo: Harvard Archives*

ter Gropius advocated a design process rather than a special "look." Restricted sites have led to simpler and more compact designs than may have been executed elsewhere by these same architects. In many cases the houses are barely visible from the street. If these first interventions seem abrupt, changing ideals have brought increasingly sensitive responses, including a growing respect for at least some of what has gone before. A chronological list of contemporary houses must include: 197 Coolidge Hill Road (1935), Howard T. Fisher; 4 Buckingham (1937), Carl Koch with Edward D. Stone; 45 Fayerweather (1940), Walter Bogner; 9 Ash (1941), Philip Johnson; 20 Follen (1949), Arthur Brooks, Jr.; 77 Sparks (1950), George W. W. Brewster; 22 Follen (1951), Carleton Richmond; 23 Lexington Avenue (1954), Carl Koch (Techbuilt); 5 Hemlock Circle (1956), James Hopkins; 64 Francis Avenue (1957), Jose Luis Sert; 61 Highland (1958), William Wainwright; 11 Gray Gardens East (1962), Frederick F. A. Bruck; 11 Reservoir (1965), Kenneth Redmond; 46 Fayerweather (1966), Peter Floyd; 199 Brattle (1966), Hugh Stubbins; 133 Brattle (1971), Hill, Miller, Friedlander & Hollander.

There have been several resourceful conversions of older houses and utilitarian structures. The most spectacular, by Paul Rudolph in 1957, transformed a concrete block garage at 144 Upland Road into an open-plan house filled with sunlight and plants. Starting in 1967, Sheldon and Annabel Dietz converted a house on Camden Street and garages on Sparks Place into an intimate complex of apartments and gardens that make the most of urban density. No. 24 Craigie Street was summarily rescued from the nineteenth century by Graham Gund in 1971. Success in blending contemporary ideas and materials with the vernacular houses of this period seems to confirm the validity of the architecture of both periods.

The oldest religious structure remaining in Cambridge is Christ Church, built in 1760. Its architect, Peter Harrison, designed King's Chapel in Boston as well as the Redwood Library and Touro Synagogue in Newport, Rhode Island. Earlier meetinghouses had doubled for commencement exercises, town meetings, and as courtrooms. In 1761, affluent Tory parishioners separated from the fourth meetinghouse to build Christ Church opposite the Common. Fourteen years later they were forced to abandon their bright Georgian edifice to the Revolution. Another splinter group built the First Parish Church in 1833 at the opposite end of the Burial Ground. They chose "Folk Gothic" to delineate their Unitarian differences. Designed by Isaiah Rogers, the interior was summarily "Federalized" in 1928, while the exterior was stripped of much expressive detail in 1954.

The remaining parishioners of the fourth meetinghouse removed to a structure on the present site of Holyoke Center, and then, in 1870, to the Gothic First Congregational Church on the Common, designed by Abel C. Martin. Two churches, both by A. R. Estey, attest the vitality of early Cambridge liturgical architecture. The brick Prospect Congregational Church (1851) combines Romanesque openings and ornament with Federal form and restraint. Estey's Gothic Revival Old Cambridge Baptist Church (1867) explores the potential of natural fieldstone and rough granite trim. Ware and Van Brunt chose Ruskin Gothic for the chapel of the Episcopal Theological School on Brattle Street (1868). Richardson Romanesque was elected by A. P. Cutting in 1891 for the Harvard-Epworth Episcopal Church near the Law School on Massachusetts Avenue.

Cambridge church structures as well as their parishioners had a tendency to wander. A Universalist church built in 1822 in Lafayette Square was first remodeled by its minister-architect Thomas Silloway, who added an Italianate spire and facade. It was then moved in 1888 to Inman Street, has since lost its steeple and most of its detail (to aluminum siding), and now serves as a Syrian Orthodox Church. A "late Georgian" edifice, designed by Isaac Melvin for the Old Cambridge Baptists in 1845 on the present site of Littauer Center, was moved to North Cambridge by Congregationalists in 1867. The Wren-like spire has been replaced with an unfortunate belfry and steeple, but the grand columnar facade remains.

Early in this century, a tiny ornament was added to Quincy Street, the Church of the New Jerusalem (1903). Its precipitous fieldstone Gothic fabric, designed by Warren, Smith and Biscoe, encapsulates with great economy of means most of what we expect from this style. In 1915, Edward T. P. Grahm designed St. Paul's Church on Arrow Street using a sturdy amalgam of Italian and French Romanesque styles. A more refined example based upon Italian

Boylston Hall, Harvard University. Schultze & Schoen; 1857. The Architects Collaborative; 1959. *Photo: Harvard Archives*

Model of Nathan M. Pusey Library. Hugh Stubbins and Associates; 1976. *Photo: Jonathan Green*

Museum of Comparative Zoology, Harvard University. The Architects Collaborative; 1972. *Photo: Carol Rankin*

Carpenter Center for the Visual Arts, Harvard University, 19 Prescott Street. Le Corbusier with Sert, Jackson & Gourley, 1961. *Photo: Harvard News Office*

Romanesque had been designed in 1904 by Maginnis, Walsh and Sullivan on Massachusetts Avenue above Porter Square. A twelfth-century Burgundian idiom was chosen by Cram and Ferguson for the Conventual Church of St. Mary and St. John (1936) on Memorial Drive above the Larz Anderson Bridge.

Contemporary church buildings since the University Lutheran Church (1950) at the corner of Winthrop and Dunster streets have lacked distinction. Two examples use urban land indifferently and cling for substance to past architectural fantasies: Latter-Day Saints (1955; neo-Georgian; Arland A. Dirlam); Holy Trinity Armenian Church (1960; twelfth-century Armenian; John Bilzerian).

The most interesting public buildings date from a single period: the library by Van Brunt and Howe (1888), and City Hall, by Longfellow, Alden and Harlow (1889). Both are a part of the Richardson tradition. In East Cambridge a scandal- and controversy-ridden superior courthouse complex threatens its betters: a courthouse by Ammi B. Young (1848) with 1814 Bulfinch parts; and a Registry of Deeds built in 1896 by Olin D. Cutter. Intensive preservation efforts are indicated to prevent what would be a serious cultural loss in exchange for marginal architectural gain.

Three contemporary schools mark progress in this field from the pioneering (for Cambridge) Morse School, as instructive today as when it was designed in 1955 by Carl Koch; the dignified Peabody School on Linnean Street (1960) by Hugh Stubbins; and the resourceful, bustling urban complex by Sert, Jackson and Associates (1970) named for Martin Luther King. Contemporary additions have been effected at the Buckingham School and at Shady Hill School by Ashley, Myer, Smith; and for the Fayerweather Street School by William Barton Associates.

With Boston just across the river and a glut of educational institutions, apart-

Gund Hall (Graduate School of Design); Harvard University, Quincy and Cambridge streets. John Andrews/Anderson/Baldwin; 1969. *Photo: Steve Rosenthal*

ments have always enjoyed a seller's market. Many private houses have long since been converted to multiple dwellings and the city is in danger of losing its invaluable stock of detached houses. Zoning laws favor a bland brick three-story "pillbox" apartment format jammed onto odd parcels of land without regard for neighborhood character or function. The larger apartment complexes dating from World War I are undistinguished, offering cloying Tudor décor and, in a few cases, a river view. Later attempts have kept pace with this marginal speculative art, but have not surpassed a Cambridge classic, 100 Memorial Drive. This 1949 landmark, designed by a team of young architects connected with MIT (Brown, De Mars, Kennedy, Koch, Rapson), combines a skip-stop elevator system and balconies in a highly livable format. Nearly every apartment has a view of the river, while lower floors open onto gardens. The expression of brick as a skin, without the pretense that it supported the building, was an innovation for both Cambridge and Boston.

HARVARD UNIVERSITY

Harvard's two oldest buildings once formed, with a third building since demolished, a courtyard facing the Common: Georgian-Colonial Massachusetts Hall (1718) and Harvard Hall (1764). Holden Chapel (1742) and Hollis Hall (1762) formed a similar court with the other side of Harvard Hall. It was not until 1889 that this relationship with the Common was severed with construction of Johnson Gate (McKim, Mead and White) and a high iron fence. Stoughton Hall (1804) is Charles Bulfinch's Federal version of Hollis Hall. Both were built, along with Harvard Hall, by the master builder and patriot, Thomas Dawes. Holworthy Hall (1811) was built by Loammi Baldwin, who oversaw construction of the Middlesex Canal, by which Chelmsford granite was transported for

Undergraduate Science Center, Harvard University
Sert, Jackson, and Associates; 1973.
Photo: Steve Rosenthal

Peabody Terrace (married students housing), Harvard University, 900 Memorial Drive. Sert, Jackson & Gourley; 1963. *Photo: Phokion Karas*

Harvard Graduate Center, 14 Everett Street. The Architects Collaborative; 1949. *Photo: Fleischer*

Larsen Hall (Graduate School of Education), Harvard University, 8 Appian Way. Caudill, Rowlett & Scott; 1965.
Photo: Caudill, Rowlett, & Scott

Charles Bulfinch's University Hall. In 1815, he offered a new planning concept that placed this granite Federal building at the center of the growing campus, surrounded by a ring of trees. The tall Ionic pilasters, collected by a balustrade at the top, were prophetic in that they effect a transition of scale from eighteenth-century brick-and-window facades to the monumental scale of Widener Library and other buildings to come.

The Old Yard was completed with buildings executed in compatible styles during the last half of the nineteenth century. Rugged, granite Boylston Hall (1857; Schultze and Schoen) was originally a science building. It received a mansard roof in 1871 and a complete renovation in 1959 by The Architects Collaborative. The introduction of plate glass in tall arched windows has set a precedent for the sympathetic treatment of many older buildings. The first mansard roof came with Grays Hall (1862; N. J. Bradlee). It was followed by Weld Hall (1870), designed by Ware and Van Brunt with what were to become the elements of brick Queen Anne. Mathews Hall favors Ruskin, the work of Peabody and Stearns in the following year. Thayer Hall, designed by Ryder and Harris, was built in 1869 to balance Hollis and Stoughton. It mixed Georgian detail with formal Academic composition. In the northwest corner, A. W. Longfellow, Jr., closed out the century by introducing the first Georgian Revival building in the Old Yard: Phillips Brooks House (1898).

Memorial Hall, a milestone in American architectural history, was dedicated to the Civil War dead. It is as much a memorial to the alumni who conceived of, built, and paid for it. Ware and Van Brunt won a competition for the design, combining a banquet hall and a theatre linked by a somber memorial transept. Today the great open-trussed hall is used for examinations, but Sanders Theatre has endeared itself to generations as an acoustically desirable setting for performances ranging from a poetry reading to a full symphony. Recently air-conditioned, its talkative radiators and open-window continuo of fire trucks and community noises will be missed. As a replacement, the inspired 195-foot copper-sheathed clock tower, destroyed by fire in 1956, should be restored to its rightful place in the daily life of the community.

Two years after the plans for Memorial Hall were completed, H. H. Richardson was asked to design a much-needed classroom building. Like Bulfinch, he thought in a larger context, establishing new directions for the land to the east of the Old Yard. Sever Hall (1818) was sited to relate to Gore Hall and Appleton Chapel, which have been replaced by Widener Library and Memorial Church, respectively. Its four engaged towers, near-continuous windows, and "whispering" elliptical arch entrance lend unassailable strength to a composition deftly lightened with delicate cut-brick ornament. Although architects who followed ignored this lesson, Henry-Russell Hitchcock, in *The Architecture of H. H. Richardson and His Times,* called it "an almost unique masterpiece of the incredibly difficult art of building in harmony with the fine work of the past and yet creating a new style for a new day."

The Classic bulk of Widener Library (1913; Horace Trumbauer) is larger than its wide steps and colonnade suggest, a feat of architectural sleight-of-hand that may have died out with the passing of architects indoctrinated in historic styles. It is "answered" by the outsized portico and "Old North" steeple of Memorial Church, designed in 1931 by Coolidge, Shepley, Bulfinch and Abbott. With University Hall, these buildings define Tercentenary Quadrangle, an outdoor amphitheatre used for graduation exercises every spring.

Monroe C. Gutman Library, Harvard University. Benjamin Thompson Associates; 1974. *Photo: Ezra Stoller*

The Garage. Conversion to retail complex: ADD, Inc.; 1973. *Photo: Steve Rosenthal*

Of the remaining Yard buildings, Robinson Hall (1900; McKim, Mead and White) and Emerson (1904; Guy Lowell) deliver a classical sermon in what had become an almost mandatory brick vocabulary; the President's House (1911; Guy Lowell) stands on borrowed Georgian dignity; and the oversimplified ornament of Houghton Library (1941; Perry, Shaw and Hepburn) suggests that the welcome "subterranean" order of Pusey Library (1975; Hugh Stubbins and Associates) was embraced a generation too late. Ivy, the architect's friend, has tempered the tentative fenestration of Lamont Library (1947; Coolidge, Shepley, Bulfinch and Abbott), which effected Harvard's long-overdue transition to more appropriate contemporary expressions.

A succession of Georgian Revival dormitories, all designed by the Shepley office in the 1920s, shelters the Yard from the twentieth century. They have been joined by Canaday (1974; Ezra Ehrencrantz), a replacement for Classical Hunt Hall (1893; William Morris Hunt). Its design offers subtly scaled window openings and forthright brick detailing, free of stylistic vanity, to this venerable, articulate collection of educational structures.

At the beginning of the North Yard, H. H. Richardson's Austin Hall (1881) incorporates many of the ideas, materials, details, and techniques for which its architect is famous. An extended examination of its imaginative Romanesque stonework, wood interior, and carved beams leaves one with the impression of having attended a deep and moving performance. Even the incised inscriptions exhort an ecclesiastical interpretation of the law. Classic Langdell Hall with its sympathetic contemporary addition designed by successive configurations of the firm of Shepley, Rutan and Coolidge, seem to suggest that law depends upon stentorian authority. In the Law Faculty Wing and Roscoe Pound Building (1967–1968), Benjamin Thompson and Associates use manganese brick and exposed concrete to resolve Austin and Langdell with their brick and brownstone neighbors. This deceptively simple assemblage of materials, surfaces, colors, furnishings, and equipment is planned down to the smallest

The Architects Collaborative Office Buildings, 46 Brattle and Story streets. The Architects Collaborative; 1966 and 1969. *Photo: Louis Reens*

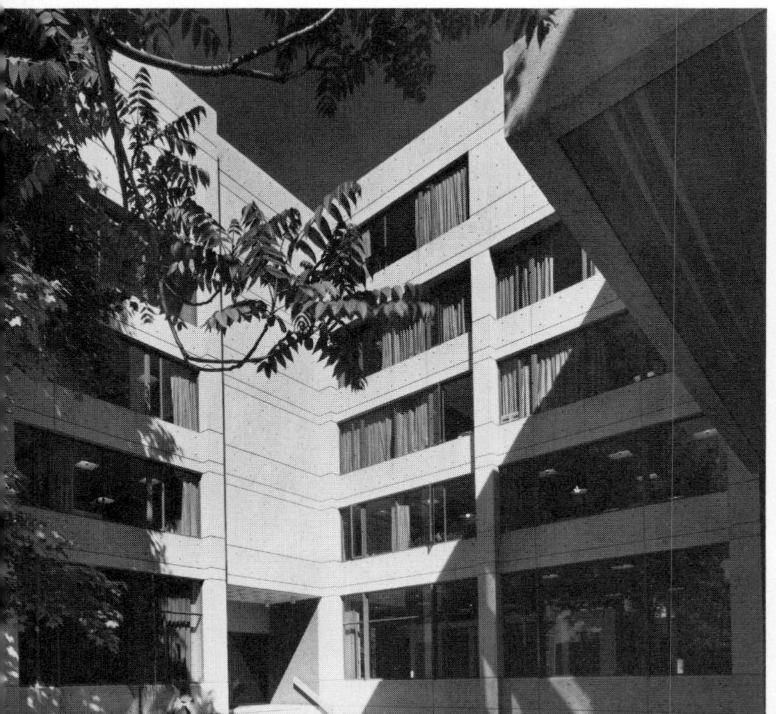

Design Research, Inc., 48 Brattle Street. Benjamin Thompson Associates; 1969. *Photo: Ezra Stoller*

Faculty Housing (Radcliffe), Linnean Street. Ronald Gourley; 1972. *Photo: Phokion Karas*

Mount Auburn Hospital. Perry, Dean & Stewart; 1974. *Photo: Phokion Karas*

Longy School of Music, Harvard University. Addition: Huygens & Tappé; 1973. *Photo: Phokion Karas*

detail, appropriate to a contemporary understanding of the law as structured experience.

The rambling University Museum, fourteen buildings by at least twelve architects, is also a laboratory of architectural compatibility. The first ten sections, built before World War I, share a common attitude toward windows and wall-bearing construction. An herbarium whose modern framing permitted wider "picture" windows interrupts this pleasant rhythm. Tozzer Library (1974; Johnson-Hotfedt), a recent addition, maintains the necessary rapport. Its reinterpretation of the masonry opening directs attention back to the parent structure. Two other wings, both by The Architects Collaborative, avoid conflict by subordinating windows to exposed structure.

The transition from the neo-Georgian Mallinckrodt Laboratories (1927; Coolidge, Shepley, Bulfinch and Abbott) to the Biological Laboratories by the same firm three years later has been compared to the stylistic breakthrough made by H. H. Richardson at Sever Hall. Its firm industrial posture accepts the carved brick frieze of animals (Katharine Ward Lane, sculptress) with dignity and delight. But it took nearly thirty years to bring this honesty to Harvard's residential structures in Quincy House and Leverett Towers.

Busch-Reisinger Museum (1914), an unexpected ornament in the disorganized North Yard, houses ancient and modern Germanic art as well as a fine baroque organ. Its narrow stone nave is just right for seeing and hearing music of the period. Across Divinity Avenue, and totally unrelated to the rest of Harvard, William James Hall (1963; Minoru Yamasaki) contains a human filing cabinet for the behavorial sciences. To provide flexible floor space, long-span girders were hung from five pairs of tapered concrete pylons, avoiding interior supports. Since in its rabbit-warren of passages and offices, columns would never have been noticed, it was unnecessary to impact the skyline with this misplaced architectural energy.

Harvard's romance with name architects produced in Carpenter Center (1961) a retrospective collection of the architectural ideas associated with its architect, LeCorbusier. As a "machine for learning" it seems to work quite well, but because the "plastic" concrete forms are scaled down, his usually rewarding spatial compositions need charitable interpretation. A slippery ramp leads to nowhere; exterior spaces, appropriate to warmer climates, are rarely habitable. Because they defy landscaping, they cannot be "used" visually either. The experience suggests that when a university invites a scholar into its midst, there is ample opportunity for a dialogue and that, when the visitor is an architect about to sire a building, the dialogue should take place before the plans are drawn.

In Gund Hall (1969; John Andrews, Anderson and Baldwin), the university has made a serious commitment to the doctrine of expressionist architecture. A multilevel drafting space under a sloping glass roof gives on to classroom floors devoted to landscape, architecture, urban design, and planning disciplines. Workshops, an auditorium, and a library share the nether regions. Admirably arranged to exclude traffic noise from a busy intersection while offering visual hospitality to Memorial Hall, it dissipates the strength of its main idea in an overcompetent preoccupation with details and connections. In keeping with current fashion, air ducts and other elements of the mechanical equipment are visually designed, whether or not they perform as intended. Design students, who can be counted on to detect physical and philosophical malfunction, have divided up their unstructured open space into personalized "environments" as if to answer the architect's explicit investigations with fantasies of their own.

Just north of the Yard, Cambridge Street has been depressed to provide a pedestrian connection as well as a setting for the new Undergraduate Science Center (1973; Sert, Jackson and Gourley). A low-lying library, stepped-back faculty offices, and a great wall of laboratories are capped by concrete-encased cooling towers sufficient to air-condition the entire university. These elements are connected with a sparkling glass skylight defining pleasant indoor "streets" and a student lounge overlooking a landscaped courtyard. Three large lecture halls, half-buried on the southwest, can be identified by the spiderlike trusses that support the roof. These aborted masses are less easy to understand than the rest of the building. Lacking scale, they become something to be circumnavigated as quickly as possible. But once inside the generous corridor system, it is clear that the art of daylit interior space has been happily advanced.

In 1960, Harvard established a new direction for the commercial area between the Yard and the houses near the river. Holyoke Center (1961, 1965; Sert, Jackson and Gourley) combines university offices, a medical center, shops, a bank, and a garage in a ten-story complex. It sets back in several places to accommodate older buildings around it and offers an all-weather pedestrian arcade linking the two districts. Forbes Plaza, with its colorful street sellers, is a timely extension of congested Harvard Square.

Peabody Terrace (1963), also by Sert, Jackson and Gourley, is a married student housing complex situated on the river. It connects high-, medium-, and low-rise elements with skip-stop elevators and bridges to achieve an economical but very livable urban density. Apartments are grouped vertically in clusters, avoiding the pigeonhole effect common to most multiple dwellings. Parking, a corner store,

Harvard Stadium; 1903. Ira Nelso Hollis, Engineer; McKim, Mead & White and George Bruno de Gersdorff, consulting architects.

MIT Chapel. Eero Saarinen; 1955. *Photo: Cambridge Historical Commission*

Kresge Auditorium, MIT. Eero Saarinen; 1955. *Photo: MIT News Service*

laundromat, nursery school, and tot lot make this a self-sufficient minicommunity. These three works by the Sert firm fulfill an important university function: to provide a laboratory for the execution of architectural and urban design concepts that can be instructive to the larger community.

Although Walter Gropius brought his revolutionary teaching methods to Harvard in 1937, it was not until 1949 that he was commissioned to design a building. The Graduate Center became a challenge to his new firm, The Architects Collaborative, in the face of a radically altered postwar economy. Planned around a tightly developed student room unit with full-width windows and built-in furnishings, its low density is almost embarrassing in light of the subsequent intensity of university development. An informal plan preserves the basic Harvard courtyard, but opens up pleasant vistas of Harkness Commons and the North Yard. Light brick and limestone trim were chosen to complement Langdell Hall. A decade later it might well have been exposed concrete, for which a technology equal to the New England climate did not exist in 1949. By far the most successful element, Harkness Commons contains meeting, lounge, and dining facilities, fortified by the provocative art of Miró, Arp, Albers, and Lippold.

The task of relating new construction to the neo-Georgian residence complex of the 1930s was more complicated. Here the eighteenth-century environment is so complete that the Indoor Athletic Building (1929; Coolidge, Shepley, Bulfinch and Abbott) seems virtually to disappear into the red brick and white woodwork. Quincy House (1968) is a more recent work by Shepley, Bulfinch, Richardson and Abbott. It uses the Harvard brick in panels framed in limestone trim reflecting the structure; windows become panels of glass. Its eight stories are "compressed" to the scale of the neighborhood by sandwiching six brick levels between two of stone and glass. A zigzag plate roof over the commons wing keeps alive the romance of the slate dormer in an otherwise flat-roofed building.

At Leverett House, increasing demand on land use would have dictated a congested low-rise solution. Twelve-story towers in brick would have mocked the already fictitious brick bearing-wall idiom of Dunster House. White limestone was chosen to explain this important structural difference and to minimize mass. An operable "standard" window is set in the framework, while bronze-tinted glass panels backed by pumpkin-colored draperies bring the composition into chromatic harmony with its neighbors.

Both Leverett and Quincy continue a landscaped experience that extends from the riverfront to the far end of the Radcliffe campus. Without this green amenity and effective planning of spaces as well as buildings, no amount of stylistic virtuosity could have succeeded. Inspired site design for the Loeb Drama Center (Hugh Stubbins and Associates) proves that a contemporary (1959) solution can be more appropriate to the residential scale of Brattle Street than cautious adherence to historic style, exemplified by the Radcliffe Graduate Center (1959; Perry, Shaw and Hepburn) at the corner of Ash Street. Loeb's functional brick massing, framed in concrete, is set off by a metal screen over the second-story windows, designed to double as a brilliantly lit "marquee" for evening performances. Prior to becoming a full partner with Harvard, Radcliffe turned to contemporary solutions in 1965 with Hilles Library (Harrison and Abramovitz). Its comfortable, well-planned interior makes it a favorite spot for study dates. In spite of fine landscaping by Diane Kostial McGuire, a nervous exterior relates neither to the older dormitories or to the private houses along Garden Street.

In Larsen Hall (1965) on Appian Way, the School of Education has acquired an introspective brick think tank designed by Caudill, Rowlett and Scott. Its romantic arches and corbeling are appropriately set off by a moatlike sunken court leading to experimental teaching facilities. Next door, extroverted Gutman Library (1974; Benjamin Thompson and Associates) proffers lively colors and human movement within its multifaceted massing to the everlasting benefit of Brattle Street and its diminishing residential ambience. It completes a decade of commercial develop-

Baker House (undergraduate housing), MIT, 362 Memorial Drive. Alvar Aalto with Perry, Shaw & Hepburn; 1947-49. *Photo: MIT News Service*

Eastgate Apartments, 100 Memorial Drive. Brown, DeMars, Kennedy, Koch & Rapson; 1949. *Photo: Cambridge Historical Commission*

Eastgate Married Students Housing, MIT, Wadsworth and Main streets. Eduardo Catalano; 1966.
Photo: MIT News Service

ment in this area that started in 1966 with construction of an office building at 46 Brattle Street for The Architects Collaborative. Adjacent multipurpose structures house, incidentally, the offices of their respective architects: Earl R. Flansburgh and Associates and Sert, Jackson and Associates. The all-glass keystone is Design Research (1969; Benjamin Thompson and Associates), a landmark retail venture that gave greater Boston its first systematic exposure to contemporary design as a way of life. Its nonexistent facade expands the streetscape and invests it with the colors, shapes, and textures of furnishings, accessories, clothing, and textiles. The *coup de grace* is the supergraphic neon "DR" sign on the back inside wall.

Connected by the Larz Anderson Bridge (1912; Wheelwright and Haven) and Weeks Footbridge (1926; McKim, Mead and White) the Graduate School of Business Administration presents its own stylistic evolution. In 1924 the University selected its architect by a competition that suggested neo-Georgian would please everybody. The New York firm of McKim, Mead and White accomplished this with splayed dormitory quadrangles supervised by Baker Library and its golden cupola. This instant nostalgia dominated successive additions until recently. While two of the buildings have incorporated innovative planning for the School's unique educational program (Aldrich and Kresge Halls; Perry, Shaw, Hepburn and Dean) they have remained architecturally neutral. The last neo-Georgian building, Cutting House (Robert S. Sturgis) was completed in 1969. Burden Hall (Phillip Johnson; 1971) slips away in contemporary anonymity, its muted interior equally, but elegantly, understated. Assimilation through contrast was tried by Kubitz and Pepi for Teele Hall, completed in 1969. Its hammered concrete and black glass enclose a post office, convenience store, and the editorial offices of the *Harvard Business Review*. Earl R. Flansburgh and Associates tackled the brick idiom again with Cumnock Hall, completed in 1975. Its crisp integrity equals that of Harvard's new buildings across the river.

Baker and McCullum Halls (Shepley, Bulfinch, Richardson, and Abbott) offer a refined version of the concrete-banded-brick style that seems to have emerged from Cambridge architectural firms over the past two decades. Nearby, an ambitious apartment complex winds inward from the river to open on pleasantly scaled interior spaces, lined with gregarious balconies and Harvard's usual fine planting. The work of Benjamin Thompson and Associates, it seems to grow out of an understanding of successful, but densely populated, areas of older cities. It is an immediate answer to the perennial problem of housing students, faculty, and employees in an already overcrowded community.

An earlier innovation, the Harvard Stadium, sleeps nine months of the year behind its classic ivy-covered facade. Built in 1903, it was the first massive reinforced-concrete structure in the world and the first permanent collegiate athletic arena. Designed under the supervision of Ira Nelson Hollis, a professor of engineering, McKim, Mead and White, and George Bruno de Gersdorff served as architectural consultants. Its open end, with a grand view of the Charles, sends cheers resounding clear to Harvard Square. In a recent design-build competition, the University selected The Architect's Collaborative to guide the development of a massive sports complex to accompany the stadium and its assorted athletic buildings. The university required that a building occupy the open space at the end of the stadium, and that the corner gate to Boylston Street be abandoned. This space and the connection to the bridge back to the Square take

Green Building (earth sciences), MIT, McDermott Court. I. M. Pei & Associates; 1964. *Photo:* Time, *Frank Lerner*

on a special importance about four or five times a year. It is a thrilling and necessary experience to be swept along behind a triumphant band in a river of people who are bent upon expressing the diminishing rite of unanimity. The wisdom of Harvard's planning will be measured annually by unforgiving multitudes.

When it became clear that the proposed presidential museum and library for the late John F. Kennedy would bring a million visitors a year to the Square, the community was prepared. Fresh from a victory over state engineers who would have widened Memorial Drive on the river at the expense of a beloved row of shade trees, it dug in again. A Harvard Square Task Force, representing the business and residential community, the university, and the city, provided input to the government study required for the project impact study required for the project. Now that the Kennedy Library is to be located in Boston, the Task Force is proceeding to implement its "Comprehensive Policy Plan" in cooperation with all concerned. This will affect growth in and around the Square and ultimately along Massachusetts Avenue in conjunction with similar efforts originating at Central Square. Another study process, this one with MIT and the industrial community, will affect the future of Kendall Square.

MIT

The Institute left its Academic beginnings in the Back Bay for newly filled land on the Cambridge shore of the Charles in 1913. In keeping with a forty-five-year tradition of architectural education, it embraced monumental Beaux Arts classicism. The McLaurin Buildings (1913), Walker Memorial (1916), and the Rogers Pavilion (1937), all by Welles Bosworth, established a challenging discipline of columns and domes. Successive additions have each attempted to reinterpret this statement in evolving contemporary terms: Hayden Li-

Frank S. MacGregor House (undergraduate housing), MIT, 450 Memorial Drive. The Architects Collaborative and Pietro Belluschi; 1970. *Photo: Phokion Karas*

Department of Transportation (formerly NASA facilities). Optics and Guidance Laboratories: The Architects Collaborative; 1970. *Photo: Burger*

brary (1949), Anderson and Beckwith with Voorhees, Walker, Foley and Smith; Metals Processing Laboratory (1950), Perry, Shaw, Hepburn and Dean; Dorrance Laboratories (1950) and Whittaker Building (1963), Anderson, Beckwith and Haible; Compton Laboratories (1955), Vannevar Bush Building (1963), Center for Space Research (1965), Skidmore, Owings and Merrill (Chicago).

Three early examples of the modern movement relieve this classical atmosphere on the other side of Massachusetts Avenue. The soaring triangular dome of Kresge Auditorium and its cylindrical consort, the MIT Chapel, were both designed in the early fifties by Eero Saarinen. Alvar Aalto's undulating brick dormitory (with Perry, Shaw and Hepburn; 1947) augments views of the river. It lost a dramatic suspended glass staircase to unsympathetic building codes. Perhaps this exciting promise will one day be realized through advanced building technology.

Linking these three buildings back to the main campus is an ingenious multi-purpose student center designed by Eduardo Catalano in 1963. It contains a specialty store, convenience shops, a bowling alley, dining room facilities, meeting rooms and offices for student activities, all topped by an undergraduate library opening onto its own roof garden. Other buildings by Professor Catalano include the Hermann Building (1964) and Eastgate (1965), a twenty-five-story concrete residence for married students.

The Alumni Swimming Pool (1937), Du-Pont Center Gymnasium (1958), Rockwell

Housing for the Elderly, Erie, Clarendon and Gore streets. Benjamin Thompson Associates; 1973.
Photo: Ezra Stoller

Cage (1947), and Pierce Boathouse (1965) all show the hand of Lawrence Anderson, who headed the Department of Architecture from 1947 until his retirement as dean in 1971. The trim boathouse, which seems to float on the river basin, is both rational and romantic, an interesting contrast to Harvard's Newell and Weld boathouses upriver (1899, 1906; Peabody and Stearns).

MIT's residential plant grew from two converted brick apartment houses on the riverfront, and the East Campus Dormitories (Welles Bosworth; Coolidge and Carlson), to include McCormick House (1962, 1967; Anderson, Beckwith and Haible), Westgate (1962; Hugh Stubbins and Associates), and McGregor House (1974; Pietro Belluschi with The Architects Collaborative). The latter uses reinforced brick construction. A third unit, constructed under the competitive "design-build" process (Sert, Jackson and Associates) provides more housing for married students.

Less complicated than Harvard's long and often enigmatic experience with architectural styles, the linear campus of the institute displays a stimulating sequence of competent, creative solutions to the requirements of its many and demanding functions. Some of this has infected nearby private development, as at Technology Square above Kendall Square (1961–1966; Cabot, Cabot and Forbes Associates, Pietro Belluschi, and Eduardo Catalano). Other projects in this area have not fared as well. A mannerist tower, constructed for NASA and now used by the federal Department of Transportation, was designed by Edward D. Stone. It has been helped somewhat with lower additions designed by The Architects Collaborative. But the tower and the self-consciously modern "Cambridge Gateway" (1968) by Emery Roth and Sons remain outside of the mainstream of the significant architectural growth common to Cambridge and Boston.

BIBLIOGRAPHY

BOOKS

Bacon, Edwin M. *Rambles Around Old Boston.* Boston: Little, Brown, and Company, 1914.

Barrows, Esther G. *Neighbors All, A Settlement Notebook.* Boston and New York: Houghton Mifflin Company, The Riverside Press, Cambridge, 1929.

Bartlett, Josiah. *Historical Sketch of Charlestown.* Boston: Massachusetts Historical Society, 1813.

Baxter, Sylvester. *An American Palace of Art, Fenway Court, The Isabella Stewart Gardner Museum in the Fenway.* Boston: The Century Magazine Publications, 1904.

Benton, Josiah Henry. *Story of the Old Boston Townhouse, 1658–1711.* Boston: Merrymount Press, 1908.

Boston Museum of Fine Arts. *Back Bay Boston: The City as a Work of Art.* 1969.

Bunting, Bainbridge. *Houses of Boston's Back Bay.* Cambridge: The Belknap Press of Harvard University Press, 1967.

Bunting, W. H. *Portrait of a Port: Boston 1852–1914.* Cambridge: The Belknap Press of Harvard University Press, 1971.

Cambridge Historical Commission. *Survey of Architectural History in Cambridge:*
Report One: East Cambridge. Cambridge: 1965.
Report Two: Mid-Cambridge. Cambridge: 1967.
Report Three: Cambridgeport. Cambridge: 1971.
Report Four: Old Cambridge. Cambridge: 1973.

Chamberlain, Allen. *Beacon Hill; Its Ancient Pastures and Early Mansions.* Boston and New York: Houghton Mifflin, The Riverside Press, Cambridge, 1925.

Crawford, Mary Caroline. *Old Boston Ways and Days.* Boston: Little, Brown, and Company, 1909.

Drake, Samuel Adams. *Historic Mansions and Highways Around Boston.* Boston: Little, Brown, and Company, 1899.

———. *Old Boston Taverns and Tavern Clubs.* Boston: W. A. Butterfield, 1917.

———. *Old Landmarks and Historic Personages of Boston.* Boston: Little, Brown, and Company, 1872.

———. *Our Colonial Houses.* Boston: Lee, 1894.

Eldredge, Joseph L. *Boston's Pictorial: Faneuil Hall Marketplace.* Boston: Friends of the Government Center, 1975.

Eliot, Charles. *Vegetation and Scenery in the Metropolitan Reservations of Boston, A Forestry Report.* Boston, New York, London: Lawson, Wolffe, and Company, 1898.

Frothingham, Richard. *History of Charlestown.* Boston: Little, Brown, 1845.

Goody, Joan E. *New Architecture in Boston.* Cambridge: The MIT Press, 1965.

Goody, Marvin E., and Walsh, Robert P. (eds.). *Boston Society of Architects, The First Hundred Years, 1867–1967. Boston:* The Nimrod Press, 1967.

Hitchcock, Henry-Russell. *The Architecture of H. H. Richardson and His Times.* New York: The Museum of Modern Art, 1936.

Hitchings, Sinclair. *Boston Impressions.* Barre, Mass.: Barre Publishing, 1970.

Howe, Mark A. DeWolfe. *Boston Landmarks.* New York: Hastings House, 1946.

———. *Boston; The Place and the People.* New York: The Macmillan Company, 1903.

Hunnewell, James Frothingham. *A Century of Town Life: A History of Charlestown, Massachusetts 1775–1887.* Boston: Little, Brown, 1888.

Jacobs, Jane. *Death and Life of Great American Cities.* New York: Random House, 1961.

Knowles, Katharine, and Whitehill, Walter Muir. *Boston: Portrait of a City.* Barre, Mass.: Barre Publishing, 1964.

Lovett, James DeWolf. *Old Boston Boys and the Games They Played.* Boston: Little, Brown, and Company, 1908.

McCaffrey, George Herbert. *The Political Disintegration and Reintegration of Metropolitan Boston.* Cambridge: Harvard University Press, 1937.

McCord, David. *About Boston.* Garden City, N.Y.: Doubleday & Company, 1949.

Morison, Samuel Eliot. *The Maritime History of Massachusetts 1783–1860.* Boston: Houghton Mifflin Company, 1961.

——— *One Boy's Boston.* Boston, Houghton Mifflin Company, 1962.

Porter, Edward G. *Rambles in Old Boston, New England.* Boston: Cupples, Upham, and Co., 1887.

Rettig, Robert Bell. *Guide to Cambridge Architecture; Ten Walking Tours.* Cambridge, The Cambridge Historical Commission (The MIT Press, Cambridge), 1969.

Ross, Marjorie Drake. *The Book of Boston, The Colonial Period 1630–1775.* New York: Hastings House Publishers, 1960.

———. *The Book of Boston, The Federal Period 1775–1837.* New York: Hastings House Publishers, 1961.

Rossiter, William S. (ed.), *Days and Ways in Old Boston.* Boston: R. H. Stearns and Company, 1915.

Shackleton, Robert. *The Book of Boston.* Philadelphia: The Penn Publishing Company, 1916.

Shurtleff, Nathaniel B. *A Topographical and Historical Description of Boston.* Boston: Published by the Order of the City Council, 1890.

Sirkis, Nancy. *Boston.* New York: The Viking Press, 1965.

Snyder, Wendy. *Haymarket.* Cambridge: The MIT Press, 1970.

Spring, James W. *Boston and the Parker House.* Boston: J. R. Whipple, 1927.

Stark, James Henry. *Antique Views of Boston.* Boston: Burdette and Company, Inc., 1967.

Stout, George L. *Treasures from the Isabella Stewart Gardner Museum.* New York: Crown Publishers, 1969.

Sullivan, T. R. *Boston, New and Old.* Boston: Houghton Mifflin Company, 1912.

Sutton, S. B. (ed.). *Civilizing American Cities; A Selection of Frederick Law Olmsted's Writings on City Landscapes.* Cambridge: The MIT Press, 1971.

Warden, G. B. *Boston; 1689–1776.* Boston: Little, Brown and Company, 1970.

Warner, Sam B., Jr. *Streetcar Suburbs, The Process of Growth in Boston, 1870–1900.* Cambridge: Harvard University Press and the MIT Press, 1962.

Weeks, Edward. *Boston, Cradle of Liberty.* New York: Arts, Inc., 1965.

Weston, George F., Jr. *Boston Ways—High, By, and Folk.* Boston: Beacon Press, 1957.

Whitehill, Walter Muir. *Boston—A Topographical History,* 2nd ed. Cambridge: The Belknap Press of Harvard University Press, 1968.

———. *Boston Public Library, A Centennial History.* Cambridge: Harvard University Press, 1956.

———. *Museum of Fine Arts, Boston, A Centennial History.* vols. 1–2. Cambridge: The Belknap Press of Harvard University Press, 1970.

Winsor, Justin (ed.). *Memorial History of Boston,* vols. 1–4. Boston: James Osgood and Co., 1880.

Wolfe, Albert Benedict. *The Lodging House Problem in Boston.* Boston and New York: Houghton Mifflin Company, The Riverside Press, Cambridge, 1906.

Woods, Robert A. (ed.). *The City Wilderness, A Settlement Study.* Boston and New York: Houghton Mifflin Company, The Riverside Press, Cambridge, 1898.

———. *The Neighborhood in Nation Building, The Running Comment of Thirty Years at the South End House.* Boston and New York: Houghton Mifflin Company, The Riverside Press, Cambridge, 1923.

ARTICLES

"Architects in the Attic." *Architectural Forum,* June 1968, 68–71.

Ayres, James. "Take a Cruise to Sunny Islands . . . Boston's." *Boston Globe,* November 3, 1972.

Campbell, Robert. "Needed: Bridge between White, Bridge Advocates." *Boston Sunday Globe,* August 17, 1975, F-2.

Canty, Donald. "Boston University Begins to Build a Vertical Campus." *Architectural Forum,* June 1964, 122–23.

"Children's Inn and Hospital Medical Center." *New England Architect,* 1971, 1–5.

Hutson, Ron. "South End Housing Debate Rekindled." *Boston Globe,* May 29, 1975, 3.

"Integrated Campus for Boston University's Landlocked Site." *Architectural Record,* May 1964, 161–70.

Kilgore, Kathleen. "Four Terrific Neighborhoods." *Boston,* August 1974, 34.

Koch, Karl. "Wharf Into Village." *Architecture Plus,* March/April 1974, 44–48.

"Long Wharf Gets an Antique Dealer." *Boston Sunday Globe,* August 17, 1975, F-1.

"Proposals." *Charlestown Patriot,* February 17, 1967.

Rodgers, David. "100% Valuation: What Will It Mean to Boston?" *Boston Globe,* June 8, 1975, A-1.

"Structural Aesthetics for Boston Garage." *Progressive Architecture,* February 1966, 160–62.

Thompson, Benjamin, and Thompson, Jane McC. "Reviving Boston's Marketplace." *Progressive Architecture,* September 1971, 157.

"Tufts New England Medical Center." *Architectural Record,* August 1974.

"Waterfront Park Will Complete Boston's 'Walk to the Sea.'" *Brookline Chronicle Citizen,* March 27, 1975, 19.

"Where Is Boston Renewal Heading?" *Christian Science Monitor,* September 21, 1972.

Yudis, Anthony J. "BRA OK's Four New Projects." *Boston Globe,* November 3, 1972, A-20.

———. "Faneuil Hall Area Now Being Restored Just as It Was in Boston of 1824–26. *Boston Sunday Globe,* October 29, 1972.

———. "'Stay' Sought for Sullivan Square." *Boston Globe,* June 1, 1975, F-1.

PROCEEDINGS

Anderson, Lawrence B. *Program for Boston City Hall Competition,* 1960.

The Bostonian Society. *Annual Meeting, 1958, 1967, 1968, 1969, 1974.* Boston: Old State House.

ADDITIONAL SOURCE MATERIAL

Books

Historical Collection. Boston Public Library, Charlestown Branch.

Historical Collection. Boston Public Library, North End Branch.

Historical Collection. Boston Public Library, South End Branch.

Articles

Press Clipping Collection 1965–1975: Boston Redevelopment Authority Library for North End, Charlestown, South Cove, South End, Fenway, Waterfront.

Press Clipping Collections: Charlestown Branch Library, North End Branch Library, South End Branch Library.

Slide Collection

Charlestown Branch Library.

REPORTS (by title)

Back Bay Residential District Guidelines for Exterior Rehabilitation and Restoration. Boston Redevelopment Authority, 1967.

Boston Architectural Drawings. Boston Public Library.

Boston Architecture and the Abdalian Collection. Boston Public Library.

Boston Architecture and the Leslie Jones Collection. Boston Public Library.

Boston Architecture and the Postcard Collection. Boston Public Library.

Boston Architecture and the Samuel Chamberlain Collection. Boston Public Library.

Charlestown History. Boston Public Library.

General Plan for Boston. Preliminary Report. Boston: December, 1965.

Look What's Happening in Charlestown. Boston Gas Company.

Private Papers of Ralph Adams Cram. Boston Public Library.

South End Walking Tour. Boston League of Women Voters. October 19, 1974.

The Boston Architectural File. Boston Public Library.

The Boston Contest of 1944. Boston University. Boston: Boston University Press, 1945.

The Boston Pictorial Archive. Boston Public Library.

The Bulfinch Collections. Boston Public Library.

The Connick Collection. Boston Public Library.

The Cram and Ferguson Collection. Boston Public Library.

The John Evans Collection. Boston Public Library.

The Maginnis and Walsh Collection. Boston Public Library.

The Peabody and Stearns Collection. Boston Public Library.

The W. G. Preston Collection. Boston Public Library.

REPORTS (by Commission)

Boston Conservation Committee and the Brookline Conservation Committee. *Charles to Charles, a Conservation and Recreation Corridor for Boston.* Dedicated to Frederick Law Olmsted 1822–1903 in the 150th year of his birth.

Boston Redevelopment Authority. *Press releases:* October 1, 1973; February 19, 1974; January 3, 1975; February 7, 1975; March 20, 1975. Public Information Center, Boston City Hall.

Boston Redevelopment Authority. *Site Description and History of the Charlestown Navy Yard.*

Boston Redevelopment Authority. *The John F. Kennedy Library, Charlestown Navy Yard Proposal.* February, 1975.

Boston Redevelopment Authority. *Urban Renewal Plans and Assorted Reports concerning:* Charlestown Urban Renewal Area; Fenway Urban Renewal Area; South Cove Urban Renewal Area; South End Urban Renewal Area; Waterfront Urban Renewal Area.

Boston Redevelopment Authority. *Work Write-up, Home Improvement Center, Charlestown.* January 12, 1967.

City Planning Board. *The North End, A Comprehensive Survey and Plan.* Boston: Printing Department, 1919.

Greater Boston Chamber of Commerce. *The Many Worlds of Boston.* 1964–1965, Annual Report. Boston: 1965.

Greater Boston Chamber of Commerce. *The New Boston, Its People, Its Places, Its Potential.* Boston: Winthrop Printing and Offset Company, 1962.

National Historic Sites Commission. *Final Report: Major Problems of Historical Preservation in the Municipality of Boston.* House Document No. 107, 87th Congress, First Session. Washington: 1961.

Subcommittee on Memorial History of the Boston Tercentenary Committee. *Fifty Years of Boston, A Memorial History.* Boston: 1932.

United Community Research Department. *Statistical Data,* concerning: Charlestown; the Fenway; the South Cove; the South End; the Waterfront. Boston: 1970.

INDEX

Numbers in italics refer to pages with illustrations or maps.